WINNING STYLES COOKBOOK

First published in the United States of America in 2004 by:

Feeding Frenzy, Inc. • 400 E. 5th North Street, Suite C • Summerville, SC 29483 • 1-888-311-8442 phn.

Publisher:	Tom Stumph	Line Editor:	Susan Cook / Kevin Cook
Writer:	Elin Jeffords	Recipe Editor:	Alice Thompson
Cover and Book Design:	Graham Walters	Recipe Testing:	Johnson & Wales University
Photography:	John Ormond	Recipe Formatting:	Cindy Parker
Copy Editor:	Dewey Webb / Roger Cook		Johnson & Wales University

Library of Congress Cataloging-in-Publication Data is on file with publisher.
2003109524

ISBN # 0-9728697-1-9

Printed & Bound in Korea
ITS Design & Printing Inc.

WINNING
STYLES
COOKBOOK

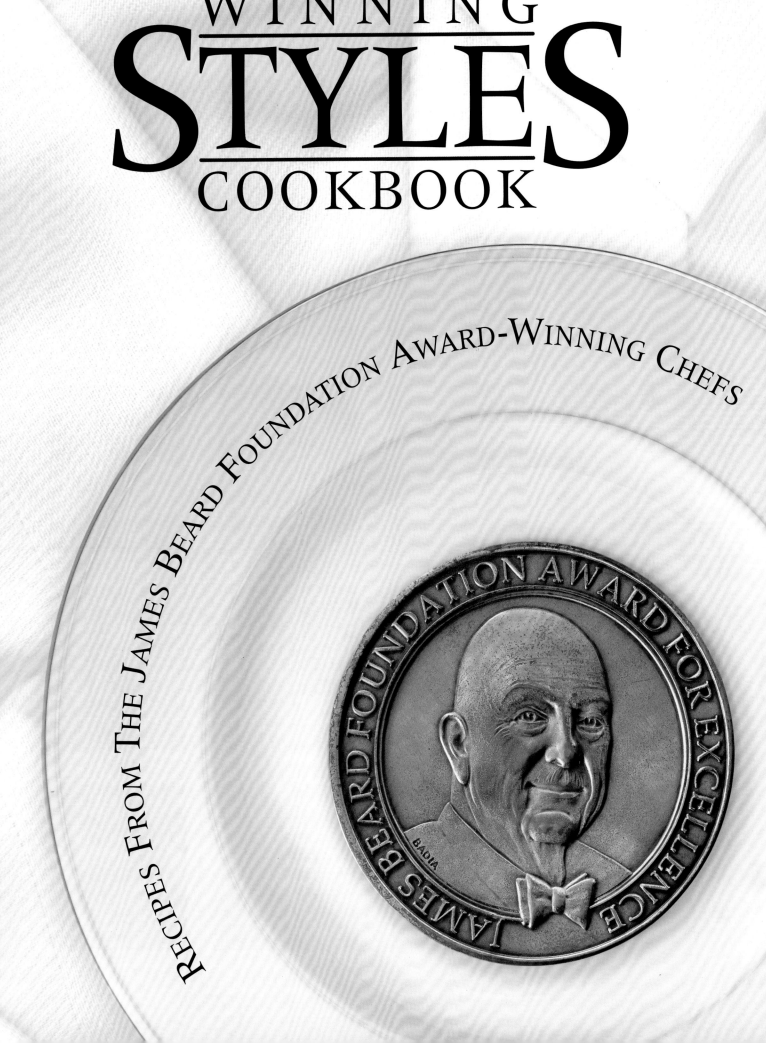

RECIPES FROM THE JAMES BEARD FOUNDATION AWARD-WINNING CHEFS

TABLE OF CONTENTS

The year 2003 marked the 100th Anniversary of James Beard's birth. This book is a tribute to the man who is considered the father of American cooking, as well as to the chefs who have been honored by The James Beard Foundation.

ACKNOWLEDGMENTS

Our sincere thanks go to everyone who participated in this book. It was a collaborative effort in every respect.

In virtually every instance, the chefs, their assistants and public relations people did what they could to ease our task.

The James Beard Foundation generously got behind the project. Without their support, this endeavor could not have happened.

America West Airlines cooperated fully in the schlepping of bags and boxes of photographic equipment during our extensive travel.

Cindy Parker and her staff at Johnson & Wales gracefully achieved the monumental chore of testing and formatting the recipes.

Phil Allen, as always, was invaluable in his research assistance, editing and computer skills, and general support.

Dewey Webb skillfully punched up text gone stodgy.

The line editing staff at The Educational Video Group made sure all the I's were dotted and T's crossed in the copy.

The recipes are more understandable and consistent thanks to the efforts of recipe editor Alice Thompson.

INTRODUCTION

Since James Beard first spread the good food gospel to hungry Americans, generations of chefs have contributed to this country's communal table in restaurants large and small, famous and obscure.

For many of those years, as Chef Robert McGrath points out in his chapter of *Winning Styles Cookbook*, professional cooking was considered "domestic labor" — despite the fact that the laboring took place in a restaurant kitchen. Little or no attention was focused on the faceless people, then mostly men, who prepared the shrimp cocktails, pommes frites and steaks Diane.

Beard himself spent little time actually cooking in a restaurant context, but the spotlight he aimed on the culinary arts through his books, columns and features, classes, consulting and television appearances changed the way Americans ate and thought about food. It also helped make the career of chef more valued and prestigious.

After Beard's death, the creation of The James Beard Foundation and the yearly awards it bestows insured that the spotlight shines even more brightly on the folks in the toques. *Winning Styles Cookbook* takes an up close and personal look at 21 of those chefs and their distinctive talents. Each of the chefs included have won top Beard Foundation honors. Some have additional awards which are not listed, such as Best TV Cooking Show or Outstanding Community Service.

How is such a cookbook born? For us, the genesis at least, was easy. What do four food-obsessed people, all in food-related professions, talk about? No surprise, primarily food, restaurants, chefs and cookbooks.

During one of those conversations the idea for *Winning Styles Cookbook* was first floated. We asked ourselves, who are the crème d' la crème of American chefs? What do they have in common? What distinguishes them from each other? How do they feel about the journey that took them to the top and the effort they must make to stay there?

The first answer was clear. While there are many excellent chefs, those who have been recognized with awards from The James Beard Foundation invariably have something very special going on both personally and culinarily. The other answers would come only when we made chef-contact.

In retrospect, the project came together quickly. First the name, *Winning Styles Cookbook*, then the plan. With the blessing of The James Beard Foundation, publisher Tom Stumph began signing up the chefs.

The rest of the crew — photographer John Ormond, art director Graham Walters and me, food writer Elin Jeffords — laid the groundwork. Before we converged on them, we did intensive research on the chefs and their restaurants. We asked each chef to provide us with six recipes: appetizer, soup, salad, two entrées and dessert. Not surprisingly, some of the chefs complied and others had their own ideas about what to contribute. Fine with us, we figured it would just make the book more interesting.

Then we headed out across the country spending long days photographing the chefs and their food, and in-between, squeezing in interviews. We watched them working in their restaurants and in most instances, sampled their food. Some of the chefs welcomed us into their homes so we could experience how they live outside of the kitchen.

As the recipes came in, they were indexed and e-mailed to Johnson & Wales for the heroic task of testing. The crew, meanwhile, enjoyed June in Seattle, September in Milwaukee and Chicago, and shivered in Boston in January. (And no, none of us experienced an appreciable weight gain.)

Answering the other questions we originally posed proved trickier. Comparing the chefs — men and women, some American, some European, some products of classic apprenticeships, some graduates of culinary academies, some self-taught — proved impossible. Each one, and the food they create, is as different and unique as a fingerprint.

What they do all have in common is a phenomenal work ethic. All believe in using the very best raw product and treating it with utmost care. Interestingly, most of the chefs made it clear to us they had no interest in preparing food they personally don't like. All expressed gratitude for what their careers have made possible and all continue to strive to excel.

These glimpses into the lives, and the intrinsically entwined culinary styles of the participating chefs, are just a snapshot. People continue to grow and change, adapting new ideas and exploring fresh directions throughout their lives. These chefs who have contributed to *Winning Styles Cookbook* are no exception.

In putting this book together, we intended for it to be enjoyed on several different levels. The gorgeous food photography makes it a culinary art book and provides a presentational blueprint for the recipes. Recipes range from those that are approachable to the average home cook to ones that take considerable skill and effort to prepare. Each chef's biography tells a riveting story of struggle and success. Finally, *Winning Styles Cookbook* is a valuable resource for those people aspiring to the professional kitchen with a wall full of awards of their own.

JENNIFER ENGLISH

FOREWORD

As James Beard observed, "food unites us," and it does so in myriad ways; by bringing us together around the table, stove or page, to share with one another our delights as well as our prejudices.

One of life's satisfactions comes from sharing food discoveries with others. Chefs do this for their guests every day. In *Winning Styles Cookbook* some of our favorite and most trusted food friends share their best, most exciting and delicious discoveries and recipes with us, just as James Beard did.

This is an ambitious, entertaining and useful cookbook. It offers original recipes, cooking tips, suggestions, advice and anecdotes from some of the top chefs from around the country, each a winner of one or more prestigious James Beard awards. They share their own winning styles; their food philosophies in innovative, educating and entertaining way. James Beard knew that epicurean excellence could be found in the big cities and smallest towns alike. Julian Serrano's cuisine shines brighter than the glow of the Vegas strip. From Gary Danko in the west to Patrick O'Connell in the east, from the dramatic, new classic cuisine of Ken Oringer and Michael Schlow in the north to the liquid Louisiana charm and sass of Susan Spicer in the south, these chefs are all

culinary stars. Each of the 21 extraordinary contributors to the book share a zealous and unwavering passion for excellence. They are united by a commitment to food and flavor, authenticity and innovation, no matter what their manner of edible artistic expression.

I love how this book is presented. Each contributing chef is profiled in a compelling, personal and intimate way. We get a glimpse into the kitchens, homes, hearts and minds of the James Beard Award-Winners as people as well as professionals. From my perspective as both a James Beard Award-Winner, and host of The Food & Wine Radio Network's nightly dinner party talk radio program where I have interviewed many of these contributors, I particularly appreciate the personal stories and beverage suggestions the chefs give with their recipes. I urge you to use and enjoy this book with gusto. Bring the recipes to life in your own home.

— Jennifer English, a 3-time Beard nominee and winner of the 2002 award for Best Radio Show About Food. Her winning radio style can be heard weeknights at www.businesstalkradio.net.

JACQUES PÉPIN
FOREWORD

I met James Beard in about 1960, not long after my arrival in New York. The food community was small then, and he was struggling to keep his rent paid by giving lessons in the kitchen of his Greenwich Village townhouse.

At that time, he was also quite willing to rent out his kitchen to help with expenses, and I would sometimes rent it to give cooking classes. Although Jim wasn't supposed to attend my classes, nothing could keep him away. I can still see him coming down the spiral staircase that connected his office and bedroom to the kitchen, smiling and puffing, to talk to the students, taste the food, and join in the fun.

With his prodigious memory, Jim once retraced for me an elaborate meal he had enjoyed at La Côte d'Or. He recounted all the dishes and the accompanying wines, describing the aroma of one dish, the texture of another, and leading me through a succession of tastes that he had experienced 20 or 30 years before. He dazzled everyone, certainly me, with his remembrances and exactness about dishes and occasions. He had extremely good food recall. The combination of all that knowledge in this simple, unaffected gentleman made it impossible not to love him. He taught me one of the most important lessons of all: to experience what I eat for what it is, to luxuriate in its aromas, flavors and textures, because tomorrow all that remains of it will be memory.

The Foundation that was created in Jim's memory has been at the forefront of a movement across America to give cuisine the respect that it has long enjoyed in France. When I moved to the United States in 1959 to work at Le Pavillon in New York, fine food in this country equaled French Food. Today, as *Winning Styles Cookbook* so amply demonstrates, American food has come of age, and it may be French, Italian, Cajun, Mexican, Asian or anything in-between. Fine dining in America encompasses root beer floats (see Michael Mina's recipe on page 247), Thai curry sea scallops with black rice cake and green papaya salad (Christine Keff, page 275), loin of lamb with crust of truffles au jus and potatoes parmesan (Julian Serrano, page 291) and so much more. For chefs cooking in the United States today, the possibilities seem limitless. James Beard, as well as the foundation established in his memory, deserve much of the credit.

— Jacques Pépin, who has plenty of winning style of his own, is a six-time James Beard Award-Winner for his many cookbooks and television shows.

THE JAMES BEARD
FOUNDATION

The James Beard Foundation is named after the man widely considered to be "the father of American gastronomy."

The Foundation headquarters is in a renovated, mid-19th century Greenwich Village townhouse that was Beard's home. Today it houses a center for promotion of the culinary arts in America, carrying on the legacy of the late chef, teacher, mentor, consultant, food writer, television personality and cookbook author. Beard died in 1985 after a half-century spent promoting fine food and American gastronomy. As he put it in his seminal book *American Cookery*, "I believe we have a rich and fascinating food heritage that occasionally reaches greatness in our own melting pot way."

James Beard was born May 5, 1903 in Portland, Oregon. His mother was a big proponent of indigenous foods, which she served at the small hotel she ran, and he grew up in an environment that stressed the best local and regional ingredients prepared in the most respectful way. It insured his lifelong appreciation for American food, and his personal winning style.

He didn't come to food professionally until his mid-thirties, when he opened a catering company to supplement the meager income from his early attempts at an acting career and teaching. He published his first cookbook in 1940, with more

than 20 others to follow. By 1955, when he established the James Beard Cooking School, his message of good food, prepared with fresh American foodstuffs, was beginning to awaken his countrymen to their own culinary heritage.

Julia Child says, "He represented the food community. He was an icon. He was Mister Cuisine." It was at her suggestion, after his death, that efforts were begun to preserve his home for historical purposes. Friends, admirers and protegés around the country engaged in a prodigious effort to raise funds that eventually would save and restore the home.

Jim, as he was called by those who knew him well, loved food and people, and delighted in mixing them together at his place on West 12th Street. That tradition continues with established celebrity chefs and promising up-and-comers from around the country presenting exquisite multi-course meals there nearly every night of the year. Through the dinners, the Foundation encourages culinary innovation, creativity and originality. The chefs invited to cook there can showcase their considerable talents, and the patrons enjoy a splendid meal. At $85

to $120 per person including wines, depending on whether you are a member or a guest, Beard House dinners are arguably one of the best culinary bargains in Manhattan.

Interesting remnants of Beard's occupation of the house remain. An elevated alcove in the front that now hosts a dining table was his sleeping area. There is a unique bathroom with all walls mirrored and no bathtub. After he had the tub removed, the corpulent culinary wizard would shower on the marble balcony of the glassed-in rear greenhouse, allegedly scandalizing (or amusing) neighbors with the view. The shower fixture remains. The walls of the main dining rooms (formerly his living area) are painted a shade of red he once described as "living in a bowl of really good tomato soup."

However, The Beard House and Foundation serves as much more than just a place to remember a great chef and to sample great food and wine in convivial company. Members receive a newsletter each month and a semi-annual "Beard House" magazine full of the best in food journalism. The Beard House library and archives contains thousands of culinary-oriented books, documents, videos and photos available for research by members, food writers and students. The Foundation publishes directories of food and beverage professionals, and restaurants. Much of the information is available on the website maintained by the Foundation at www.jamesbeard.org.

In its on-going effort to promote the culinary arts, the Foundation holds seminars on a wide variety of subjects at the house and helps organize similar events around the country. The James Beard Foundation Scholarship Program provides some $400,000 per year to help aspiring food professionals hone their skills. Some of the most popular events are designed for children, especially during the holidays. The latest project is "The Greens," an opportunity for 25- to 40-year-olds to get together to sample fine wines and cuisine at locations all around Manhattan in a relaxed, informal atmosphere.

The Foundation year ends and begins with a two-week series of events centered around Beard's birthday in the spring, culminating with The James Beard Foundation Awards. Dubbed the industry's biggest party, this event honors chefs, restaurants, winemakers, journalists, and cookbook authors in a ceremony often called the "Oscars of the food world."

Through these efforts and many others, The James Beard Foundation succeeds admirably in its efforts to continue and advance the tradition of its namesake. No doubt, Jim would be pleased.

J AMIE S HANNO N

N E W   O R L E A N S ,   L A

American Express Best Chef: Southeast 1999

"My mother prefers to think of death as a gathering in the 'tavern in the sky' of all her favorite people." So wrote Ti Adelaide Martin in her introduction to *Commander's Kitchen* cookbook, which was published, to great acclaim in 2000.

Sadly, just a year later, her co-author Jamie Shannon, executive chef of Commander's Palace in New Orleans, joined that gathering. The Garden District gastronome was only 40 years old.

Shannon left behind his wife Jeannette, young son Tustin, as well as a legion of co-workers and colleagues who greatly admired and respected him.

Ti Adelaide Martin, daughter of Ella Brennan and one of the extended Brennan clan that more or less rules the Crescent City's restaurant world, expressed some of the sentiments of those closest to Shannon as well as her own personal feelings for him when she gave his eulogy.

In it, Martin said she had loved being Shannon's friend because he worked so hard and never felt entitled to things. She also noted he sincerely wanted to see others succeed and helped young cooks do exactly that. Martin went on to say Shannon was a good son, husband, father and friend, as well as chef and leader.

Shannon was brought up not in the famed Garden District, but in the Garden State — New Jersey. Like so many award-winning chefs, his intense interest in food began at a young age. His great-grandparents had left Russia and Austria in the early 1900's and brought an Old Country love of food with them to America. At one time they owned a restaurant in Philadelphia, and after that lived on a farm near Jamie's family. Growing up,

he spent summers with them, learning and internalizing their respect for raising and preparing food.

In his brief lifetime, Shannon graduated from the prestigious Culinary Institute of America and climbed swiftly to top rung at one of the United States' best restaurants (Commander's Palace was recipient of James Beard Awards for Best Service in America in 1993 and America's Most Outstanding Restaurant in 1996). Shannon won his own share of awards along the way, and most importantly acted as mentor to a generation of younger chefs. For that, Shannon gave full credit to Emeril Lagasse, who had been *his* mentor when he came on board at Commander's and Lagasse was executive chef.

He called his method "the extensive career ladder" and it requires everyone in the kitchen to become familiar with every station and every step in the process, and for 16 years at Commander's, 11 of them as executive chef, he prepared his crew to go out and kick butt, just as he did.

There is no better insight into Shannon's culinary style than to read *Commander's Kitchen*. His cooking tips at the end of each recipe demonstrate both his deep and wide knowledge of the process of cooking. You also get a sense from the assured, conversational tone, that he must have been not only a great chef but a good man as well.

Oyster and Artichoke Cakes

Serves: 4

Artichokes:

4 each artichokes, large,
 stems trimmed

1 tablespoon kosher salt

Sauce:

1-1/3 tablespoons unsalted butter

1 tablespoon minced garlic

1 each medium shallot, diced

4 each green onions, sliced thin

3/4 cup Pernod or other
 licorice-flavored liqueur

2/3 cup heavy cream

1/2 pint shucked oysters,
 with their liquid

Kosher salt and freshly ground
 black pepper to taste

Cakes:

2 tablespoons unsalted butter

3 tablespoons minced garlic

1 each medium shallot, diced

1 cup assorted chopped wild
 mushrooms, cleaned

2 each green onions, sliced thin

1/2 pint shucked oysters,
 with their liquid

1/2 cup fresh bread crumbs

1 each large egg, beaten lightly

1/2 cup all-purpose flour

2 tablespoons olive oil

For the Artichokes:

- Arrange the artichokes upside down in a large steaming basket set in a large pot over 2 inches of water and the kosher salt. Cover and bring to a boil over high heat. Reduce the heat to moderate and steam the artichokes until they are tender when pierced with a knife, or until the large leaves pull off easily, about 25 minutes. Drain, run the artichokes under cold water to stop the cooking, and transfer to a platter. When cool enough to handle, remove and discard the artichoke leaves. Using a small spoon, scrape out and discard the hairy chokes. Cut each artichoke bottom into eighths, like a pie.

For the Sauce:

- Place a medium skillet over medium-high heat until hot but not smoking. Add 1 teaspoon (*1/3 tablespoon*) of butter and melt. Add the garlic and shallot and cook for 30 seconds, or until golden. Add the green onions and cook for about 1 minute. Carefully add the 3/4 cup of Pernod (*it will flame*) and cook for 30 seconds, or until flame dies. Add the cream and boil the mixture until it is reduced by half, about 1 minute. Add the oysters and cook until the edges curl, about 1 minute. Remove the skillet from heat and add the remaining 1 tablespoon of butter, stirring, until butter is completely melted. Season the sauce with salt and pepper to taste. Set the sauce aside and keep warm.

For the Cakes:

- Place a large skillet over medium-high heat until hot but not smoking. Add the butter and melt. Add the garlic and shallot and cook for 30 seconds, or until golden. Add the mushrooms and green onions and cook for about 2 minutes, or until the mushrooms are cooked through. Add artichoke pieces and cook for 30 seconds. Add the oysters, and cook until the edges curl, about 1 minute.

- Transfer the mixture to a bowl and chill in the refrigerator until cool, about 30 to 45 minutes. Stir the bread crumbs and the beaten egg into the chilled oyster mixture.

- Place the flour in a shallow bowl. Divide the cake mixture into four balls and press the mixture into disks about 1 inch high. Dredge the cakes in the flour.

- Place a large skillet over medium-high heat until hot. Add the olive oil and heat until hot but not smoking. Add the cakes and cook for about 1-1/2 minutes per side, or until golden and heated through. Drain on paper towels.

To Finish and Serve:

- Divide the cakes among four appetizer plates and top with the poached oysters and sauce.

Catfish Pecan with Lemon-Thyme-Pecan Butter

Serves: 6

Pecan Flour:
3/4 cup pecan halves
1-1/2 cups all-purpose flour
Creole seafood seasoning to taste

Catfish:
1 each medium egg
1 cup milk
6 each catfish fillets, 6 ounces each *(may substitute flounder, trout, bass or other small, non-oily fish)*, free of bones and scales
Creole seafood seasoning to taste
4 tablespoons butter

Lemon-Thyme-Pecan Butter:
8 tablespoons butter
1-1/2 cups pecan halves
3 each lemons, cut in half
1 teaspoon Worcestershire sauce
6 each large sprigs of thyme
Kosher salt and pepper to taste

Finish:
3/4 cup pecan halves
1/4 pound crabmeat
1 cup mixed greens

For the Pecan Flour:

- Place the pecans, the flour, and the Creole seasoning in the bowl of a food processor. Process until finely ground. Transfer the pecan flour to a large bowl.

For the Catfish:

- Whisk the egg in a large mixing bowl and add the milk. Season both sides of the fish fillets with Creole seasoning. One at a time, place the fillets in the egg wash. Remove one fillet from the egg wash, let excess fluid drain back into the bowl. Dredge the fillet in the pecan flour and coat both sides, shaking off any excess. Transfer to a dry sheet pan, and repeat with the remaining fillets.

- Place a large sauté pan over high heat and add 2 tablespoons of the butter. Heat until the butter is completely melted and starts to bubble. Place three fish fillets in the pan, skin-side up, and cook for 30 seconds. Reduce the heat to medium, and cook for another 1-1/2 to 2 minutes, or until the fillets are evenly brown and crisp. Turn the fish over and cook on the second side for 2 to 2-1/2 minutes, or until the fish is firm to the touch and evenly browned.

- Remove the fish and place on a baking rack. Wipe the sauté pan clean with a paper towel. Add the remaining 2 tablespoons of butter and repeat the sautéing process with the remaining pieces of fish.

For the Lemon-Thyme-Pecan Butter:

- When all the fish fillets are cooked, wipe the pan clean once again and place it over high heat. Melt the butter and, just as the butter starts to turn brown, add the pecans and sauté for 2 to 3 minutes or until the nuts are toasted, stirring occasionally. Put the lemon halves face down in the pan, first squeezing a little juice from each half. Add the Worcestershire and thyme, season with salt and pepper, and cook for 30 seconds more or until the thyme starts to wilt and becomes very aromatic.

To Finish and Serve:

- Place one fish fillet and a lemon half on each of six dinner plates. Spoon some pecan butter around each piece of fish, and use the wilted thyme, crabmeat, mixed greens and pecan halves to garnish the plates.

Jamie Shannon's Beverage Recommendations

Oyster and Artichoke Cakes
A very enthusiastic recommendation for the Chardonnays from Chassagne-Montrachet. They are a bit more expensive but a perfect match with this dish. These wines have a bit of a licorice flavor.
page 7

Catfish Pecan with Lemon-Thyme-Pecan Butter
Chardonnay with a toasted almond *(or any nut flavor)*, specifically from the Meursault region of France.
page 9

Garlic-Crusted Redfish with Creole Succotash and Sweet Potato Hay
Chardonnay that is light-bodied and floral that can stand up to the sweetness of the succotash; specifically from the Russian River Valley.
page 11

Garlic-Crusted Redfish with Creole Succotash and Sweet Potato Hay

Serves: 4

Sweet Potato Hay:

3 cups canola oil

1 each large sweet potato, peeled and cut into julienne *(about 2-1/2 cups)*

Kosher salt and freshly ground black pepper to taste

Creole Succotash:

1 each medium turnip, peeled, cut into medium dice *(about 1-1/2 cups)*

1 each medium sweet potato, peeled, cut into medium dice *(about 1-1/2 cups)*

1 each small butternut squash, peeled, cut into medium dice *(about 1-1/2 cups)*

1 cup lima beans, fresh or frozen

1 tablespoon olive oil

3 cloves garlic, minced

2 each medium leeks, cut into medium dice *(about 1-1/2 cups)*

3/4 cup vinegar

8 tablespoons cold unsalted butter, cut into small pieces

Kosher salt and freshly ground black pepper to taste

1 tablespoon minced parsley or fresh tarragon

Garlic-Crusted Redfish:

4 each redfish fillets, 6 ounces each, boned, scaled, skin on

Kosher salt and freshly ground black pepper to taste

1 cup flour

1/3 cup minced garlic

2 each large egg whites, whisked lightly

1/2 cup olive oil

For the Sweet Potato Hay:

- Heat the canola oil in a deep skillet or deep fryer until a deep-fry thermometer registers 350 degrees. Fry the julienne sweet potatoes in batches until golden, about 2 to 3 minutes. Drain on paper towels. While still hot, form into small balls that resemble tumbleweeds and season with salt and pepper. Keep warm.

For the Creole Succotash:

- Blanch the turnip, sweet potato, squash and lima beans in boiling salted water in a large saucepan until just tender when pierced with a fork, about 7 minutes. Drain in a large colander.

- Heat a large skillet until hot but not smoking and add the olive oil. Add the garlic and sauté until golden, about 30 seconds. Add the leeks and cook until translucent, about 2 minutes. Add the vegetable mixture and the vinegar, and cook until the liquid is reduced by half, about 2 minutes. Reduce heat to medium and add the butter, stirring until butter is emulsified, about 2 minutes. Season with salt and pepper and stir in parsley or tarragon. Set the succotash aside and keep warm.

For the Garlic-Crusted Redfish:

- Check the fish pieces, removing all visible scales and bones. Season each piece of fish with salt and pepper on both sides. Combine flour, garlic, and salt and pepper to taste in a shallow bowl. Place egg whites in another shallow bowl. Dip the skin side of each fish piece only into the egg whites, and then dip into flour mixture. Shake off excess flour mixture.

- Place a skillet with 1/4 cup of the olive oil on the stove over medium heat. When the oil is hot but not smoking, place half of the fish pieces, skin-side down, into the skillet and cook until golden brown, about 2 minutes. Reduce the heat to medium-low. Cover the skillet and cook the fish for another 2 minutes, or until done *(be sure not to let skin get too dark)*. If skin gets too dark remove cover and place skillet in 350 degree oven until cooked. Remove the fish to drain on a paper towel. Wipe out the skillet and repeat with the remaining fish and remaining 1/4 cup oil.

To Finish and Serve:

- Divide the succotash among each of four dinner plates. Arrange a fish fillet over the succotash on each plate and top each with sweet potato hay.

ROBERTO DONNA

WASHINGTON, DC

American Express Best Chef: Mid-Atlantic, 1996

After almost 25 years in Washington, D.C., Roberto Donna is part of the fabric of the city, but his roots are still firmly planted in the Piedmont region of Italy. Born in a small town near Torino, food always played an integral role in his life.

His mother owned a grocery store. There was a restaurant just next door and Donna spent summers in Asti with his grandparents who grew vegetables. "Grandfather would carry rock salt in his pocket, so he could pick, season and eat a ripe tomato anytime. My early memories are all of food," he says.

He would accompany his grandfather to market where they sold the homegrown produce. "There was a bakery nearby and I knew there would be fresh pizza coming out of the oven at seven in the morning and again at ten, and I'd be right there," reminisces Donna.

At home in Torino, he hung out at the next-door restaurant. "I'd come from school and eat lunch and then go over to the restaurant and eat again. I spent so much time there the cooks started giving me chores to do to keep me out of the way. Soon I was working Saturdays and Sundays."

It surprised no one when at the tender age of 13 Donna enrolled in the esteemed culinary academy, Instituto Alberghiero di Torino. He graduated five years later with the highest marks in the school's history. Intending to expand his professional horizons, he worked in England, France and Switzerland but says, frankly, the experiences just made him believe even more deeply that Italian food was the best in the world and he was determined to spread the word about it.

When the opportunity to take a job as sous chef at Romeo and Juliet restaurant in Washington came along, Donna jumped at it. He worked there for a year and then returned to Italy; but the District had gotten under his skin, and shortly thereafter he got an offer he couldn't refuse to take over as head chef of Romeo and Juliet.

He opened the first restaurant of his own, Galileo, in 1984 with a firm purpose in mind.

"Essentially, at the time there was no truly authentic Italian restaurant in the area. Italian wines weren't respected. I brought in great wines no one had ever heard of and introduced quail, risotto and tiramisu to D.C. I wanted to do it right."

In Donna's book, doing it right means making bread and fresh mozzarella daily, growing herbs behind the restaurant, patronizing local growers for the best seasonal produce and going directly to the Mother Country for cheeses, olive oil, canned tomatoes, pasta and wines. It means using the ingredients that Piedmont is known for such as game, rice, truffles, milk fed veal. It also means taking the time-honored traditional dishes of Piedmont, reproducing them with integrity and sometimes putting his own personal spin on them.

Galileo's wine list tops out at around 2000 selections and it has earned the prestigious Wine Spectator Grand Award of Excellence, one of only 94 in the world. When the restaurant was redecorated a few years ago, Donna installed a temperature controlled cheese cellar which holds up to 75 different varieties, many of them little known in the U.S.

The educational process doesn't end with diners; Donna is also well known in the culinary community for mentoring young chefs. Mike Nayeri, his general manager for the past 18 years says, "He allows his staff to grow while he is teaching and training them. There is a whole generation of people who have gone on to own restaurants after working with Roberto."

If "a whole generation" sounds like hyperbole, it's not. That group of chefs is a direct result of Donna's incredible energy and enterprise. In the years since he opened Galileo, he has owned as many as 12 restaurants in the Washington area. The number is now down to a relatively modest five, four of which are run by partners.

What slowed Donna down? Very simply, while creating and administrating restaurants provided it's own thrills, he missed cooking. At first, he considered opening a small gourmet restaurant, but decided it would not be financially feasible. The answer presented itself when the tenants next door to Galileo moved out. Donna moved right in, creating a restaurant within a restaurant, which he calls his Laboratorio. It fits in Galileo like a sausage in its skin.

The spacious, spare yet elegant interior of Galileo includes a cozy bar in front, a rare-as-hens-teeth-in-the-big-city outdoor dining area in back and rooms for private parties. Architectural detailing, swooping arches and cozy nooks, along with massive floral arrangements and walls covered with Donna's framed awards and commendations lends character and color.

Totally enclosed, but visible from the main dining room through a glass wall, Il Laboratorio del Galileo stars a stage-like kitchen with a commodious granite work station for Donna to perform in full view of the seven tables. Kibitzing with the chef, by the way, is encouraged. Done in shades of lemon and cream, the room exhibits paintings by Piedmontese artists and graceful bronze sculptures by Joanne Nuss.

the menu also changes daily and diners are encouraged to build their own four or six course meals from the available selections.

If his schedule weren't already hectic enough, Donna also participates in a wide array of community services that include D.C. Central Kitchen, which provides both food and restaurant training opportunities to the homeless. He serves on the board of The American Institute of Wine and Food and The James Beard Foundation, preparing one or two dinners at the Beard House in New York each year and several more Beard benefit dinners around the country. In addition, Donna is a member of Share Our Strength as well as vice-president of Gruppo Ristoranti Italiani, a consortium of restaurants around the country dedicated to promoting authentic Italian food culture. Although he has curtailed his travel schedule, he is on the road at least twice a month and gets back to Italy to reconnect six or eight times a year.

Donna lives almost directly behind the restaurant which means he is virtually always on call. He spends the little free time he does have enjoying long distance biking, martial arts and karate and other vigorous forms of exercise, thus hoping to balance out the heroic eating and drinking that goes along with being a chef and restaurateur.

Ask Donna where he goes from here and he answers without hesitation, "My goal is to continue to make my customers feel comfortable with the food. Every ethnic restaurant should do that. We are the ambassadors of our cuisine."

Donna holds court there most nights depending on his travel schedule. Each evening some 30 fortunate diners experience a 12 course tasting menu that may include a hot and cold appetizer, soup, stuffed pasta, rolled pasta, risotto, a seafood entrée, a poultry or meat entrée followed by the cheese course, pre-dessert and dessert. Guests can opt for wines especially chosen for each course. When making reservations, guests are encouraged to express preferences, dislikes and dietary restrictions. Donna keeps track of each evening's menu by computer and never exactly repeats any except for the signature ending of bomboloni, irresistible little hot-from-the-fryer Italian doughnuts.

The Laboratorio doubles as an interactive cooking school in the spring and fall with Donna teaching everything from basic risotto techniques to a five course meal highlighting various regions of Italy to students who end the session enjoying the fruits of their labor along with a glass of wine.

Meanwhile, in Galileo proper, it is business as usual, lunch Monday through Friday and dinner seven nights a week. Here

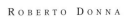

Asparagus and Mozzarella Bocconcini Salad in a Black Truffle Dressing

Serves: 4

Black Truffle Dressing:

1 ounce black truffles (*quantity of the truffles is personal*), cut into julienne

3 ounces roasted Vidalia onions, cut into fine julienne

2 tablespoons balsamic vinegar

6 tablespoons olive oil

Salt and pepper to taste

Asparagus:

16 spears medium asparagus

4 each Mozzarella Bocconcini

For the Black Truffle Dressing:

- Place the onions in a bowl with the julienned black truffles. Add the balsamic vinegar and olive oil and adjust with salt and pepper. Let it rest at least 24 hours to allow the black truffles to transfer flavor to the dressing.

For the Asparagus and Mozzarella Bocconcini Salad:

- Wash and clean the asparagus. If necessary, peel them. Steam until tender. Place them on a serving dish around the bocconcini and top with the black truffle dressing. Serve warm for best results.

Octopus Salami with a Potato and Basil Salad

Serves: 8-10 as an appetizer

Octopus:

3 pounds fresh octopus

1 pound red bliss potatoes, cut into 3/4-inch cubes

Octopus Cooking Liquid:

7-1/2 cups dry white wine

1 each onion, large

1 each carrot

4 each celery stalks

1/2 cup chopped flat-leaf parsley

1 each bay leaf

1 teaspoon black peppercorns

1 each lemon

2 each wine bottle corks

2 tablespoons salt

Dressing:

1 cup olive oil

Juice of two lemons

1 clove garlic

14 each fresh basil leaves

4 teaspoons chopped flat-leaf parsley

1 slice white bread, crust removed

1 each egg, hard-boiled

5 each gherkins

1/4 cup chopped Kalamta black olives

Salt and pepper to taste

Finish:

Olive oil to taste

Oregano to taste, dried or fresh

Salt and pepper to taste

4-5 sprigs fresh basil for garnish

For the Octopus:

- Rinse the octopus in fresh water several times and then remove the mouth and the eyes. Holding the octopus by the head, smash the head a few times on the countertop in order to break up some of the hard fibers within. This will help ensure that the octopus will be tender after cooking.

For the Octopus Cooking Liquid:

- Place all of the ingredients for the cooking liquid in a large stockpot. The corks are included to help keep the octopus tender while cooking. Add the octopus. Bring the mixture to a boil, reduce heat and simmer for 45 minutes. Remove the stockpot from the heat and allow to cool for 10 minutes. Remove the octopus from the liquid and place into a tube shaped cylindrical bag. Squeeze as much liquid out of the octopus as possible. Tie it well at 1-inch intervals. Place in the refrigerator with a heavy weight on top of it. Refrigerate for at least 6 hours.

- Remove the corks from the cooking liquid in the stockpot and discard. Put the cubed potatoes into the stockpot. Bring to a boil, reduce heat and simmer for 10 minutes, or until potatoes are crisp-tender. Drain the potatoes and place in a large bowl.

For the Dressing:

- Place all of the dressing ingredients except the black olives in the blender. Blend for 1 minute on medium speed. Mix the olives with the potato cubes in a bowl. Add the dressing and toss gently. Put the mixture into a ring mold and refrigerate until needed.

To Finish and Serve:

- Slice the octopus very thinly and place on serving platter. Season lightly with olive oil, oregano, salt and pepper. Turn the molded potato salad mixture out onto the serving platter over the octopus. Garnish with fresh basil leaves.

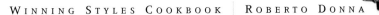

Escarole Soup with Potato and Meatballs

Serves: 4

Meatballs:

1/2 **pound** pork sausage

1/2 **pound** ground veal

2 **each** eggs

1/4 **cup** pine nuts

1/4 **cup** raisins

1/4 **cup** grated Parmesan cheese

Escarole Soup:

6 **tablespoons** olive oil

2 **cloves** garlic, minced

1 **each** small onion, finely
chopped

3-1/2 **pounds** escarole, cleaned,
dried and chopped

2 **each** potatoes, cut into
1/2-inch cubes

Salt and pepper to taste

Finish:

1/4 **cup** grated Parmesan cheese

4 **sprigs** fried parsley *(optional)*

For the Meatballs:

- In a large bowl, combine the pork, veal, eggs, pine nuts, raisins and Parmesan cheese and mix well. Shape the mixture into meatballs approximately the size of hazelnuts and fry them in a heavy bottom sauté pan over medium heat until golden brown. Remove from pan, drain well, and refrigerate.

For the Escarole Soup:

- Heat the olive oil in a soup pot or stockpot over medium-low heat. Add the minced garlic and the finely chopped onion and cook until the onion is translucent. Add the escarole. Sauté for 2 minutes. Add the potato cubes. Add just enough water to the pan to fully cover the mixture *(approximately 1 quart)*. Simmer over low heat for 20 minutes. Add the meatballs and cook over low heat for an additional 10 minutes. Adjust seasonings to taste.

To Finish and Serve:

- Garnish with Parmesan cheese and fried parsley, if desired.

Warm Salad of Shrimp, Porcini and Potato

Serves: 4

Salad:

1 **head** frisée lettuce

1 **cup** potatoes, cut into
1/2-inch cubes

8 **ounces** cremini mushrooms

1 **recipe** court bouillon
(see page 21, side bar)

1 **pound** medium head-on
shrimp or prawns, or 2/3 pound
shrimp without heads

1/2 **cup** olive oil

4 **tablespoons** smashed garlic

5 **each** basil leaves, chopped

1 **teaspoon** chopped flat-leaf
parsley

Salt and pepper to taste

Finish:

1 **each** lemon, cut into
eight wedges

For the Shrimp Salad:

- Cut the root from the frisée lettuce and separate the leaves. Rinse, dry thoroughly and place in refrigerator to chill.

- Boil the cubed potatoes in salted water for 8 minutes. Drain the potatoes and set aside.

- Thoroughly clean the cremini mushrooms and cut them in half and set aside.

- Prepare the court bouillon using the recipe *(see page 21, side bar)*. Put strained bouillon in a saucepan.

- Peel and devein the shrimp, saving the heads for garnish. Place the shrimp in the court bouillon over low to medium heat and cook for 2 to 3 minutes. Immediately remove shrimp from the bouillon and plunge into an ice-water bath. Drain the shrimp and set aside.

- In a sauté pan, heat 1/4 cup of the olive oil over medium-low heat. Add the garlic and cook until the garlic is golden, taking care not to burn. Remove the pan from the burner and add the basil and parsley.

- Place the potatoes and the mushrooms in a bowl. Add the hot seasoned olive oil, the remaining 1/4 cup of olive oil and the shrimp and stir together gently. Add salt and pepper to taste.

To Finish and Serve:

- Place a small bunch of frisée on each of four serving plates. Squeeze one wedge of lemon over the frisée on each plate. Put 1/4 of the salad mixture on top of the frisée on each plate. Garnish each plate with an additional lemon wedge, and 1 or 2 shrimp heads, if desired.

Lobster Risotto

Serves: 2

Lobster:
1 each 4-pound lobster

Lobster Broth:
1/4 cup olive oil
2 cloves garlic, crushed slightly
1 each carrot, cut into
  small pieces
1/2 cup brandy
1/4 cup dry white wine
2 tablespoons tomato paste
1/2 cup chopped parsley sprigs
1 each thyme sprig
2 quarts water

Risotto:
1/4 cup olive oil
1 each medium onion,
  very finely chopped
1-1/2 cups Italian Arborio rice
1/4 cup dry white wine
12 each clams
12 each mussels
12 each shrimp
1 pound squid, thoroughly
  cleaned and, if large, chopped

Finish:
3 tablespoons butter
2 teaspoons chopped parsley
2 teaspoons chopped basil
Salt and pepper to taste

For the Lobster:

- In a large pot, cook the lobster in boiling water for 3 minutes. Remove them from the boiling water and plunge into ice-cold water for 1 minute. Drain and let cool until the lobster can be handled without burning your fingers. Crack the body and claws, split the tails, and remove all of the lobster meat from the carcass, setting the meat aside. Crack or chop the lobster carcass into small pieces.

For the Lobster Broth:

- In a stockpot, heat the olive oil. Add garlic, chopped lobster carcass and the carrot. Sauté until the vegetables start to sweat. At this point, add the brandy and cook until it is completely reduced. Then add 1/4 cup of the white wine, and again let it reduce completely. Add the tomato paste, parsley sprigs, thyme and water. Bring to a boil and then reduce heat and simmer for 25 minutes, skimming impurities from the top as needed. Strain the broth and set aside, discarding the solids.

For the Risotto:

- In a large sauté pan, heat the olive oil and add the finely chopped onions. Cook until the onions are translucent. Add the rice to the pan and toast for a few minutes until lightly browned. Add the white wine and cook until wine is completely reduced. Start adding the strained lobster broth 1/2 cup at a time, stirring constantly until all liquid is absorbed before adding additional broth. There should be approximately 3-1/2 cups of lobster broth to be incorporated into the risotto.

- Once all of the lobster broth has been absorbed, reduce to low flame and add the clams. Cook for 5 minutes. Then add the mussels, shrimp and squid. Cook for 3 or 4 minutes, and then add the lobster meat, cut in small pieces, and finish cooking for approximately 4 minutes.

To Finish and Serve:

- Remove the pan from the flame and add the butter, chopped parsley and basil. Stir for 2 minutes, season with salt and pepper to taste and serve while still very hot.

Court Bouillon

For the Warm Salad of Shrimp,
Porcini and Potato Recipe, see page 19

1-1/2 quarts water
1/4 cup lemon juice
1/4 cup white wine
1 each celery stalk, chopped
1 each small onion, peeled and
  chopped
1 each leek, white part only,
  cleaned and chopped
1 teaspoon white peppercorns
2 each bay leaves
1 bunch parsley stems
1 teaspoon dried thyme

Place all ingredients in stockpot and heat to a boil. Reduce heat to low and simmer for 25 minutes. Strain.

Braised Tuna Fish, Sicilian Style

Serves: 2

Sauce:

1 **clove** garlic

1 **each** onion, cut into julienne

1/4 **cup** olive oil

1 **tablespoon** sliced green olives

2 **each** celery stalks,
  cut into julienne

1 **tablespoon** capers

1 **pound** canned Italian peeled
  tomatoes, chopped

1 **each** bay leaf

2 **tablespoons** raisins

2 **tablespoons** pine nuts

1 **pinch** oregano

2 **tablespoons** red wine vinegar

1 **tablespoon** sugar

Tuna:

1/4 **cup** olive oil

4 **pieces** tuna steak, each
  3/4-inch thick and cut into
  2-inch squares

Finish:

2 **each** toasted focaccia wedges
  (optional)

For the Sauce:

- In a heavy-bottom sauté pan over medium heat, sauté the garlic and onion for 2 minutes in the olive oil. Add the olives, celery, capers, tomatoes, bay leaf, raisins, pine nuts, oregano, red wine vinegar and sugar to the pan and cook for 10 minutes, or until the vegetables are tender.

For the Tuna:

- In a saucepan over medium-high heat, heat the olive oil and sear the fish steaks for 2 minutes on each side. Add the sauce mixture to the saucepan with the fish, lower the heat to medium, and cook for an additional 5 minutes.

To Finish and Serve:

- Divide the vegetable mixture evenly between two serving plates. Place two tuna squares on top of the vegetable mixture on each plate. Garnish with toasted focaccia wedges, if desired.

Ravioli Alla Donna

Donna still uses a ravioli press that was presented to him by the chefs he worked for as a boy in his hometown of San Raffaele Cimena. One of his favorite raviolis has a boiled potato and sautéed leek filling mixed with Parmesan cheese. It is served with a sauce of heavy cream, Parmesan cheese and butter.

Sweet Italian Fennel Tart with Star Anise Ice Cream

Serves: 4

Ice Cream:

1-1/2 cups milk
1/2 cup heavy cream
1/2-inch piece vanilla bean
4 each star anise
8 each egg yolks
1/2 cup granulated sugar

Crispy Disk:

3 sheets phyllo dough
1/4 cup butter, melted
1/2 cup powdered sugar

Fennel:

12 ounces fresh fennel,
  bulb only, diced
3/4 cup granulated sugar
1 cup water
1/4-inch piece vanilla bean
1/2 each fresh lemon, sliced

For the Ice Cream:

- Bring milk, cream, vanilla bean and star anise to a boil in a saucepan. Remove the pan from the heat, set aside, and allow the mixture to steep for 2 hours.

- Beat together the egg yolks and sugar in a bowl until lemon colored and smooth. Put the egg and sugar mixture in a large saucepan. Remove the vanilla bean and star anise from the milk mixture and combine it with the egg yolks and sugar. Cook the mixture over medium heat, stirring constantly, until it coats the back of a spoon *(about 180 degrees – do not boil or mixture will curdle)*. Cool to 60 degrees. Freeze in an ice cream maker according to manufacturer's directions.

For the Crispy Disk:

- Preheat oven to 350 degrees. Place one sheet of the phyllo dough on a cookie sheet that has been brushed with melted butter. Brush the sheet of dough with more melted butter and sprinkle with approximately 1/3 of the powdered sugar. Place second and third sheets of phyllo dough on top of the first, brushing with melted butter and dusting with powdered sugar between each sheet. Cut the phyllo dough into 2-1/2-inch squares. Bake at 350 degrees until golden brown. Cool, place in an airtight container, and set aside.

For the Fennel:

- Place all ingredients in a saucepan and cook over low to medium heat approximately 45 minutes, or until tender. Drain fennel.

To Finish and Serve:

- Place a crispy disk on the center of each of four serving plates. Layer the fennel and two more crispy disks on each plate, Napolean-style. Serve with a scoop of star anise ice cream on the side.

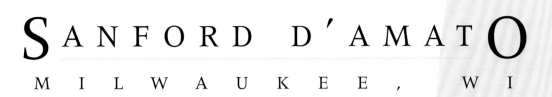

SANFORD D'AMATO

MILWAUKEE, WI

American Express Best Chef: Midwest, 1996

Though he is an admitted "baseball sap," the Brewers weren't the only thing that brought Sanford D'Amato back home to Milwaukee. In his words, "It was about having a life as well as a career."

Not that the New York restaurant scene wasn't plenty alluring. D'Amato graduated from the Culinary Institute of America in 1974, where Peter Van Erp mentored him. D'Amato describes Dutch-born Van Erp's approach as "True to each cuisine he cooked. It had an enormous influence on me."

After an extra year at the Institute on a fellowship, D'Amato worked at the famed Waldorf Astoria, but he was restless and still wanted to learn more. "In the early seventies, French restaurants in New York hired only French chefs and I wanted to apprentice in one," says D'Amato.

He struggled to breach the Gallic wall, and with an introductory letter from Van Erp in hand and typical quiet determination, D'Amato finally progressed through a procession of prestigious French restaurants including Le Chantilly and Le Veau d' Or. "I learned how a classic French kitchen operates, and Roland Chenous, the best fish chef I ever met, taught me about seafood."

After a stint working with New York pastry chef Dieter Schorner, who he calls "brilliant," D'Amato took a long hard look at where he wanted to go next.

"It is so difficult to balance your life when you are caught up in that big city thing. I came back to Milwaukee intending to open a restaurant, knowing I could have a good lifestyle as well," says D'Amato.

Milwaukee was where his family lived and where his career had started. He grew up working in his grandparents' neighborhood grocery store and before long he was preparing to-go items like olive salad. "My grandparents lived next door to the store and we'd go over for dinner. Grandpa was a great cook, and he'd make pasta and meat-balls and speidini."

Before long, Sandy was cooking at home along with his father who, taking note of his son's interest and talent in the kitchen, arranged, through a beer salesman that serviced the store, to get the younger D'Amato a job in a German restaurant specializing in fish fries.

D'Amato was so serious about preparing for a culinary career he signed on for an apprenticeship in a work release program for prisoners. The director commented that D'Amato was obviously committed to educating himself since he was the only voluntary participant in the program.

Upon his homecoming, D'Amato worked at John Byron's restaurant where he both built a local reputation and met and married Angie, his wife of the past 24 years. He says, "I'd set a goal for myself that I'd have my own restaurant by the time I was forty."

He accomplished that goal in a surprising and touching way. Explains D'Amato, "In 1989, my dad decided to sell the family grocery store. Angie and I thought, 'Well, let's go for it. We can be our own landlords and live upstairs from the restaurant. At least we'll always have something to eat.'"

His father was worried about the location, which was near a freeway under construction. However, it was also only eight blocks from downtown and the major hotels, and since the D'Amatos intended it to be a destination restaurant, they didn't think it mattered.

It didn't. Once the sleek oriental-contemporary dining room was completed, the national spotlight soon was trained on D'Amato and his namesake Sanford restaurant. "We started the restaurant as a labor of love rather than a business," says

Angie. "We wanted to have food that tasted good, great service and to make people happy. We'd visited France a few years before and took notes on all the niceties that give a place pizzazz, like replacing silver from a clean, folded napkin rather than from the servers hand."

Serendipitously, D'Amato's self-described modern ethnic culinary style was right at home in Milwaukee, a city which has always valued ethnicity. His multi-course prixe fix menus contain dishes with Mediterranean and Asian influences but the chef prefers not to cross or combine culinary cultures. "For me, mixing the flavors doesn't work; the most I will do is give the dish a contemporary twist."

His sparkling seafood preparations and sumptuous desserts reflect his apprenticeships in those specialties. D'Amato's quest to focus on French cuisine bore fruit when the couple opened casual Coquette Cafe in 1999.

The D'Amatos live in a 100-plus year-old Victorian decorated with a charming mix of antiques and contemporary furnishings across the street from the Sanford restaurant. They share quarters with lop-eared bunnies Walt and Frankie. (And, no, rabbit is not featured on Sanford's menu.)

They finally have the time and ability to have that life outside of the restaurants. "It took a lot of effort,"

says D'Amato. "We had to make sure our team at Sanford could handle things without us there every minute before we opened Coquette. Now, both restaurants are firmly established."

The D'Amatos play tennis and are avid bikers, practicing for touring France by bicycling along Lake Michigan. Both are dedicated moviegoers and have a permanent Monday night movie date. Of course, living in Milwaukee means Brewer season tickets for baseball fanatic Sandy.

The couple owns a compact RV and travels the country visiting chef friends. A tour of the South gave Sandy a chance to sample various styles of barbecue and Angie is looking forward to her first trip West.

Discussing the future, D'Amato says "I'm living my goal, so I need a new one. In addition to my weekly column for the *Milwaukee Journal Sentinel*, I'll probably do more writing."

Along with more of his extraordinary cooking, it's something to which we can all look forward.

Mussel Timbale with Green Olives and Romesco Sauce

Serves: 8

Romesco Sauce:

1/4 cup regular olive oil

1 each large shallot, peeled and sliced *(about 2 tablespoons sliced)*

2-3 cloves garlic, peeled

1/2 cup raw almonds, blanched

2 medium dried New Mexico chiles, seeded, stems removed, and cut into 1/4-inch strips

1 can plum tomatoes in juice, drained *(12 ounces)*

2 each bay leaves

1 teaspoon kosher salt

1/4 teaspoon fresh ground black pepper

2-1/2 tablespoons red wine vinegar

1/4 cup dry white wine

2 tablespoons water

Mussels:

2 pounds mussels, scrubbed, beards removed

2 tablespoons olive oil

1 tablespoon sliced shallots

1/2 tablespoon sliced garlic

2 each thyme sprigs

10 each peppercorns, crushed

1 cup dry white wine

Potatoes and Olives:

1 pound russet potatoes, peeled and diced small

1/2 pound green olives, pitted, cut into small pieces *(Sicilian or Manzanillo)*

2 tablespoons flat-leaf parsley

Kosher salt and freshly ground pepper to taste

Finish:

1 tablespoon almond or walnut oil

1 tablespoon grapeseed oil

1 teaspoon lemon juice

1 tablespoon chopped flat-leaf parsley

Kosher salt and freshly ground pepper to taste

Salted almonds, sliced and toasted *(optional)*

For the Romesco Sauce:

• In a non-reactive sauté pan over low to medium heat, add the oil, shallot, garlic and almonds and cook slowly for 10 minutes. Mixture should lightly brown but not get too dark. Add the chiles and sauté for 1 minute. Add the tomatoes, bay leaves, salt and pepper and cook slowly for 3 to 4 minutes. Add the vinegar, white wine and water and bring to a boil. Remove the bay leaves, and carefully pour the sauce into a blender. Pulse and blend until smooth. Strain the mixture through a medium-mesh strainer. Adjust seasoning if needed. Refrigerate until needed. Warm up slowly before serving.

For the Mussels:

• Open mussels that do not close immediately when tapped should be discarded

• Place a pot large enough to hold twice the amount of mussels over medium heat. Add the oil. When the oil is warm, add the shallots, garlic, thyme and peppercorns and sauté for 30 seconds. Add the mussels and wine and cover. Cook until all of the mussels have opened. Halfway through the cooking process, stir the mussels so they cook evenly. Drain into a colander, reserving the liquid for the potatoes. Allow the mussels to cool. Once cooled, remove the mussels from the shells and refrigerate the meats until needed.

For the Potatoes and Olives:

• Blanch the potatoes in boiling salted water until they are tender. Drain potatoes, and while still warm, cover with the reserved mussel cooking liquid. Allow the potatoes to cool slightly and then refrigerate. Once the potatoes are fully chilled, remove them from the refrigerator, drain and discard the mussel liquid. Add the olives, 1/4 cup of the romesco sauce, and parsley to the potatoes. Season to taste with salt and pepper.

To Finish and Serve:

• Toss mussel meats with almond oil, grapeseed oil, lemon juice, parsley and 1 tablespoon of the romesco sauce. Season to taste with salt and pepper. Place a 3- to 4-inch ring mold with no bottom on each of eight serving plates. Divide the mussel mixture between the molds, packing lightly. Top each portion with potato and olive mixture. Pack down and remove the molds. Garnish with romesco sauce and almonds.

Chickpea, Escarole and Eggplant Salad with Smoked Paprika Vinaigrette

Serves: 8

Chickpeas:

1-1/2 cups chickpeas
1 each small onion, peeled
1 each carrot
1 each stalk of celery
3 quarts salted water
1/2 tablespoon ground
  black pepper
6 cloves garlic
1 each bay leaf
1 each ham shank, smoked
  (optional)

Eggplant:

4 each Japanese eggplants
  (approximately 8 ounces each),
  cut into 1/4-inch slices
2 tablespoons chopped garlic
1/4 cup olive oil
Kosher salt and freshly ground
  black pepper to taste

Escarole:

4 heads escarole, rinsed, cored
  and cut into large dice
1/4 cup olive oil
Salt and pepper to taste

Smoked Paprika Vinaigrette:

1/4 cup grapeseed oil
1/4 cup finely chopped shallots
3 each bay leaves
2 tablespoons finely chopped
  garlic
1 tablespoon hot smoked
  paprika*
1 tablespoon sweet smoked
  paprika*
2 teaspoons kosher salt
3/4 teaspoon freshly ground
  black pepper
1/4 cup sherry vinegar
1/4 cup extra-virgin olive oil
2 tablespoons walnut oil

For the Chickpeas:

- Rinse the chickpeas and soak them in 6 cups hot tap water at room temperature until cooled. Stir, cover and refrigerate overnight.

- Drain chickpeas and rinse. Place all the ingredients in a saucepan and bring to a boil. Reduce heat and simmer, half-covered, for about 25 to 30 minutes until chickpeas are tender. Drain and remove vegetables, optional ham shank and herbs. Refrigerate until needed.

For the Eggplant:

- Toss the eggplant with the garlic, oil, and salt and pepper and let sit for 10 minutes. On a very hot grill pan or char broiler, grill the eggplant slices for 20 seconds on each side. Remove and refrigerate until needed.

For the Escarole:

- Toss the escarole with the olive oil, salt and pepper. In a very hot sauté pan, scald the escarole in small batches about 20 seconds for each batch, until slightly wilted. Refrigerate until needed.

For the Smoked Paprika Vinaigrette:

- In a sauté pan over medium-high heat, heat the grapeseed oil. Add the shallots and bay leaves and sauté for 1 minute. Add the garlic and sauté for 30 seconds. Add the hot and sweet paprika and sauté for 30 seconds. Add the salt, pepper and remove from the heat. Add the vinegar, olive oil and walnut oil. Let cool to room temperature before using. Refrigerate any unused dressing.

To Finish and Serve:

- Bring all the vegetables to room temperature. Divide the eggplant slices between eight plates, laying them in circles. Mix the escarole and the chickpeas together with enough paprika vinaigrette to lightly coat. Place in the center of the eggplant slices. Garnish the eggplant with more paprika vinaigrette and serve.

* Available from gourmet specialty shops and spice purveyors

Coquette Café

"I wanted a more casual restaurant where we'd see customers twice a week instead of twice a year," says Sanford D'Amato. "The kind of place where I'd feel comfortable out on the floor. At Sanford's I feel I should be in the kitchen."

When he and wife, Angie, were approached by the owner of an early 20th-century brick building in Milwaukee's historic Third Ward, they grabbed the opportunity to open a place there.

A coquette is defined as, "a girl who flirts with men to win their affection." The décor of this aptly named café quickly captures the diner's affection while its fare flirts with the taste buds.

It is a big, comfortable space, warmly lit and buzzing with people enjoying a glass of wine and a bowl of cheese-capped French onion soup, a charcuterie plate, quiche, salad Nicoise, coq au vin or steak with frites.

And, true to form, with his devotion to a variety of ethnic culinary styles, D'Amato always features "Coquette's Travels" — a variety of dishes from other countries such as Greece and Italy.

Sweet Potato Soup with Seared Tomatillos

Serves: 8

Sweet Potato Soup:

2 tablespoons grapeseed oil

1 pound smoked pork
   bones or ham

1 pound onions, peeled and
   diced medium

1 each jalapeño, seeded and diced

2 each bay leaves

1 each cinnamon stick,
   4 inches long

3 cloves garlic, sliced

1/4 pound poblano peppers,
   seeded and diced

1 tablespoon ground coriander

1 cup dry white wine

2 pounds sweet potatoes,
   peeled and diced medium

7 cups chicken stock

Kosher salt to taste

2 teaspoons freshly ground
   black pepper

Tomatillo Garnish:

1-1/2 pounds tomatillos, husked
   and cut into small wedges

2 tablespoons grapeseed oil

Salt and pepper to taste

2 each jalapeño peppers, seeded
   and very finely diced

2 tablespoons lime juice

2 tablespoons sugar

Finish:

1 cup coarsely chopped
   cilantro leaves

For the Sweet Potato Soup:

- Heat the grapeseed oil over medium-high heat. Add the smoked pork bones and render for 3 minutes. Add the onions, jalapeño, bay leaves, cinnamon stick, garlic and poblanos and sweat for 5 minutes. Add the coriander and sauté for an additional minute. Add the wine and cook until mixture is reduced by 2/3. Add the potatoes and stock and bring to a boil. Reduce heat and simmer for 25 to 30 minutes, until the potatoes are very tender. Remove bay leaves, cinnamon stick and pork bones. *(Pick meat from pork bones and reserve as an additional garnish if desired.)* Purée the soup mixture in a blender. Add salt and pepper to taste. Keep warm while preparing tomatillo garnish.

For the Tomatillo Garnish:

- Heat a sauté pan over high heat. In a large bowl, toss the tomatillos with the oil and then season with salt and pepper. Add the tomatillo mixture to the heated pan and sear for 1 minute. Add the jalapeños and cook for 30 seconds. Add the lime juice and sugar and cook until the mixture is reduced by 1/2.

To Finish and Serve:

- Divide the tomatillos between eight serving bowls. Sprinkle the cilantro leaves in each bowl. Ladle the hot soup over the leaves and around the tomatillos and serve.

Optional:

- Use meat from pork bones, minced finely, as an additional garnish for the soup.

Seared Striped Bass on Green Papaya Salad with Green Curry Sauce

Serves: 4

Sea Bass and Marinade:

3/4 cup corn oil

1/4 cup lime juice

1 tablespoon chopped garlic

2 tablespoons brown sugar

4 each skinless fillets of striped bass *(approximately 7 ounces each, 1 to 1-1/2-inches thick)*

Green Papaya Salad:

1 teaspoon tamarind concentrate*

1/2 teaspoon chile paste with garlic

1-3/4 tablespoons buckwheat honey *(may substitute plain honey)*

1-3/4 tablespoons lime juice

1/4 cup grapeseed oil

1 teaspoon fish sauce, preferably nam pla*

1/4 teaspoon kosher salt

1 teaspoon ground ginger

1/8 teaspoon freshly ground black pepper

4 each scallions, trimmed, rinsed and sliced very thin

1 each green papaya, peeled, seeded and cut into long julienne strips *(approximately 2 cups)*

2 each nest of vermicelli *(bean thread noodles, comes 8 nests per package)* * covered with hot water for 15 minutes, drained and reserved

Green Curry Sauce:

2 teaspoons sesame oil

1/4 cup chopped ginger root

2 cloves garlic, sliced

1/4 cup dry white wine

1 tablespoon lime juice

2 teaspoons green curry paste*

1 can coconut milk, 13-1/2 ounces

1/2 teaspoon fish sauce, preferably nam pla*

1/2 cup cilantro leaves

Kosher salt and freshly ground black pepper to taste

For the Sea Bass and Marinade:

- Mix together all ingredients except bass. Place bass in marinade, cover, and refrigerate for 4 to 6 hours.

For the Green Papaya Salad:

- Mix all ingredients together except papaya and noodles. Add papaya and mix. Add the noodles and mix. Let set for 15 minutes before serving.

For the Green Curry Sauce:

- In a small saucepan, heat oil. Add the ginger and garlic and sauté for 30 seconds. Add the white wine and the lime juice and cook until reduced to almost dry. Add the curry paste, coconut milk and fish sauce and cook until reduced to 1 cup of liquid. Place in a blender with the cilantro leaves and carefully pulse, then blend until well blended, about 20 to 30 seconds. Strain through a medium-mesh strainer and keep warm.

To Finish and Serve:

- In a hot pan, season the bass fillets with salt and pepper and sear about 4 to 5 minutes per side depending on the thickness of the fillets. They should have a golden caramelized color *(do not over cook)*. Divide the papaya salad between each of four plates. Place bass on top and garnish with the green curry sauce.

* Available at Asian markets

Chef Tip:

Preheat the pan *before* adding butter, oil, etc. Then sauté over medium in order to get proper caramelization.

Salmon on Seared Rapini with Saffron Lima Bean Broth

Serves: 4

Saffron Lima Bean Broth:

1 cup dry lima beans, rinsed
  (6 ounces)

1/4 each onion

1/2 each small leek

1/2 each celery stalk

1 each herb sachet
  (see side bar recipe)

2 tablespoons kosher salt

1/2 teaspoon saffron threads

1 quart cold water

1-1/2 cups unsalted
  chicken stock

Seared Rapini:

1 bunch rapini
  (approximately 12 ounces)

2 tablespoons olive oil

3 cloves garlic, chopped

1/2 teaspoon chopped shallots

Salt and pepper to taste

**Glazed Garlic and
Orange Garnish:**

8-10 large cloves garlic,
  sliced and julienned

Zest from 1 large orange,
  removed in long strips

1 teaspoon olive oil

1 teaspoon sugar

1 pinch salt

1 tablespoon chopped
  flat-leaf parsley

Salmon:

4 each skinless salmon fillets
  (6-7 ounces each), preferably
  4 x 4 x 1-inch thick

Salt and black pepper to taste

1/2 cup flour for dredging

1/4 cup regular olive oil

Finish:

2 tablespoons flat-leaf parsley,
  cut into chiffonade

For the Lima Bean Broth:

- Place the lima beans in a container and cover with 4 cups of very hot water. Cover and refrigerate overnight.

- Drain the beans and place in a 3-quart saucepot. Add the vegetables and the herb sachet. Add salt, saffron and water. Bring to a boil and cook at a semi-rapid simmer, partially covered, for about 35 to 40 minutes, until beans are tender and creamy inside but not falling apart. Drain the beans, reserving liquid. Cool liquid and add 1-1/2 cups of chicken stock. Adjust seasonings and reserve.

For the Seared Rapini:

- Peel tough rapini stems. Chop stems about 1/8-inch thick. Keep stems separate from tops. Chop tops 1/2-inch thick. Heat a 12-inch sauté pan until very hot. Add oil and rapini stems. Sauté 20 seconds. Add garlic and shallots and sauté for 10 seconds. Add tops and sauté for 45 seconds to 1 minute, until tender but still crisp. Add salt and pepper to taste. Place in refrigerator to chill until needed.

For the Glazed Garlic and Orange Garnish:

- Place garlic and orange zest in a pan of water. Bring to boil for 5 seconds and strain. Refresh in cold water. Strain again well. Bring a non-stick sauté pan up to high heat. Add olive oil, garlic and orange mixture. Add sugar and salt and sauté for 30 to 45 seconds over high heat. Add parsley. Remove to a plate and cool. Reserve.

For the Salmon:

- Season the fillets with salt and pepper. Lightly dredge in flour. Pat off excess flour. Sauté in a 12-inch hot sauté pan in olive oil for 3 to 4 minutes per side for 1-inch-thick fillets, or until golden.

To Finish and Serve:

- Heat the lima beans and broth. Add the chiffonade of flat-leaf parsley to the beans. Warm the rapini and divide between each of four large soup bowls. Place cooked salmon fillet on top of rapini. Surround with beans and pour broth over salmon. Garnish with glazed garlic and orange zest.

Herb Sachet

8-inch square cheesecloth

6 cloves garlic, large

2 whole cloves

3 whole star anise

1 tablespoon peppercorns

2 sprigs fresh thyme

2 whole bay leaves

Green onion stem or twine

Lay out the cheesecloth square and place the next 6 ingredients in the center. Gather up the cheesecloth into a sack and tie with a green onion stem or piece of twine. Use as directed.

Chargrilled Loin of Elk on Summer Vegetable Sauté with Tart Cherry Essence

Serves: 4

Elk Loin:
4 **each** 6-ounce medallions elk loin

Marinade:
1 **cup** dry red wine
2 **tablespoons** red wine vinegar
2 **each** shallots, sliced
2 **cloves** garlic, sliced
1 **each** bay leaf
2 **each** thyme sprigs
2 **tablespoons** extra-virgin olive oil
1 **teaspoon** juniper berries
1 **teaspoon** black peppercorns, crushed
1/4 **cup** tart cherries, pitted

Tart Cherry Essence:
1 **tablespoon** olive oil
1/4 **cup** sliced shallots
12 **ounces** tart cherries, pitted *(8 ounces for sauce; save 4 ounces for garnish)*
1 **cup** dry red wine
1/4 **cup** marinade *(see above)*
1-1/2 **cups** elk or veal stock *(may substitute low-sodium beef stock)*
1 **tablespoon** balsamic vinegar
Kosher salt and freshly ground black pepper to taste

Parsley Oil:
1/2 **cup** parsley leaves
1/4 **cup** extra-virgin olive oil
Kosher salt and freshly ground black pepper to taste

Finish:
3 **tablespoons** olive oil
Kosher salt and freshly ground black pepper to taste

For the Marinade:

- Mix all marinade ingredients together and marinate elk loin medallions for 3 hours. Remove elk. Put the marinade in a small saucepan and bring to a boil. Reduce heat and cook until mixture is reduced to 1 cup of liquid. Strain the mixture through three layers of cheesecloth. Return to saucepan and again bring to a boil. Reduce heat and cook until mixture is reduced to 1/4 cup of liquid. Set aside and reserve for use in sauce.

For the Tart Cherry Essence:

- Sauté shallots in oil for 1 minute over medium heat. Add 8 ounces of the cherries and the wine and cook until reduced to 2 tablespoons of liquid. Add 1/4 cup of the reserved marinade, the elk or veal stock, and the vinegar and cook until reduced to 1 cup of liquid. Strain. Season with salt and pepper to taste. Add the remaining 4 ounces of cherries for garnish and set aside, keeping warm.

For the Parsley Oil:

- To make oil, put all ingredients in a blender and blend until smooth. Strain, if desired.

To Finish and Serve:

- Toss elk medallions in olive oil and season with salt and pepper. Grill over medium-high fire for 2 to 3 minutes per side, until medium rare. Divide summer vegetable sauté between four serving plates. Place one elk loin on each bed of vegetables. Spoon tart cherry essence and cherries over elk. Spoon a little parsley oil around the plates and serve.

* Available at specialty baking and/or health food stores

Summer Vegetable Sauté

3 **tablespoons** clarified butter
3 **tablespoons** olive oil
4 **ounces** Yukon gold potatoes, diced small and blanched
4 **ounces** small pattypan squash, halved or quartered depending on size
6 **ounces** wild mushroom mix *(chanterelles, morels, etc.)*, cut into small dice
Kosher salt and freshly ground black pepper to taste
1 **tablespoon** finely chopped shallot
1 **teaspoon** finely chopped garlic
2 **ounces** cherry essence*

Over high heat, add clarified butter and olive oil to large sauté pan. When the oil is hot, add the blanched potatoes. Sauté for 1 to 2 minutes until golden in color. Add squash and sauté until colored. Add the mushrooms and sauté until browned. Add salt and pepper to taste. Add the shallot and garlic. Sauté for 30 seconds. Add cherry essence and mix. Keep warm.

Lemon Pound Cake with Caramelized Apricots

Serves: 6

Lemon Pound Cake:

8 tablespoons butter,
  at room temperature

1/2 cup sugar

3 each eggs, separated,
  at room temperature

1 tablespoon dark rum

1/2 tablespoon lemon reduction
  (2 tablespoons lemon juice and zest
  of lemon reduced three-fourths over
  medium heat to 1/2 tablespoon)

2/3 cup flour, sifted

Scant 1/2 teaspoon
  baking powder

Caramelized Apricots:

1/2 cup sugar

3 tablespoons water

1/2 cup heavy cream

12 each apricots, pitted and cut
  into 1/4-inch pieces

Ground pepper to taste

For the Lemon Pound Cake:

- Preheat oven to 325 degrees. Cream the butter and 2/3 of the sugar until light and lemon colored. Beat in the egg yolks one at a time. Add rum, lemon reduction, flour and baking powder and mix until just combined. In a separate bowl, whip the egg whites with the remaining sugar until soft peaks form. Fold 1/2 of the egg whites into the butter and sugar mixture. Repeat with remaining egg whites. Pipe the mixture evenly into six non-stick molds or six regular molds that have been buttered and floured and have a piece of parchment paper on the bottom *(you could also use custard cups or ramekins)*. Bake for about 11-12 minutes, until firm.

For the Caramelized Apricots:

- Mix the sugar and water in a small saucepan and cook over medium heat until deep golden. Slowly and carefully mix in the heavy cream. Bring to a boil and add the apricots and pepper. Cook until the apricots are tender. Remove the apricots and set aside. Simmer the sauce for an additional 7 to 10 minutes until thick and syrupy.

To Finish and Serve:

- Warm the cakes in the molds in a 350-degree oven for 5 minutes. Remove the cakes from the molds onto each of six serving plates. Serve with the apricots, the caramel sauce and your favorite ice cream.

D'Amato's Favorite Desserts

Plum Tart Atop Roasted Plums with
Spiced Plum Consommé

Caramelized Fig Spice Cake, Caramel
Sauce and Basil Ice Cream

Warm Lemon Pound Cake
with Lemon Curd and
Sour Cream/Anise Ice Cream

Banana Toffee Tart,
Banana Rum Ice Cream

Bittersweet Chocolate Tart,
Coffee Ice Cream

Warm Chocolate Espresso Cake
with Mocha Cream

Orange Crème Brûlée

Tart Cherry Clafoutis,
Morello Cherry Ice Cream

Macadamia Nut Tart,
Coconut Ice Cream

Pear or Apple Tart,
Vanilla Ice Cream

Flourless Chocolate Cake,
Vanilla Ice Cream

Gratin of Fruits —
Mangoes, Strawberries,
Cherries and Raspberries
— topped with
Macadamia-Coconut Crisp

Frozen Lime Soufflé

Raspberry and
Passion Fruit Sorbet

PATRICK O'CONNELL

WASHINGTON, VA

All-Clad Metalcrafters Outstanding Chef, 2001

American Express Best Chef: Mid-Atlantic, 1992

Washington, Virginia is located one and one half-hours from the District of Columbia. It's a quaint, picture-book village five blocks long and two blocks wide. Populated by just 180 inhabitants, it is one of the world's premiere food and lodging destinations.

A visit to The Inn at Little Washington in the Shenandoah Valley, whether for a sumptuous dinner or a leisurely stay, is the contemporary equivalent of a grand pilgrimage. Every aspect of the operation is ravishing and a reflection of chef/owner Patrick O'Connell's amazing attention to detail. Along with his partner, Reinhardt Lynch, O'Connell has created the most fantastic and intensely personal of environments and invites everyone else to share it.

Referring to The Inn's over-the-top Victorian decor, O'Connell says with a smile, "There is definitely personality behind all this. A writer once said to me, 'it's not my taste but at least it's somebody's taste.'"

In a world of cookie-cutter hotel and restaurant chains, O'Connell correctly took this as a compliment. His culinary style draws unqualified raves from critics and customers alike, and O'Connell has snagged virtually every award the food and travel community has to bestow.

In view of this, it's interesting that O'Connell did not take the usual career route for a chef. Raised in the Maryland suburbs of D.C., he had no inclination toward cooking for a living, apart from a high school job working in a diner. In fact, he intended to go into the theater, and studied acting and speech at Washington's Catholic University.

After graduating, O'Connell headed for Europe. "It was during the sixties, a turbulent time, and I wanted to disconnect from American culture."

After a year, he returned home, planning to wrap up his affairs and go back overseas to settle permanently. To his surprise, he found enormous changes had taken place in the United States during his absence.

"Energy was percolating on every level, especially on a culinary level. Until that point, there was no respect for the culinary arts in America like there was in France. In Paris you would see people elbowing each other to get a glimpse of the food displayed in Fauchon's window. Here there was none of that awe of food."

Americans were beginning to understand and appreciate ethnic food, the hippie contingent was promoting natural and organic foods, and according to O'Connell, those like him who were interested dove right in. "All of a sudden I felt completely different about a career in the food business. I knew that it could be an artistic pursuit that would engage all my talents and capacities."

O'Connell was earning extra money painting houses and mentioned to some friends he was looking for help. They introduced him to Lynch. Shortly thereafter, the two packed up, moved to a farm in rural Virginia and began growing and selling vegetables. They fell into catering after helping out at local parties and in the beginning did it the hard way. "We had a wood stove, a garage sale electric frying pan and we bought all our ingredients at Safeway," O'Connell laughs.

When the business took off, the pair decided instead of taking their food on the road, they would have their customers come to them. So, 25 years ago, they opened a restaurant in a 100 year-old building that had previously done duty as a garage, community center and craft shop.

The menu was simple, the food inexpensive but excellent, and word spread fast. A DC restaurant critic

wrote a glowing review and from then on it was onward and upward for O'Connell and Lynch who have never stopped refining both the cuisine and the property.

Over the years, the two have refurbished, expanded and, with the help of London stage and set designer Joyce Evans, decorated The Inn in a style that can only be described as elegant excess. (Evans' renderings of the completed rooms have been lovingly framed and hung throughout The Inn.) The design of the sun-lit kitchen is based on the dairy at Windsor Castle, the main sitting room is floored with 400 year-old parquet, and the bar and lounge painted with murals featuring playful monkeys capering in human guise.

In the process, they have created a vibrant community in Washington. Buying local properties, they have been able to add guest quarters, retail space and staff housing. Long-time members of The Inn's 100-person staff have settled in the town to raise families. O'Connell and Lynch have developed a barter system with townspeople that assures them of a constant supply of the regional foodstuffs that play such an important role in O'Connell's culinary style.

On the subject of style, he shies away from labels. "When you are invited to a friends house for dinner, would you ask them what kind of food do you cook? Of course not, no one cooks the same thing every day. And for a chef, once you're nailed to a certain schtick, you burn out."

As close as he will get to defining his style is saying, "I enhance our regional ingredients and offer a taste of something people cannot get anywhere else in the world. It's American haute cuisine."

Those ingredients include wild morels, fresh herbs and heirloom tomatoes, locally raised beef and rabbits, grits, artisanal cheeses, Virginia ham and wines (from a wine cellar that includes 14,000 bottles). Dishes are prepared with meticulous French technique and the best of the best luxury product; seafood, foie gras, caviar, white and black truffles and imported produce.

O'Connell despises the idea of a restaurant "concept." "I never think in those terms. I cook what I feel like cooking at the time. It should be like a dinner party every night."

That spontaneity is matched by his sense of ongoing refinement. "It is an evolutionary process. Each time I cook a dish I try to elevate it, adding a new dimension or, simplifying it to enhance the essence."

Grand as the food and surroundings are, O'Connell never loses his sense of humor. He underscores his devotion to the two house Dalmatians with the black-and-white spotted trousers and aprons the kitchen crew wears; appro-

priately, the doggy bags have the same pattern. Even the names of his dishes exhibit sly wit — Lucky Duck: Braised Duck and Seared Foie Gras Sailing on a Raft of Wilted Watercress in an Aromatic Broth. Then there are The Seven Deadly Sins, a flight of desserts that might include, according to the season, apple tart, lemon meringue pie, coconut ice cream, panna-cotta and three chocolate desserts ranging from lightest to richest.

The cheese tray arrives on top of a rolling fiberglass cow complete with realistic moo. A signature serving of soup with each meal is presented in a demitasse cup, a reminder of the early days when there were literally not enough bowls. Miniature ham biscuits are a nod to Southern tradition, and meals end with a tiny wicker picnic basket holding a treasure of equally petite sweets.

Everything is geared to pleasing guests. Says O'Connell, "We keep trying to elevate every aspect. When we inch up in one area, we then strive to pull everything else up to match."

Projects in the works for The Inn are a full-service spa and more rooms to accommodate increased business. O'Connell is also working on a second cookbook which will be published in 2004. It's about "grandma food," he says, taking dishes like macaroni and cheese and pineapple upside down cake and bringing them forward without allowing them to lose essential character.

Says O'Connell, "The gifts that most good restaurateurs have are understanding people, caring for people while being in control of their own lives."

The man has accomplished exactly that.

Green Beans Tempura with Asian Dipping Sauce

Serves: 4

Asian Dipping Sauce:

1 tablespoon rice wine vinegar

7 tablespoons nuoc nam
fish sauce*

2 tablespoons sugar

1/2 cup cold water

Juice of 1 lime

2 tablespoons finely
julienned carrot

1/4 cup minced cilantro

2 cloves garlic, large,
peeled and minced

2 each jalapeño peppers, ribs and
seeds removed and discarded,
finely chopped

Green Beans Tempura:

1/4 pound French green beans

2 quarts vegetable or peanut oil
(for deep frying)

1 cup cake flour

7 ounces club soda, very cold

Salt and black pepper to taste

Finish:
Salt to taste

For the Asian Dipping Sauce:

- Mix all of the ingredients together in a medium-size bowl, stirring until the sugar is dissolved. Store in the refrigerator until ready to use.

For the Green Beans Tempura:

- In a deep fryer or heavy pot, heat the oil to 350 degrees. Using a knife, cut off the tips of the green beans. Using a fork, gently combine the flour and the club soda. The batter will appear slightly lumpy and should have the consistency of heavy cream. Season with salt and pepper to taste. *(The bubbles in the club soda help keep the tempura light and crispy, therefore it is important to make the batter just before using it.)*

- One at a time, dip each green bean into the tempura batter and shake off any excess. Carefully drop the beans into the hot oil and fry for about 1-1/2 minutes, turning them with a slotted spoon until they are just golden and crisp. Remove the beans from the fryer and drain them on paper towels.

To Finish and Serve:

- Season the beans with salt and serve immediately with the Asian dipping sauce on the side.

* Available at Asian markets

Melange of Virginia Country Ham, Pear, Parmigiano-Reggiano and Baby Arugula

Serves: 4 to 6

Melange:

6 ounces Virginia country ham,
sliced as thinly as possible

2 to 3 each Anjou pears, thinly
sliced on a mandoline *(you may
use a hand-held or table-top slicer)*

8 ounces Parmigiano-Reggiano

1/2 cup baby arugula, well
cleaned and picked over

1/2 cup pine nuts, lightly toasted

Freshly cracked black
pepper to taste

1 cup extra-virgin olive oil,
good-quality

For the Melange:

- Delicately layer all of the ingredients in a mound in the center of four to six 6-inch plates. Sprinkle with pepper and drizzle with olive oil.

Crab Salad with Mango, Avocado and Tropical Fruit Purée

Serves: 4

Tropical Fruit Purée:

1 each small cantaloupe, peeled, seeds discarded

1/2 each fresh pineapple, peeled and cored

2 tablespoons lemon juice

2 tablespoons roughly chopped cilantro

Sugar to taste

Crab Salad:

2 cups jumbo crabmeat, carefully picked over

1-1/2 tablespoons minced jalapeño pepper

2 tablespoons lemon juice

1-1/2 tablespoons nuoc nam fish sauce*

1/2 cup halved fresh avocado, with the pit removed

1/4 cup diced fresh mango

For the Tropical Fruit Purée:

- Purée the melon in a food processor fitted with a metal blade and pour the mixture into a medium-size bowl. Purée the pineapple and add it to the melon purée. Add lemon juice and mix the purée thoroughly. Tie up the chopped cilantro in a 5-inch square of cheesecloth. Add the cilantro sachet to the purée. Cover and refrigerate at least 1/2 hour or overnight. Before serving, add a pinch of sugar if necessary.

For the Crab Salad:

- Combine crabmeat, jalapeño, lemon juice and fish sauce in a medium-size mixing bowl. Fold carefully with a rubber spatula to prevent breaking up the lumps of crabmeat. Place a ring mold *(or a round cookie cutter that is about 2 inches tall and 2-1/2 inches wide)* on each of four chilled plates. With a teaspoon, scoop 2 tablespoons of avocado from the shell and place at the bottom of the mold. Pack down lightly with the back of the spoon. Place 1 tablespoon of mango on top of the avocado, and press it down gently. Place a final layer of the crabmeat mixture and smooth off the top with the flat side of a knife. Lift the ring mold off carefully. Repeat this process on the remaining plates.

To Finish and Serve:

- Ladle the tropical fruit purée around the edges of the crab mold and serve chilled.

* Available at Asian markets

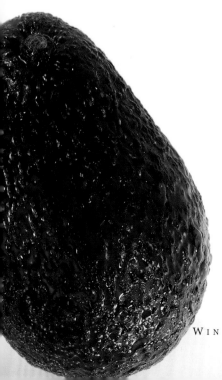

Patrick O'Connell's Beverage Recommendations

Tempura Green Beans
A white Rhône, specifically something that is predominantly Marsanne, such as Hermitage Blanc.
page 49

Ham, Pear, Parmigiano-Reggiano and Baby Arugula Melange
A very light and delicate Manzanilla sherry shows off this dish in an almost tapas style.
page 49

Crab Salad with Mango, Avocado and Tropical Fruit Purée
A classic New Zealand Sauvignon Blanc with nuances of pink grapefruit and passion fruit makes for a perfect food-and-wine partnership with its slight natural sweetness.
page 51

Black Truffle Pizza
A big, fat Chardonnay, something that has seen some significant new wood and malolactic fermentation.
page 53

Chocolate Mint Fantasy
Banyuls is traditionally considered to be one of the few wines that matches well with dark chocolate and also holds up well to the assertive flavors of the mint ice cream.
page 57

Pizza with Black Truffle and Country Ham

Serves: 6

Shallot Fondue:

4 tablespoons unsalted butter

2 cups peeled and sliced shallots

Salt and freshly ground black
 pepper to taste

Pizza Dough:

2 ounces compressed yeast

2/3 cup warm water

1/4 cup milk

2 tablespoons olive oil

1-1/2 pounds all-purpose flour

1 teaspoon salt

Black Truffle Pizza:

1 recipe pizza dough

Cornmeal for dusting

1 recipe shallot fondue, at room
 temperature *(see above)*

1 cup freshly grated Parmigiano-
 Reggiano cheese *(about 3 ounces)*

4 ounces black truffles, sliced
 1/16-inch thick

2/3 cup grated Fontina cheese
 (about 3 ounces)

Finish:

2 thin slices country ham,
 well-trimmed, cut into
 thin strips

Chopped red onions to taste
 (optional)

Chopped shallots to taste
 (optional)

For the Shallot Fondue:

- In a heavy-bottomed saucepan, melt the butter over medium heat and add the sliced shallots. Reduce the heat to low and cook, stirring occasionally, for 30 minutes or until golden brown. Season with salt and black pepper and cool to room temperature.

For the Pizza Dough:

- In a mixing bowl, combine the yeast, water and milk. Mix well. Add the oil. In a clean mixing bowl, combine flour and salt. Mix, then make a well in the center. Add the yeast mixture and blend into a dough. Knead for 4 to 5 minutes. Form the dough into a ball and place the dough in an oiled bowl. Cover with a clean damp towel, and allow the dough to rise in a warm place until doubled in size.

For Black Truffle Pizza:

- On a floured board, roll out the pizza dough to about 1/8-inch thick. Lay a bowl about 5 inches in diameter upside down on the dough and, using the rim as a pattern, cut out six circles with a sharp paring knife. Dust the back of a cookie sheet with cornmeal and place the pizza rounds on top of it.

- Place a pizza stone in the oven and preheat to 450 degrees. Spread a thin layer of the shallot fondue onto each pizza round leaving a 1/2-inch border of dough showing around the edge.

- Lightly sprinkle the Parmigiano-Reggiano over the shallot fondue. Arrange the sliced black truffles in slightly overlapping concentric circles on top of the shallot fondue and sprinkle with Fontina cheese.

- Using a spatula, carefully slide the pizzas onto the hot stone and bake until the crusts are crisp and golden brown.

To Finish and Serve:

- Remove from the oven and sprinkle with country ham. Garnish with red onions and shallots to taste if desired. Serve immediately.

Virginia Ham

"Country Folks' Caviar." That's what some connoisseurs call Virginia ham, a robust regional delicacy that is one of the specialty ingredients used at The Inn at Little Washington.

Deep-red in color, with a smoky, salty flavor far more assertive than its pink Easter-dinner cousin, the Virginia ham *(or "country ham," if it hails from elsewhere)* is a meal more than a year in the making. In the fall, the butchered hog haunches are covered with a curing rub, then hung in smoke houses where burning hardwood does its part in the 12-month aging process.

While huge, high-volume operations have largely taken over what was once a back woods business, traditionalists like Patrick O'Connell feel the best hams still come from farmers or small slaughterhouses. That's why The Inn at Little Washington's supplier is Calhoun Country Hams in nearby Culpepper, Virginia.

"Tom Calhoun is a ham artist," O'Connell says. "His hams are moist, less salty and low on preservatives."

Calhoun Country Hams
540-825-8319
1-877-825-8319
www.calhounhams.com

Sole Fingers with Green Herb Sauce

Serves: 4 to 5

Green Herb Sauce:

1 **cup** roughly chopped dill

1 **cup** roughly chopped parsley

1 **cup** roughly chopped watercress

1/2 **cup** roughly chopped tarragon

2 **tablespoons** capers

2 **tablespoons** Dijon mustard

2 **cups** mayonnaise

1-2/3 **tablespoons** lemon juice

1 **teaspoon** kosher salt

1/4 **teaspoon** freshly ground
black pepper

1/2 **cup** water

Seasoned Cornmeal:

2 **cups** yellow cornmeal

2 **tablespoons** kosher salt

1/4 **teaspoon** freshly ground
black pepper

Crispy Collard Greens:

Oil for frying

1/2 **cup** thinly sliced collard
green leaves, washed and
thoroughly dried

Salt to taste

Sole:

Oil for frying

12 **ounces** Dover sole, lemon sole
or flounder, cut into 3-inch
strips, 1/4-inch wide

1 **cup** buttermilk

For the Green Herb Sauce:

- Wash and pat dry all of the fresh herbs. Combine all of the ingredients in a food processor and purée. Strain the sauce through a fine-mesh sieve and store covered in the refrigerator until ready to use.

For the Seasoned Cornmeal:

- Combine all the ingredients. Set aside until ready to use.

For the Crispy Collard Greens:

- In a deep fryer, bring the oil to 350 degrees. Have ready a plate covered with paper towels. Add collard greens to the hot oil and fry just long enough to make them curl, about 30 seconds. Remove from the oil and drain on the paper towels. Lightly salt to taste.

For the Sole:

- Using a deep fryer, heat oil to 350 degrees. Soak the sole in the buttermilk for about 2 to 3 minutes. Remove the pieces of fish from the buttermilk and roll in the seasoned cornmeal. Shake off the excess cornmeal and carefully drop the pieces one at a time into the hot oil. Fry the fish in small batches until golden brown. Remove from the oil and drain on paper towels.

To Finish and Serve:

- Serve the sole on a bed of crispy collard greens with the green herb sauce on the side.

Chef on the Spot

What was your worst cooking experience?

"I dread and loathe Thanksgiving. In the early days we knew we had to serve it. I had never cooked a turkey or wanted to; I'd only seen my mom do it. It was a total disaster and took seven or eight years before it got better."

If you're not doing the cooking what is your favorite cuisine?

"Vietnamese. I love all the raw ingredients and it's so textural, fragrant, fresh and interesting."

What is your favorite comfort food?

"Pasta with olive oil, pine nuts, black pepper, parsley and Parmesan."

Do you have a guilty food pleasure?

"Nacho and Cool Ranch Doritos®. I like that vibrantly fake taste."

Chocolate Mint Fantasy

Serves: 6

Mint Ice Cream:

2 cups whole milk

2 cups heavy cream

1 cup granulated sugar

1/4 pound fresh peppermint
(about 2 bunches)

8 each egg yolks, lightly beaten

2 tablespoons crème de menthe

Chocolate Ribbons:

1 pound semisweet chocolate,
finest quality

For the Mint Ice Cream:

- In a 2-quart heavy-bottomed saucepan, combine the milk, cream, sugar and mint over medium heat. Bring to a boil, then remove from heat and allow to steep for approximately 1 hour or until the cream mixture has a peppermint flavor. Remove the peppermint. Bring the cream mixture back to a simmer.

- Place the egg yolks in the top of a double boiler or in a large stainless steel bowl and slowly whisk in the hot cream mixture. Set the mixture over a pot of simmering water and whisk until the mixture thickens enough to coat the back of a spoon.

- Remove from heat and strain through a fine-mesh sieve. Stir in the crème de menthe. Chill in the refrigerator, then freeze in an ice cream machine according to the manufacturer's instructions.

For the Chocolate Ribbons:

- Roughly chop the chocolate with a chef's knife and place it in a stainless steel bowl. Place the bowl over a pot of barely simmering water, making sure that no moisture comes in contact with the chocolate. Stir the chocolate occasionally until it is about half melted. Remove from heat and whisk until all of the chocolate has melted and is very smooth. The chocolate should be between 85 to 92 degrees. Test by dipping a wooden spoon into the chocolate and bringing it to your lower lip. The chocolate should feel cool to the touch.

- Using a metal cake spatula, spread 1/2 cup of the melted chocolate out onto a marble slab or the back of a cookie sheet. The chocolate should be only 1/8-inch to 1/16-inch thick.

- Allow the chocolate to set up slightly and just begin to dry. Using a knife, cut the chocolate into 2-inch wide ribbons. Push a wide putty knife or metal pastry scraper held at a 45 degree angle under the chocolate and scrape the ribbons off of the marble slab or cookie sheet, forming irregularly shaped curls.

- Allow the chocolate curls to solidify for a few more seconds, then place them in a sealed container and store in the freezer.

To Finish and Serve:

- Several hours before serving, smooth the mint ice cream into the walls of six pre-frozen soup plates or serving bowls and return them to the freezer. Just before serving, remove the chocolate curls from the freezer and mound them on top of the ice cream.

ROXSAND SCOCOS

PHOENIX, AZ

American Express Best Chef: Southwest, 1999

Talented, innovative and nationally acclaimed, Roxsand Scocos is an icon for aspiring women chefs. The route to the top has meant unrelenting hard work and personal sacrifice for this owner of the Phoenix restaurant, Roxsand.

As with most people who have made food their life, Scocos' upbringing played a big part in determining her eventual career. Growing up in a small, lakeside community in Michigan, she attests to an ideal childhood. "It was like living at a perpetual camp with year-around activities like swimming, water-skiing, cross country skiing and ice skating. We had an orchard in the back yard and blackberry bushes grew alongside the railroad tracks."

She spent a lot of her formative years in the company of her Italian grandmother and Spanish grandfather. "Food was totally huge in that house," recalls Scocos. "They lived to eat. I remember sitting at the table watching grandma cook. She was a true matriarch. I could taste, but she was in charge and wanted no help."

Grandpa provided his share of food memories. When Roxsand hosted an ice skating party for friends, he made it a point to drive into Detroit to stock up on supplies from an Italian deli, and then grilled savory sausages in the fireplace for the hungry youngsters.

As well as being an enthusiastic athlete, Scocos took private art lessons throughout high school, and after graduation was accepted at the prestigious Center for Creative Studies in Detroit. When an opportunity arose to visit Paris where a friend worked at La Varenne culinary academy, her life took a different, but equally artful, turn.

"I had figured out that I was never going to make a living with art, and in Paris I became totally immersed in food,"

Hawaii, she shifted into high gear, opening her first restaurant at age 24. During the time she spent in Honolulu, Scocos ended up owning a catering company and a second restaurant.

"That is where it all came together for me," she explains. "I was French trained, in the Island environment, part of the Chinese community and my chef, Haggi, was Moroccan. I designed the food and he executed it. He taught me so much and without even being conscious of it, the French, Asian and Moroccan came together and formed the basis for my culinary style."

The Hawaiian experience was hugely gratifying. With a wealthy, international clientele, Scocos soon boasted the highest-grossing restaurant per square foot in the Pacific basin. She says, "The sky was the limit. My job was to dream up dazzling, unbelievable fetes for people like designer Bill Blass and his entourage."

When the relationship with her boyfriend ended, Scocos set out for her next stop — Arizona.

She and new husband Spiros, whom she'd met before leaving the Islands, moved to Phoenix where he owned a condo. The couple opened a small restaurant in the nearby resort community of Scottsdale that became an immediate hit. "It was the first time I was on my own in the kitchen, formulating my ideas about food," Scocos says. "We were driven to make it work, doing it all alone and putting in 20 hour days, six days a week."

The eclectic, imaginative menu was a revelation to customers and critics, and in order to describe it, Roxsand coined the term "Transcontinental Cuisine." Her lavish line-up of desserts and pastries became the gold standard among area restaurants.

Soon the restaurant was too small for the crowds of eager customers and the couple opened a larger, more sophisticated place on Phoenix' restaurant row.

After the birth of their first daughter, Tatiana, the couple bought a restaurant in Moscow, Idaho where Spiros had gone to school and were considering Seattle as another possible location. When daughter Theo was born several years later, the enormous challenge of balancing family life with an unrelent-

says Scocos. "I went through dozens of cookbooks — Pépin, Fisher, Child — studied them like textbooks."

Back in Detroit, at the age of 20, she started a company that catered for film production crews and, to make ends meet, she waited tables at night. "I was determined to make a living at it and I did."

Scocos then opened a wholesale bakery, and when enough money was available she'd go back and forth to Paris, continuing her culinary education.

Her relationship with a Chinese-American boyfriend determined the next career step. Moving together to ing work schedule and long distance-commutes became too much, and the couple divorced.

Scocos focused her attention on her original restaurant. Spiros opened a different kind of dining establishment across town. They remain good friends and devoted parents.

Using her flawless taste and artistic sensibility, Roxsand's dramatic, contemporarily furnished restaurant with intimate balcony dining is a gallery for the art and artifacts collected on her travels. Scocos has also furnished her home with an appealing combination of ethnic and contemporary furniture and art that she has acquired over the years. Art remains important in her life. A homebody, Scocos cooks simply for her family, and there is always fruit and feta cheese in the refrigerator for after-school snacks.

Meanwhile, she continues to evolve professionally. Deeply committed to the sustainable agriculture movement, she says that supporting local growers has caused her to rethink and

redefine her culinary philosophy. "I live in the Southwest, but my culinary repertoire is not necessarily Southwestern, so how can I reconcile my belief in supporting local produce?" she reflects. "I discovered I needed to look at the latitude of what grows here: pomegranates, figs, dates, pistachios, olives, citrus. It's no contradiction; my food has always had Persian, Turkish, Moroccan inclinations."

Scocos also says that she continues to simplify and distill her culinary philosophy, and that goes hand in hand with how she shapes her life. She hikes and works out regularly, something that is obvious from her trim figure. Travel is important. She and Tatiana visited India recently, and China and Spain are favorite vacation destinations.

Scocos has an almost Eastern life view. "Historically, when I have been at a crossroads, which seems to be about every ten years, I think through my past experiences and try to understand where they are taking me next," she observes. "Then things start germinating."

Asian Pear and Fig Slaw with Lime-Curry Vinaigrette

Serves: 6

Lime-Curry Vinaigrette:
(makes approximately 1-1/2 cups or 12 ounces)

4 cloves garlic, mashed and chopped

4 each Roma tomatoes, skinned, seeded and diced

2 each jalapeños, seeded and diced very finely

2 tablespoons chopped mint leaves

2 tablespoons chopped basil

2 teaspoons curry powder

7 tablespoons fish sauce*

1/4 cup lime juice and zest

2 tablespoons sesame oil

3 tablespoons rice vinegar*

3 tablespoons soy sauce

Slaw:

3 each Asian pears

3 each figs, fresh

Finish:

6 ounces Chinese pine nuts, roasted*

12 ounces Lime-Curry Vinaigrette

3 ounces wild mesclun greens

Lime zest for garnish

For the Lime-Curry Vinaigrette:

• Combine all ingredients in a bowl. Whisk until well blended (*use fish sauce sparingly to taste — it can be overpowering*). Chill until ready to use.

For the Slaw:

• Shave the pears and figs thinly. The pears and figs must be shaved on a Japanese mandoline to get the necessary thinness. The fruit must be kept extremely cold; hold in acidulated ice water. Drain very well before assembling salad.

To Finish and Serve:

• Toss both fruits and pine nuts together. Place 1/2 ounce lightly dressed greens on six chilled 12-inch dinner plates. Stack the tossed fruits on top. Drizzle the fruits and plate with the vinaigrette. Do not toss fruits in the dressing — it will overpower the flavor of the fruits. Garnish the rims of the plates with lime zest.

* Available at Asian markets

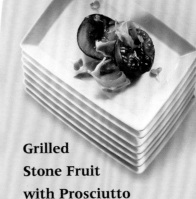

Grilled Stone Fruit with Prosciutto

Serves: 4

4 each ripe peaches, apricots, nectarines or plums, halved and pitted

Hoisin sauce*

8 pieces prosciutto, thinly sliced

Spread cut side of fruit with hoisin sauce and broil or grill briefly. Wrap with prosciutto slices. Place 2 halves on each plate and serve.

Carrot-Corn Soup with Forbidden Black Rice

Serves: 8

Rice:

1 cup forbidden black rice**

Carrot-Corn Soup:

2 each bacon slices, finely chopped

1 each onion, finely chopped

2 teaspoons curry powder

1 teaspoon crushed dried chiles

1 teaspoon ground cumin

2 each thin carrots, peeled and cut into 1/4-inch slices

1/2 pound corn kernels

2 cans coconut milk
(14 ounces per can)

2 cups water

Salt and pepper to taste

2 tablespoons chopped cilantro

2 tablespoons chopped mint

2 tablespoons chopped scallions

For the Rice:

• Prepare rice according to package directions. Pack the cooked rice into eight greased timbales. Keep warm.

For the Carrot-Corn Soup:

• While the rice is cooking, prepare the soup. Sauté the bacon until the fat is completely rendered. Add the onion and spices. Cover and cook gently until very aromatic and the onion is tender. Add the carrots, corn, coconut milk and water. Simmer for a few minutes. Season to taste with salt and pepper. At the very end, add the chopped herbs and scallions.

To Finish and Serve:

• Unmold each of the rice timbales into a soup plate. Gently ladle soup around timbale in each plate.

** Available at Asian markets and speciality stores. If unavailable, substitute sticky purple or Jasmine rice.

Malanga and Leek Terrine

Serves: 6

Malanga and Leek:

1 **each** malanga (*may substitute one large potato*)

Corn oil for sautéing

1 **pound** leeks, whites only, rinsed well and diced

Salt and pepper to taste

1 **cup** heavy cream

Zest from 1/2 orange (no white pith)

Finish:

6 **each** blood oranges

Mesclun greens (*optional*)

For the Malanga and Leek:

- Peel the malanga and hold in ice water. Sauté the diced leeks in corn oil until completely translucent. Season with salt and pepper. Add the heavy cream and cook over low to medium heat until reduced completely. Stir in orange zest to taste and correct seasonings. Set aside and let cool.

- Preheat oven to 350 degrees. Slice malanga (*or potato*) paper thin using a mandoline. Grease a loaf pan or rectangular mold with butter and line with parchment paper. Lay down a layer of sliced malanga and cover thinly with leek mixture. Continue alternating malanga with leek until the mold is filled to the top. Cover tightly with plastic wrap and then with foil. Bake for 1-1/2 hours, or until cooked through. Remove from oven and let cool.

To Finish and Serve:

- Prior to serving, juice the oranges and warm the juice gently. Do not boil. Unmold the terrine onto a serving platter when cool. Slice terrine with a knife dipped in hot water. Serve with blood orange broth. Garnish with mesclun greens.

Duck Confit with Raisin-Balsamic Reduction

Serves: 4

Dry Spice Rub:

1/4 **cup** ground cumin

1/4 **cup** ground cinnamon

1/4 **cup** ground coriander

3 **tablespoons** ground allspice

2 **tablespoons** ground cardamom

1/2 **tablespoon** ground nutmeg

1 **tablespoon** ground cloves

3 **tablespoons** ground thyme

2 **tablespoons** ground ginger

12 **each** bay leaves, chopped in a spice grinder

6 **cloves** garlic, smashed on a counter

Duck:

2 **each** whole ducks, quartered

Duck fat or canola oil

Raisin-Balsamic Sauce:

1 **cup** sugar

1 **cup** port

2 **cups** balsamic vinegar

1 **cup** raisins

2 **cups** duck stock or chicken stock

Salt and pepper to taste

2 **tablespoons** butter

For the Spice Rub:

- Combine all ingredients in a bowl.

For the Duck:

- The thighs and legs will be used for the confit and the breasts will be seared and sautéed. Rub the spice mixture over duck pieces. Cover and refrigerate overnight.

- Next Day: Sear the duck thighs, in rendered duck fat or canola oil. Once seared, remove the thighs to an ovenproof container suitable for slow oven cooking. Cover the seared thighs with canola oil or duck fat and place in a 250 degree oven. Allow to cook very slowly until meat is cooked and nearly falling off of the bone, approximately 3 to 4 hours. Remove from the oven and cool to room temperature in the fat.

- Lightly score the skin on the breast pieces in a crisscross pattern for better fat extraction. Sear the duck breasts over medium-high heat until rare to medium rare. Reheat the duck thighs. Blot the sautéed breast on a towel to remove excess fat, and slice on the bias as thinly as possible.

For the Raisin-Balsamic Sauce:

- Place sugar in heavy-bottomed pan and melt. Cook until caramelized and golden brown. Carefully add the port and balsamic vinegar (*the mixture will sputter*). The sugar will seize up, but it will melt as it heats. Simmer until smooth. Add the raisins and cook until reduced by 2/3. Add the duck or chicken stock and reduce to a napping consistency, usually a 1/2 reduction. Season to taste with salt and pepper. Add butter and whisk until blended. Keep warm.

To Finish and Serve:

- Arrange the sliced duck breasts on serving plates. Place a heated duck thigh alongside the breast. Spoon the warm sauce over the meats.

Roast Monkfish Tails with Warm Olive Sauce

Serves: 4

Monkfish Tails:

4 each monkfish tails, 8-ounces
  each, cleaned weight

1 cup olive oil

1/2 cup chopped parsley

1/4 cup chopped garlic

2 teaspoons cumin

1/2 cup lemon juice

1/2 cup chopped cilantro leaves

1 tablespoon paprika

1/2 teaspoon cayenne pepper

Salt and pepper to taste

Warm Olive Sauce:

1/2 pound olives,
  pitted and split*

4 ounces anchovy fillets

4 tablespoons capers

2 cups extra-virgin olive oil

1/2 cup lemon juice

1 tablespoon hot mustard

Salt and pepper to taste

For the Monkfish:

- Clean the monkfish tails of the membrane in which they are encased. Place all of the remaining ingredients in a food processor and pulse until well mixed. Place the monkfish in a pan and cover completely with marinade, ensuring that the fish is fully immersed. Marinate overnight in the refrigerator, turning occasionally to ensure full flavor.

- Preheat oven to 350 degrees. Remove the fish from marinade, drain and dry. Sear on all sides in a small amount of oil in a hot sauté pan, then cover the pan with a lid and place in the oven for about 25 minutes.

For the Warm Olive Sauce:

- Mix all ingredients together in a saucepan and warm them gently over low heat. Keep warm.

To Finish and Serve:

- Remove the fish to a serving platter. Reduce the pan juices down to syrup over low to medium heat. Drizzle the reduction over the fish and then spoon the warm olive sauce around the plate.

* It is always nice to use an assortment of high-quality olives.

Smoked Slow-Roast Pork Butt with Mole

Serves: 8

Pork Butt:

3 pound pork butt
1/2 cup kosher salt
1/4 cup dried Mexican oregano
Corn oil

Mole:

4 tablespoons lard
3 each ancho chiles, seeded, stemmed and soaked in warm water, drain and reserve the soaking water
2 each corn tortillas
1/2 each onion, diced
1-1/2 each Roma tomatoes, chopped
2 tablespoons sesame seeds
1 each bay leaf
1/2 teaspoon ground cinnamon
1/4 teaspoon ground cumin
1/2 teaspoon cayenne pepper
1/2 teaspoon dry oregano
1/2 teaspoon ground pepper
1/2 teaspoon salt
1/4 cup raisins
1/4 cup cashews
6 cups chicken stock
1 bunch cilantro, leaves only

Finish:

16 each corn tortillas, steamed

For the Pork Butt:

• Cover the pork butt with kosher salt and Mexican oregano. Cold smoke the meat, ideally over wood. Once smoked, rub with corn oil and place in a covered ovenproof pan with a small amount of water. Roast in a 300 degree oven until the meat is fork tender, approximately 3 to 4 hours. Remove from the oven and shred the meat, pulling it apart with 2 forks. Reserve on a covered platter.

For the Mole:

• Fry the chiles in the lard and set aside. Fry the corn tortillas in the same lard and set aside. Purée the fried chiles and the tortillas in a food processor, adding enough of the chile soaking water to form a smooth, loose paste.

• Sauté the onion, tomatoes, sesame seeds and spices together for 3 to 4 minutes in the lard left over from frying the chiles and tortillas. Add the chile and tortilla paste to the sautéed onions in the pan. Stir constantly to bring all the favors together. Add the salt, raisins and cashews, stirring constantly. Finally, add the chicken stock and simmer for approximately 1 hour. Transfer the mixture to a food processor and purée. Add the cilantro and continue to pulse until smooth.

To Finish and Serve:

• Serve the sauce with the roasted pork along with fresh steamed corn tortillas.

Roxsand's Desserts

Known for her desserts, Roxsand always has a wide variety of scrumptious treats available.

Adult Kit Kat crunchy hazelnut chocolate bottom and a lighter chocolate top dusted with French dark cocoa.

B-52 Torte three layers of rich truffle cream, one layer with Bailey's Irish Cream®, one with Grand Marnier®, one with Kahlúa®, topped with crushed pistachios.

Berliner moist flourless chocolate poppyseed walnut cake topped with raspberry preserves.

Marjolane multi layers of japonaise *(a crispy hazelnut meringue)*, praline, chocolate ganache, and chantilly cream.

Florentine Cookies two caramelized almond honey cookies painted with chocolate.

Fresh Fruit Tart organically grown seasonal berry or fruit tarts in a variety of pastries.

Raspberry Engadine a buttery walnut pastry bande, painted with raspberry preserves, and baked with coconut and walnut filling.

Tarte au Citron bracingly tart and buttery curd baked in a ginger pastry.

Chocolate-Raspberry Pâté

Makes: 1 loaf pan

Pâté:

1 tablespoon melted butter

18 ounces bittersweet chocolate

1/2 cup unsalted butter

12 each egg yolks*

6 tablespoons sugar, divided

3 each egg whites*

3/4 cup heavy cream

2 tablespoons sour cream

2 cups fresh berries
(raspberries or other fresh berries)

1-1/2 cups Bittersweet Chocolate
Glaze (recipe follows)

Bittersweet Chocolate Glaze:

2 tablespoons butter or
margarine

1 ounce unsweetened
baking chocolate

4 tablespoons milk

2-1/3 cups powdered sugar

1/2 teaspoon vanilla

For the Pâté:

- Butter a loaf pan with the melted butter. Line the pan with parchment paper.

- Melt the bittersweet chocolate and the butter in a pan over very low heat. Set aside. In a bowl, beat the egg yolks and 4 tablespoons of the sugar until mousse-like in consistency.

- Fold 1/3 of the yolk mixture into chocolate mixture just until combined. Then fold remaining yolk mixture into chocolate mixture. Return the mixture to a heat-proof bowl. Whisk over a double boiler until a whisk run through the bowl leaves a trail *(or slight trough)* in the mixture. Remove from heat; set aside to cool.

- In a separate bowl, whip the egg whites with 1 tablespoon of the sugar until stiff. Fold 1/3 of the egg whites into the chocolate/egg mixture just until combined. Then gently fold in the remaining egg whites.

- In a separate bowl, whip the heavy cream and the sour cream with the remaining 1 tablespoon of sugar until mousse-like in consistency. Fold 1/3 of the cream mixture into the chocolate/egg mixture just until combined. Then very gently fold the remaining cream mixture into the chocolate/egg mixture.

- Pour 1/3 of mixture into the prepped loaf pan, placing a layer of the fresh berries on top, being careful not to place any berries too close to the sides of the pan. Pour another 1/3 of the mixture on top, and place an additional layer of the fresh berries on top of the second layer. Cover with remaining 1/3 of mixture and freeze overnight.

For the Bittersweet Chocolate Glaze:

- Combine butter or margarine with chocolate in a microwave-safe bowl. Microwave on high power for 2 minutes or until melted.

- Remove from microwave. Stir in milk alternately with powdered sugar. Beat until blended and smooth either by hand or with an electric mixer. Combine until the glaze is smooth and only slightly runny. Stir in the vanilla and mix well.

To Finish and Serve:

- Unmold pâté onto serving platter. Pour or spread bittersweet chocolate glaze over the loaf, slice and serve.

* Use pasteurized eggs only, available pasteurized in the shell at some grocery stores or in bulk in cartons in most stores.

THIERRY RAUTUREAU

SEATTLE, WA

American Express Best Chef: Northwest/Hawaii, 1998

Five minutes with Thierry Rautureau and the image of a stern, humorless chef, wielding his whisk over a crew of cowed minions vaporizes like a drop of water on a hot stove.

With his jaunty trademark fedora, his ever present smile and witty rapid-fire conversation, he more resembles a Gallic cabaret comic or character actor in a French film than the proprietor of a much-lauded restaurant.

Rautureau describes his cuisine as, "French contemporary with a Northwestern flair," which in essence, sums up the odyssey that took him from his birthplace in Saint Hilaire de Loulay in the Muscadet region of France to the front of the American culinary pack.

The oldest of three children, Thierry was the one mom left with instructions on preparing dinner after school. "It was `Pick the haricot verts, put the water on the fire and cook them, peel and chop, and add the turnips and carrots to the pot au feu.' — I hated it, I wanted to play with my friends."

Yet something must have clicked during all that time spent in the kitchen, because when Rautureau graduated from high school he decided that instead of going on for an academic degree, he would train to be a chef. "It was a combination of things," he says. "My cousin was an apprentice cook and my mother told me that as a chef I could travel the world and always have a meal and a roof over my head."

She turned out to be prescient. Completing a two-year apprenticeship in Anjou, Rautureau worked in Mont St. Michel in Normandy, Chamonix in the French Alps and Hendaye in the Basque region. "I took influences from each place, picking up a style without knowing it. In the Basque, it was bell peppers, eggplant and zucchini — in the Alps, cheese, potatoes and cream. In Normandy, it was mussels, lamb and flageolets."

WINNING STYLES COOKBOOK | THIERRY RAUTUREAU

73

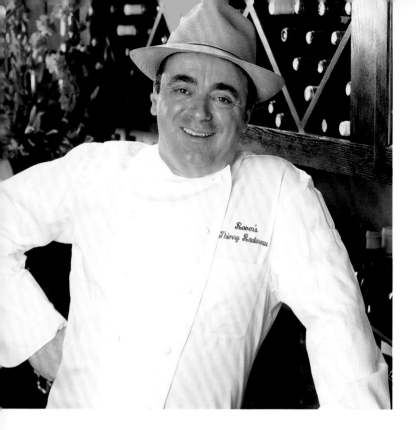

After a stint in the French army, Rautureau went to the United States to work, planning to stay six months. That was 25 years ago.

He met wife-to-be Kathleen when both were working at The Seventh Street Bistro in Los Angeles. The pair searched for a restaurant property in the area, but the prohibitive prices were discouraging to the young couple. In 1987, they took a fortuitous trip to Seattle to visit Rautureau's longtime friend Cyril Frechier who took them to dinner at Rover's, a local restaurant. The timing could not have been better. Rover's owners wanted to sell and Kathleen says, "We were ready. We wanted a business, a house and a place to raise kids, and the Madison Valley area of Seattle is a real community within the city."

Rautureau adds, "We visited Pike Place Market and I could just picture myself shopping and then coming back to the restaurant and cooking. We truly have the bounty of America here."

They subsequently bought a house two blocks from the restaurant and their sons Adrian and Ryan attend the local school. In a neat turnabout, Frechier — the catalyst of their settling in Seattle — is now Rover's manager and sommelier.

"At first I didn't make too many changes in the restaurant; it wouldn't have worked here then," says Rautureau. "We did pasta, beef, chicken. It was a la carte. Slowly, over six to eight years, we changed into what we are today."

Today, Rover's effortlessly meshes Rautureau's classic French training with the incredible abundance of foodstuffs available in the Pacific Northwest. "I don't follow trends. I'm not even always sure what the trends are," he laughs.

Nor does he need to chase the new and way-out. Situated away from Seattle's prime tourist area, Rover's is a genuine dining destination. Two-thirds of the clientele are visitors from the East Coast. Entering through an intimate courtyard under mature trees, diners find a series of small rooms painted soft daffodil yellow and hung with bright whimsical paintings by French-born artist Isa D'Arleans. Lighting is warm and indirect, tables meticulously set and lavish floral arrangements, courtesy of Kathleen, give the sense of dining in someone's home. Providing the home-cooked dinner consists of a choice of three prix fixe menus, a six or nine course menu degustation, as well as the vegetarian menu that has become a Rautureau signature. "The vegetarian thing was just getting popular in L.A. in the mid-eighties and when we moved to

Seattle I immediately recognized with the abundance of produce available and the growing customer interest, it was a natural direction."

Even non-vegetarians crave creations like Rautureau's ultra whipped egg and lime fraiche scrambled, served in the shell and topped with snapping crisp, briny sturgeon caviar. His deeply flavorful pinot noir sorbet with complex notes of clove, cinnamon, orange and lemon zest is the ideal palate cleanser. A woven basket of bright green avocado slices cradles sweet scarlet and saffron teardrop tomatoes and crunchy corn kernels in a subtle, lemon vinaigrette. It is as beautiful as it is satisfying.

Seafood preparations shine. Local salmon, crab, mussels, clams, oysters and scallops all get the Rautureau touch, and he fearlessly marries sweetbreads, foie gras and fava beans. (No jokes about a "nice Chianti," please.)

Menus change daily to some extent, and considerably with the season. Each dish is prepared with the precision of a surgeon, the eye of an artist and phenomenal attention to detail. The restaurant crew makes its own vinegar, duck prosciutto and confit. Every summer the kitchen staff, headed up by the self-described "Chef In The Hat" and his Sous Chef Adam Hoffman, preserves more than 350 pounds of cherries, apricots and nectarines. Says Rautureau, "In January, there is no dessert better than those ripe, sweet cherries on vanilla ice cream. It's a taste of summer."

At home, Kathleen does most of the cooking, preparing simple healthful food like roast chicken and corned beef and cabbage.

When they entertain, the chef does the honors, popping over to the restaurant to see what's available in the walk-in. The couple doesn't dine out often, preferring to spend time at home as a family.

Rautureau's out-of-the-restaurant schedule is hectic. He is completing a cookbook, guest chefs at national culinary events and does a lot of fundraisers around the country.

Relaxation for Rautureau is not necessarily quiet time. He is a proficient, self-taught drummer who has had his own kit since 1979. What's the attraction? "I go down in the basement, put on a CD and pound away. I like the noise and it's a tension releaser," he explains.

After 16 years of working in a space no bigger than the average home kitchen, Rautureau remodeled and enlarged both the restaurant's kitchen and the formerly pocket-sized foyer. A wine cellar of 5,500 bottles was also built which increased Rover's wine list to 600 labels with more than 100 half-bottles, all evenly divided between French and American vintages.

When asked what's next, his answer is direct, "Over the next ten years, you are going to see Rover's and me carrying on our tradition, and then you will find me retired in Provence somewhere between Grasse and Vence in the hills behind Nice."

You'll recognize him by the hat.

Smoked Salmon and Crispy Potatoes with Crème Fraîche

Serves: 4

Salmon:

4 ounces smoked salmon, sliced in julienne

1 teaspoon finely chopped shallot

1/4 teaspoon finely chopped parsley

1/4 teaspoon finely chopped chives

1 tablespoon crème fraîche

1 tablespoon walnut oil

Potatoes:

2 each Yellow Finn potatoes, finely diced

1 each shallot, finely chopped

1 tablespoon clarified butter

1 tablespoon sliced chives

1 tablespoon crème fraîche

Salt and pepper to taste

Finish:

4 tablespoons basil and tomato oil *(optional)*

Crème Fraîche

Chopped chives to taste

For the Salmon:

- In a bowl, toss the salmon ingredients together until well-mixed. Set aside.

For the Potatoes:

- In a sauté pan, sauté the diced potatoes and the shallot in clarified butter until the potatoes are crisp-tender. Remove from heat and stir in the sliced chives and the crème fraîche. Add salt and pepper to taste.

To Finish and Serve:

- Pack 1/4 of the salmon mixture into each of four 3-inch round molds. Top each with 1/4 of the potato mixture, packing well. Place each on a serving plate and remove from mold. Drizzle basil and tomato oil around each. Top with a dollop of crème fraîche and chopped chives.

Wild Mushroom Salad with Micro Greens and Aged Balsamic Vinegar

Serves: 4

Dressing:

2 tablespoons unsalted butter *(may substitute Moroccan olive oil)*

3 cups wild mushrooms *(chanterelle, lobster, coral, matsutakes)*

1/4 cup minced shallots

1 teaspoon minced garlic

1 teaspoon chopped thyme

2 tablespoons aged balsamic vinegar *(ideally 25-year-old)*

1/4 cup olive oil

Salt and pepper to taste

Salad:

3 cups micro greens or garden greens *(red oak leaf preferred)*

Finish:

Salt and pepper to taste

For the Dressing:

- In a small sauté pan, heat the butter *(or oil)* until golden brown over medium to high heat. Add the mushrooms and sauté until colored.

- Add the shallots, garlic and thyme and lightly brown. Add the balsamic vinegar. Incorporate the olive oil into the mixture with a whisk.

- Season the dressing with salt and pepper to taste and remove from heat and reserve. Remove and set aside some of the mushrooms for garnish.

For the Salad:

- Toss greens with the vinaigrette.

To Finish and Serve:

- Arrange the tossed salad on serving plates and place reserved mushrooms on top and around the greens. Season with salt and pepper to taste.

Red Bell Pepper Flan with Green Lentils and Rosemary Beurre Blanc

Serves: 4

Red Bell Pepper Flan:
3 each red bell peppers
2 each eggs
1/3 cup cream

Green Lentils:
1 tablespoon extra-virgin olive oil
1 each shallot, chopped
1 sprig fresh rosemary, chopped
1 clove garlic, chopped
1/2 cup green lentils
1 cup vegetable stock
Salt and pepper to taste

Rosemary Beurre Blanc:
1 tablespoon butter
6 each shallots, sliced
2 bunches fresh rosemary, chopped
1 cup white wine
1 tablespoon heavy cream
6 tablespoons butter, cut into cubes

For the Red Bell Pepper Flan:

- Preheat oven to 300 degrees and heat water for hot water bath. Over an open flame, roast bell peppers until skin is charred black. Peel off the skin and remove seeds and discard. Purée the peeled roasted peppers in a blender. Mix 1/2 cup of the pepper purée with the eggs, then add the cream. Butter four 4-ounce ramekins. Place molds in baking pan. Pour bell pepper mixture into remekins. Fill the baking pan with the preheated hot water to reach halfway up the sides of the ramekins. Cover the baking pan tightly with foil. Bake for approximately 15 minutes. Keep warm until ready to serve.

For the Green Lentils:

- Heat olive oil in a skillet. Add the shallot, rosemary and garlic and let sweat for 2 minutes over low to medium heat. Add the lentils and vegetable stock. Bring to a boil. Reduce heat and cook until tender, about 25 minutes. Season to taste with salt and pepper.

For the Rosemary Beurre Blanc:

- Heat butter in a skillet. Add the shallots and rosemary and let sweat about 1 minute. Add the white wine. Cook over low to medium heat until reduced by 3/4. Add the heavy cream. Continue cooking until again reduced by 3/4. Incorporate the butter slowly with a whisk, one cube at a time. Strain the sauce and keep warm.

To Finish and Serve:

- Arrange the lentils in a circle on one end of each of four serving plates. Unmold a flan next to the lentils. Spoon the beurre blanc around each flan. Serve hot.

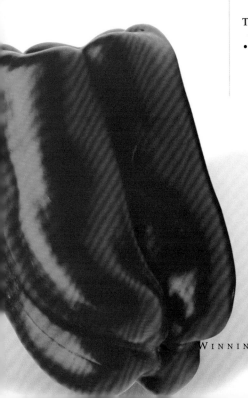

Thierry Rautureau's Beverage Recommendations

Smoked Salmon and Crispy Potatoes with Crème Fraîche
Sancerre Les Cailottes, Etienne Riffault 2000
page 77

Wild Mushroom Salad with Micro Greens and Aged Balsamic Vinegar
Pouilly Fumé Silex, Didier Dagueneau 1999
page 77

Red Bell Pepper Flan with Green Lentils and Rosemary Beurre Blanc
Margaux Pavilon Blanc 1998
page 79

Roast of Scottish Venison with Soybeans and Huckleberry Sauce
St.-Emilion Château Cheval Blanc 1985
page 81

Ellensburg Lamb Loin with Nectarine Chutney and Bing Cherry Sauce
Hermitage John Louis Chave 1997
page 83

Chilled Yakima Peach Soup
Muscat de Beaume de Venise, Coteau de Coyeaux 1999
page 85

Chocolate Crème Brûlée
Illy Coffee Double Espresso
page 85

Roast of Scottish Venison with Soybeans and Huckleberry Sauce

Serves: 4

Huckleberry Sauce:

5 tablespoons butter

1 pound venison bones,
  broken into small pieces

1 each carrot, finely diced

6 each shallots, chopped

1 clove garlic, chopped

5 sprigs fresh thyme

3 each bay leaves

3/4 cup raspberry vinegar

1/2 cup huckleberries

3 cups veal stock

1/4 cup sugar

1/2 cup water

4 tablespoons red wine vinegar

Soybeans:

3 tablespoons butter

2 tablespoons shallots, chopped

1 pound fresh soybeans

Salt and pepper to taste

Scottish Venison:

3 tablespoons butter

16 ounces venison roast, boned
  out *(ask your butcher for Denver
  cut or substitute venison loin)*

For the Huckleberry Sauce:

- In a hot pan, melt 3 tablespoons of the butter and brown the venison bones. Add the carrot, shallots, garlic, thyme and bay leaves and cook until browned and roasted. Add the raspberry vinegar and cook until reduced by 2/3. Add the huckleberries and cook for 3 to 4 minutes. Then add the veal stock and continue cooking until reduced again by 2/3.

- Make a caramel by combining the sugar and water in a saucepan and cook over medium heat until brown. Carefully stir in the red wine vinegar, cooking and stirring until smooth. Add the caramel sauce to the veal stock sauce. Strain and finish the sauce with the remaining 2 tablespoons of the butter.

For the Soybeans:

- In a sauté pan, melt the butter. Add the shallots to the pan and sauté for 2 to 3 minutes. Add the soybeans and cook slowly until tender. Season to taste with the salt and pepper.

For the Scottish Venison:

- Preheat oven to 375 degrees. In a hot sauté pan, melt the butter. Sear the venison. Finish the venison in the preheated oven for a few minutes until medium rare, an internal temperature of 130 degrees on an instant-read meat thermometer. Take the roast out of the pan and let it rest for at least 15 minutes.

To Finish and Serve:

- Slice the venison roast. Place on serving plates, top with sauce and serve soybeans on the side.

Chef Tip

"When working on a dish, don't cut your own taste short. Try it. If you really like it, there is no way in the world the person across the table isn't going to like it, too."

Ellensburg Lamb Loin with Nectarine Chutney and Bing Cherry Sauce

Serves: 4

Bing Cherry Sauce:

12-16 ounces lamb bones, broken into small pieces (*drizzle with 2 tablespoons of vegetable oil*)

1 each carrot, finely diced

6 each shallots, chopped

1 clove garlic, chopped

5 sprigs fresh thyme

3 each bay leaves

1 cup raspberry vinegar

1 cup Bing cherries, pitted

3 cups lamb stock
   (*may substitute veal stock*)

1/4 cup sugar

1/2 cup water

4 tablespoons butter

Salt and pepper to taste

Lamb:

2 each lamb loins
   (*about 12 ounces each or four each lamb loins, approximately 6 ounces each, boned out and silver skin removed*)

Salt and pepper to taste

Chutney:

4 halves nectarine

1 each red onion, finely diced

1/4 cup red wine vinegar

For the Bing Cherry Sauce:

- Brown lamb bones in a hot pan. Add carrot, shallots, garlic and herbs and cook until shallots and carrots are roasted and browned. Add 3/4 cups of the vinegar and cook until reduced by 3/4. Add the cherries and cook for approximately 5 minutes. Add the lamb stock and cook until reduced by 2/3. Remove from heat and set aside.

- Make a caramel by combining the sugar and water in a saucepan and cooking over medium heat until browned. Carefully stir in the remaining 1/4 cup of raspberry vinegar, cooking and stirring until smooth. Add the caramel sauce to the browned lamb stock mixture. Strain the sauce and whisk in the butter. Season with salt and pepper to taste. Remove from heat and keep warm.

For the Lamb:

- Season lamb with salt and pepper to taste.

- Preheat oven to 350 degrees. In a hot sauté pan, sear the lamb loin. Finish the lamb in the oven for 5 to 7 minutes, or until pink. Allow the lamb loin to rest for at least 5 minutes, then slice it.

For the Chutney:

- Place the nectarines, red onion and red wine vinegar in a hot sauté pan. Cook slowly for approximately 5 minutes. Remove from heat and keep warm.

To Finish and Serve:

- Place the sliced lamb loin on serving plates. Pour sauce over lamb. Place a mound of chutney to the side of the lamb. Excellent served with fava beans and/or a potato mousseline.

Rautureau's Favorite Tool

A Swedish fish spatula with a tip customized by Rautureau with a slight bend at the widest part. "It's practical, well-made, flexible. It fits nicely in the hand and picks things up without breaking them."

Chilled Yakima Peach Soup

Serves: 4

Yakima Peach Soup:
1/4 cup granulated sugar
1-1/2 cups water
2 each ripe peaches,
    cut in half and pitted
5 leaves lemon verbena

For the Yakima Peach Soup:

- In a wide pot, bring the sugar and water to a boil over medium heat. Place the peaches and the lemon verbena leaves into the boiling mixture, covering with a towel to keep the peaches immersed in the water. Return to a boil, reduce heat and poach the peaches for about three minutes. Remove the peaches and the lemon verbena leaves from the syrup, discarding the verbena leaves and put the peaches immediately into an ice water bath to make peeling easier. Remove peels and reserve. Let peaches and peels cool. Set syrup over an ice bath to cool. Once both are cool, put the peaches and the peels back into the syrup. In a blender, mix the peach and syrup until very smooth.

To Finish and Serve:

- Chill thoroughly in refrigerator.

Chocolate Crème Brûlée

Serves: 5

Crème Brûlée:
5 each egg yolks
1/4 cup sugar
2 cups heavy cream
1/2 pod vanilla bean
4-1/2 ounces bittersweet
    chocolate, chopped fine

Finish:
2 tablespoons granulated sugar

For the Crème Brûlée:

- Preheat oven to 325 degrees and heat water for water bath.

- In a stainless steel bowl, whisk the egg yolks with the sugar. Place the heavy cream in a medium-size, heavy saucepan. Split the vanilla bean lengthwise and scrape the seeds into the saucepan with the cream. Toss the vanilla bean pod in with the cream as well. Bring the cream just to a boil, and remove from the heat. Add the chocolate and stir until it is melted.

- Whisk the cream into the egg mixture, then strain through a fine-mesh sieve. Skim the foam off the top with a ladle or spoon. Ladle the custard into each of five 5-ounce ramekins and place in a hotel pan or roasting pan. If there are any remaining bubbles or foam, scoop them off the surface of the ramekins. Pour the preheated water into the pan to a depth of about 1/2 to 3/4 inches. Cover the pan with foil and prick the foil with a knife, lifting gently with the tip of the knife to form a tent.

- Bake for 20 to 30 minutes, or until the custards have a gelatinous, rather than a watery, jiggle. Refrigerate until thoroughly chilled.

To Finish and Serve:

- Sprinkle granulated sugar over each custard, place under the broiler until the sugar bubbles and browns. Cool before serving.

CHARLIE TROTTER

CHICAGO, IL

All-Clad Metalcrafters Outstanding Chef, 1999

American Express Best Chef: Midwest, 1992

When asked how his culinary style has developed, Charlie Trotter observes dryly, "All of that has been very well documented." Indeed it has.

Reams of material has been written about the Chicago-based celebrity chef and he has generated quite a bit of paper himself with over a dozen cookbooks to his name.

He says that his cooking style is Western European-derived — Italian, French and Spanish with Asian nuances — and likens it to jazz, an appropriate comparison since his father named him after saxophonist Charlie Parker. He points out that the greats, like Miles Davis and John Coltrane, never perform a piece of music the same way twice. Similarly, spontaneity and improvisation are hallmarks of Trotter's food.

Growing up in suburban Chicago, Trotter showed no evidence of his future vocation. He majored in political science in college and for relaxation, began cooking for his roommates at the University of Wisconsin.

"I enjoyed the process and thought, I'll try and find out if I'd like doing this. If it doesn't work out I can always go back to my original plan. Meanwhile I'll learn how to feed my family and friends," he says.

In his typically focused fashion, Trotter grabbed a job as a waiter at Chicago's Sinclairs restaurant and eventually convinced Chef Norman Van Aken that he actually belonged in the kitchen. Says Trotter, "It was love at first sight. It has never seemed like work to me. I set out on this path; reading, working, traveling and dining in Europe."

He pursued the path for five years, eventually cooking for people in their homes on weekends. He says modestly, "At that point, I thought, I don't know if I know everything, but I feel comfortable opening a restaurant."

In 1987 the eponymous Charlie Trotter's debuted to instantaneous acclaim. The restaurant is located in a turn-of-the-last-century brownstone in Chicago's colorful Lincoln Park neighborhood. (Trotter also owns the adjoining building which includes a ravishingly furnished studio kitchen where Trotter's PBS television series, *The Kitchen Sessions with Charlie Trotter* is taped). The complex includes four temperature and humidity controlled redwood wine cellars that hold 1,600 different selections from around the globe.

From the cozy bar through the three dining rooms, the restaurant has a feel that is at once both elegant and very intimate. Why is this relatively small (100 seats) restaurant the gastronomic equivalent of Mecca? Very simply, Trotter is a single-minded perfectionist. For ingredients, he draws from a network of close to 100 purveyors with an emphasis on naturally raised and/or free-range meat and game, line-caught seafood and organic produce. Everything from bread to dressings and sauces are made in-house. Trotter uses sauces that are vegetable juice-based rather than butter or cream-based.

CHARLIE TROTTER'S

Thursday, September 5, 2002
Grand Menu

Mille Feuille of Squashes, Roasted Eggplant, Heirloom Tomatoes
with Swan Creek Farm Ricotta & Gazpacho Sorbet
~Seresin Sauvignon Blanc, Marlborough 2000~

Olive Oil Poached Scottish Salmon with Cauliflower,
Cucumber, Salmon Roe & Dill Vinaigrette
~Bordeaux Chateau Talbot "Caillou Blanc" 1999~

European Daurade with Yellow, Round & Red Carrots,
Sunchoke & Black Cardamom Infused Carrot Emulsion
~Bourgogne Blanc F. Jobard 1993~

Slow Poached Breast of Squab with Napa Cabbage, Foie Gras
& Spiced Squab Consomme
~Ancien Pinot Noir, Carneros 1999~

Roasted White Trumpet Royale, Lobster & Cauliflower Mushrooms
with Japanese Kumai Jasmine Rice Cake & Kalamata Olive Sauce
~J.C. Cellars "Ventana Vineyard" Syrah, Monterey 1999~

Pistachio Crème Anglais & Frozen Pistachio Nougat
Huet 1997~

The restaurant is 100 percent smoke-free and amazingly, cocktails, a huge profit-center for most restaurants, are not served. Says the chef, "I don't want guests feeling they have over-indulged. I want them to feel stimulated and alert."

Dinner à la Trotter can be enjoyed one of three ways. The Grand Degustation menu features seven courses, but optional add-ons can bring it up to ten or more. For a complete blow out, The Kitchen Table Menu averages about 15 courses. The Vegetable Menu, meanwhile, may sound abstemious but in Trotter's hands it becomes a symphony of pure, intense flavors and varying textures.

One of the reasons for Trotter's incredible success is that he never ceases driving himself. "Any creative person is obliged to evolve," he says. "But, if you want to keep on growing, it has to happen in a natural way. My cooking grows lighter and I rely more on subtlety. As I mature, I find there are more and more Asian references in my cuisine."

"Until recently," says Trotter, "I've concentrated on vertical rather than horizontal growth. I haven't been interested in proliferating more restaurants and just wanted to make sure this one is the best it can possibly be."

Having accomplished that goal, the still driven Trotter is opening a new restaurant in Los Cabos, Mexico which features Latino Caribbean-accented seafood.

Trotter has also developed a popular product line that includes prepared meals, sweet and savory sauces, cured salmon and coffee. Along with completing his three most recent cookbooks

and a fourth television series, Trotter travels extensively as a teacher, consultant and motivational speaker. His most noteworthy out-of-the-kitchen activities though, are of a charitable nature. He created the non-profit Charlie Trotter Culinary Education Program. The program awards scholarships to students seeking careers in the culinary arts and promotes the quest for education and the development of interest in cooking and food among Chicago-area school kids. Every week, Trotter hosts a dinner for students from around the city. They tour the restaurant, dine and speak with restaurant employees about different foods, organic farming, running a restaurant and dining etiquette.

Given such a non-stop schedule, what he does for fun? When asked, Trotter sounds amazed at the question. "I have fun everyday. I feel guilty because I've never had a 'job.'"

He does find time for some leisure activities. A high school gymnast, Trotter is still athletic and now runs marathons. His favorite is the Medoc Marathon, run in the Bordeaux region of France in celebration of the harvest. Trotter is devoted to his son Dylan and the two play chess together as well as face off on the tennis court and ski in season.

His final summation of a style of cuisine that has become world famous is, "My food is extremely personal to me. I serve exactly what I want to eat."

Mille-Feuille of Squashes, Roasted Eggplant, Heirloom Tomatoes with Swan Creek Farm Ricotta and Gazpacho Sorbet

Serves: 4

Puff Pastry:

3 each pieces of puff pastry,
each 1/4-inch thick,
6 x 8 inches in size

Ricotta Mixture:

1 cup ricotta

2 tablespoons olive oil

2 teaspoons white wine vinegar

2 tablespoons chopped chives

Salt and pepper to taste

Eggplant Purée:

1 each small eggplant, rubbed
with olive oil

3 cloves garlic,
peeled and quartered

3 each bay leaves

1 tablespoon olive oil

2 teaspoons balsamic vinegar

1 teaspoon sherry vinegar

Oven-Roasted Tomatoes:

8 each red tomatoes, cut into 1/8-
inch wedges, seeds and pulp
removed from each wedge

8 each yellow tomatoes, cut into
1/8-inch wedges, seeds and
pulp removed from each wedge

1-1/2 tablespoons olive oil

1-1/2 teaspoons chopped thyme

Salt and pepper to taste

Squash Blossoms:

12 each squash blossoms,
cleaned and thistles removed

2 teaspoons olive oil

1 teaspoon white wine vinegar

Additional Items:

Zucchini Slices:
Recipe on page 102

Tomato Powder:
Recipe on page 102

Gazpacho Sorbet:
Recipe on page 102

Finish:

3 tablespoons chopped
fresh basil

4 teaspoons micro chervil
*(may substitute with lightly
chopped chervil)*

For the Puff Pastry:

- Line a sheet pan with parchment paper. Lay the pieces of pastry on the pan. Top with another layer of parchment paper, and add another sheet pan on top. Repeat this process until all the pastry used. Bake at 315 degrees for 15 minutes.

For the Ricotta Mixture:

- Combine all ingredients in a mixing bowl and season to taste with salt and pepper. Refrigerate until needed.

For the Eggplant Purée:

- Preheat the oven to 400 degrees. Cut slits in the eggplant with a paring knife, and insert the garlic slices and bay leaves. Wrap in aluminum foil and bake for 45 minutes to 1 hour, or until tender. Scrape the eggplant meat from the skin, and discard the bay leaves and garlic pieces. Purée the eggplant meat until smooth and place on a non-stick sheet pan. Reduce oven temperature to 315 degrees and bake the purée for 20 minutes. Season the purée with the olive oil, balsamic vinegar and sherry vinegar. Season to taste with salt and pepper. Refrigerate until needed.

For the Oven Roasted Tomatoes:

- Preheat oven to 275 degrees. Lay the tomato wedges on a rack set over a sheet pan. Lightly brush the tomato wedges with the olive oil and sprinkle with the thyme. Roast for 30 minutes. Pat dry with a towel. Season with salt and pepper.

For the Squash Blossoms:

- Open up the squash blossoms and discard the stems. Brush the squash blossoms with the olive oil and vinegar and lay flat.

To Assemble the Mille-Feuille:

- Place 1 piece of the puff pastry on an even surface and spread a thin layer of the ricotta mixture over the puff pastry. Continue to layer with the following ingredients: zucchini slices *(see recipe on page 102)*, oven-roasted red tomatoes, chopped basil, eggplant purée, another puff pastry sheet, ricotta mixture, squash blossoms, oven-roasted yellow tomatoes, and eggplant purée. Top with a final layer of the puff pastry.

To Finish and Serve:

- Slice the mille-feuille with a very sharp knife into 1-inch thick slices. Carefully transfer slices to each of four serving plates. Spoon the reserved red bell pepper mixture reserved when making the gazpacho sorbet *(see recipe on page 102)* in two lines on the top and bottom sides of the mille-feuille. Sprinkle with the tomato powder *(see recipe on page 102)* and micro chervil. Spoon a quenelle *(an oval scoop shaped like a football — to shape, use two warm spoons to form the sorbet)* of the gazpacho sorbet *(see recipe on page 102)* over each serving of the mille-feuille.

Olive Oil Poached Scottish Salmon with Cauliflower, Cucumber, Salmon Roe and Dill Oil

Serves: 4

Lime Zest:

2 teaspoons lime zest

Poached Salmon:

4 cups olive oil

1 each 13 x 6-inch long piece of Scottish salmon, skin removed, and sliced into twelve 1/2-inch-thick pieces

Salt and pepper to taste

Cauliflower Purée:

1 cup steamed and chopped cauliflower

1 tablespoon olive oil

2 tablespoons heavy cream

Salt and pepper to taste

Cauliflower Florets:

1/4 cup tiny cauliflower florets, steamed

2 teaspoons olive oil

1 teaspoon white wine vinegar

Salt and pepper to taste

Salmon Roe:

1/4 cup salmon roe *(available from fish mongers, also called Keta)*

2 teaspoons olive oil

2 teaspoons soy sauce

1 teaspoon yuzu lemon juice*

Finish:

8 teaspoon dill oil**

4 teaspoons thinly sliced pickled radish

1/4 cup #10 Parisian *(very small melon baller)* scooped English cucumber, skin removed

4 each micro cucumbers *(may substitute thin slices of cucumber cut with a decorative cookie cutter)*

2 tablespoons micro mâche***

4 teaspoons micro parsley or sprouts

1/2 teaspoon powdered togarashi*

1/2 teaspoon ground Japanese citrus tree spice*

For the Lime Zest:

- Place lime zest on a cookie sheet lined with parchment paper and place in a 200 degree oven for 2 hours. Set aside until needed.

For the Poached Salmon:

- Place the olive oil in a wide, shallow saucepan. Heat the olive oil until it reaches 105 degrees. Place the salmon slices in the oil and cook for 15 minutes on each side. The salmon should be submerged in the olive oil. The salmon will appear bright pink once it is cooked, not pale pink like you would expect. Remove the salmon from the oil and season with salt and pepper.

For the Cauliflower Purée:

- Purée the cauliflower with the olive oil and heavy cream until smooth. Season to taste with salt and pepper.

For the Cauliflower Florets:

- Toss the steamed florets with the olive oil and vinegar and season to taste with salt and pepper.

For the Salmon Roe:

- Gently mix the salmon roe with the olive oil, soy sauce and yuzu lemon juice.

To Finish and Serve:

- Spread a 4-inch square of the cauliflower purée in the center of each of four serving plates. Place three slices of the salmon over the purée. Spoon the salmon roe over the salmon slices and around the plates. Drizzle the dill oil around the plates and arrange the remaining garnishes and lime zest around the salmon.

* Available at Asian markets
** Available in gourmet and specialty markets
*** Available at some health food stores

Charlie Trotter's Beverage Recommendations

Mille-Feuille of Squashes, Roasted Eggplant, Heirloom Tomatoes with Swan Creek Farm Ricotta and Gazpacho Sorbet
Seresin Sauvignon Blanc, Marlborough 2000
page 91

Olive Oil Poached Scottish Salmon with Cauliflower, Cucumber, Salmon Roe and Dill Oil
Bordeau Chateau Talbot "Caillou Blanc" 1999
page 93

Steamed European Turbot with Yellow, Burgundy, Round and Red Carrots, Sunchokes and Black Cardamom Infused Carrot Emulsion
Bourgogne Blanc F. Jobard 1993
page 95

Slow Poached Breast of Squab with Napa Cabbage, Foie Gras and Spiced Squab Consommé
Ancien Pino Noir, Carnjeros 1999
page 97

Steamed European Turbot with Yellow, Burgundy, Round and Red Carrots, Sunchokes and Black Cardamom-Infused Carrot Emulsion

Serves: 4

Steamed Turbot:

4 each turbot or halibut fillets,
  3-ounces each, skin removed

1/4 cup Serrano ham cut into
  tiny dice *(may substitute
  any cured ham)*

1/4 cup diced salt-cured pork fat,
  blanched in water

1/4 cup toasted and chopped
  pecans

1 teaspoon chopped thyme

1/2 teaspoon ground fennel seed

1/4 teaspoon ground cardamom

1 teaspoon finely grated
  orange zest

1/2 teaspoon grated ginger

Salt and pepper to taste

Carrots:

8 each tiny yellow carrots or baby
  carrots, peeled and cooked

4 each tiny round orange carrots,
  peeled and cooked

1 each small burgundy carrot,
  peeled, cooked and sliced into
  bite-size pieces

2 teaspoons olive oil

2 teaspoons yuzu lemon juice*

Salt and pepper to taste

Sunchoke Purée:

1/2 cup peeled and chopped
  sunchokes, blanched
  (also called Jerusalem artichokes)

1/4 cup vegetable stock

2 teaspoons yuzu lemon juice*

2 tablespoons olive oil

Salt and pepper to taste

Cardamom-Carrot Emulsion:

2 teaspoons toasted
  black cardamom seeds**

1 cup sliced carrots

3 cups vegetable stock

1 tablespoon white wine vinegar

2 teaspoons chile vinegar

1/4 cup butter

Salt and pepper to taste

Finish:

8 teaspoons basil oil

12 each micro carrot tops or
  dill sprigs

For the Steamed Turbot:

- Bring a few inches of water to boil in a pot fitted with a steamer insert. Place fillets on the steamer insert. Cover the pot and steam until fish is opaque and firm to the touch, approximately 3 to 4 minutes.

- Place the ham and pork fat in a sauté pan and heat for 3 minutes. Add the pecans, thyme and spices and continue to cook for 1 minute. Season to taste with salt and pepper. Just prior to serving, place this mixture as a crust on the warm steamed turbot. Dish should be served warm, not room temperature.

For the Carrots:

- Place all the carrots in a sauté pan with the olive oil and yuzu lemon juice and cook until just hot. Season the carrots to taste with salt and pepper.

For the Sunchoke Purée:

- Purée the sunchokes with the vegetable stock, yuzu lemon juice and olive oil until smooth. Season to taste with salt and pepper and warm just prior to use.

For the Cardamom-Carrot Emulsion:

- Place the cardamom seeds, sliced carrots and vegetable stock in a saucepan and cook over medium heat until the carrots are tender. Purée the mixture and pass it through a fine-mesh sieve. Return the carrot purée to the saucepan and add the vinegars. Whisk in the butter and season to taste with salt and pepper. Froth with a hand-held blender just prior to use.

To Finish and Serve:

- Spoon the sunchoke purée in a horizontal line in the center of each of four serving plates. Place a piece of the turbot at 9 o'clock on each plate and arrange the carrots at 3 o'clock. Spoon the froth from the emulsion over the turbot and carrots. Drizzle the basil oil around the plate and sprinkle with the micro carrot tops.

* Available at Asian markets
** Available at gourmet specialty shops and spice purveyors

More of Charlie Trotter's Beverage Recommendations

Roasted White Trumpet Royale, Lobster and Cauliflower Mushrooms with Japanese Kumai Jasmine Rice Cake and Kalamata Olive Sauce

J.C. Cellars "Ventana Vineyard" Syrah, Monterey 1999

page 99

Napoleon of Chocolate-Hazelnut Cream, Strawberries and Blueberries with White Chocolate Gelée

Banyuls Chapoutier 1996

page 101

Slow-Poached Breast of Squab with Napa Cabbage, Foie Gras and Spiced Squab Consommé

Serves: 4

Poached Squab:

1-1/2 quarts squab or chicken stock

3 cloves garlic

1 each bay leaf

2 each sprigs thyme

4 each squab breasts, skin removed *(may substitute game hens)*

12 each 1/2-inch squares of foie gras

Salt and pepper to taste

Napa Cabbage:

3 tablespoons foie gras trimmings

3 cups Napa cabbage, cut into a fine chiffonade

1/2 teaspoon minced ginger

2 tablespoons butter

2 teaspoons balsamic vinegar

Salt and pepper to taste

Spiced Squab Consommé:

1-1/2 quarts squab consommé or game hen or chicken consommé *(see side bar recipe)*

1 piece star anise

1/2 each jalapeño, seeded

1 teaspoon coriander seeds

1 tablespoon hot pepper vinegar*

Elephant Garlic:

4 pieces elephant garlic, peeled

1/2 cup olive oil

Additional Items:

Preserved Ginger::
Recipe on page 102

Finish:

1 cup braised black-eyed peas

8 each tiny candy-striped beets, cooked and cleaned

8 each tiny golden beets, cooked and cleaned, or baby beets

4 tablespoons preserved ginger

1 teaspoon chopped sage

1 teaspoon chopped parsley

32 pieces micro celery sprouts *(may substitute alfalfa sprouts)*

Ground black pepper to taste

For the Poached Squab:

• Place the stock in a saucepan and add the garlic, bay leaf and thyme. Heat to 160 degrees *(use an instant-read thermometer)*. Add the squab breasts to the stock. Cook the squab breasts for 12 minutes and remove from the liquid. Add the foie gras to the stock and cook for 1 minute or until just medium rare. Remove the foie gras from the stock *(discard or save the stock for another use)* and season the foie gras with salt and pepper. Thinly slice the squab just prior to serving and season to taste with salt and pepper.

For the Napa Cabbage:

• Cook the foie gras scraps in a pre-heated sauté pan until they melt. Add the cabbage, ginger and butter. Cook over medium heat for 3 minutes or until the cabbage is wilted. Add the balsamic vinegar and season to taste with salt and pepper.

For the Spiced Squab Consommé:

• Place the squab consommé in a saucepan with the star anise, jalapeño, coriander and vinegar. Bring to a boil, reduce heat and simmer for 3 minutes. Strain. Season the consommé to taste with salt and pepper.

For the Elephant Garlic:

• Preheat oven to 325 degrees. Blanch the garlic in water 3 times. Place the blanched garlic in an oven-proof pan with the olive oil and cover. Bake for 30 minutes or until tender. Remove the garlic from the olive oil and slice each piece in half.

To Finish and Serve:

• Spoon some of the black-eyed peas in the center of four shallow bowls. Arrange the beets, 1 tablespoon preserved ginger *(see recipe on page 102)*, poached foie gras, and napa cabbage around each bowl. Place the sliced squab over the black-eyed peas. Ladle in the remaining spiced squab consommé and sprinkle with the chopped sage, parsley and micro celery sprouts. Top with freshly ground black pepper.

* Available in gourmet or salad dressing sections of grocery stores

Squab Consommé

Yield: 1-1/2 quarts

2 quarts squab stock *(you may substitute chicken or game hen stock)*

6 each egg whites

1/2 cup finely diced Spanish onion

1/3 cup finely diced carrot

1/3 cup finely diced celery

1/4 cup finely diced tomato

1 pound ground squab meat *(or chicken or game hen — same type as the stock)*

Salt and pepper to taste

Place the stock in a large saucepan and cook over medium heat for 10 minutes, or until warm. Whisk together the egg whites, onion, carrot, celery and tomato in a medium bowl until slightly frothy. Whisk in the ground meat. Whisk the egg mixture into the hot stock. Stir constantly in one motion with a wooden spoon for about 10 minutes, or until a raft begins to form. Stop stirring and reduce to a slow simmer. After the raft forms, break a small hole in the raft and continue to simmer for 45 minutes, or until the liquid appears crystal clear. Strain through a fine-mesh sieve lined with cheesecloth, being careful not to break the raft. Discard the raft and season the consommé to taste with salt and pepper.

Roasted White Trumpet Royale, Lobster and Cauliflower Mushrooms with Japanese Kumai Jasmine Rice Cake and Kalamata Olive Sauce

Serves: 4

Kohlrabi:

1 head kohlrabi

1 cup vegetable stock

1 clove garlic

2 teaspoons olive oil

Salt and pepper to taste

Endive:

2 heads Belgian endive

2 tablespoons butter

2 tablespoons sugar

1 cup mirepoix

1 cup port wine

1/2 cup red wine

1 cup vegetable stock

Roasted Mushrooms:

1/2 cup white trumpet royale
mushrooms

1/2 cup cauliflower mushrooms
*(may substitute oyster or wild
mushroom mix)*

1/2 cup lobster mushrooms

2 tablespoons butter

1 tablespoon minced shallot

1/2 teaspoon minced garlic

1/2 cup mushroom stock

1 teaspoon chopped sage

1 teaspoon chopped thyme

2 teaspoons lemon juice

Kalamata Olive Sauce:

1/2 cup chopped, pitted
kalamata olives

1-1/2 cups red wine

1/4 cup hot Meat Stock Reduction
(see side bar recipe)

Additional Items:

Rice Cake:

Recipe on page 103

Pearl Onions:

Recipe on page 103

Finish:

4 teaspoons micro kohlrabi
(may substitute sprouts)

4 teaspoons 25-year-old balsamic
vinegar *(or reduce a good quality
balsamic vinegar until syrupy)*

For the Kohlrabi:

- Cut the kohlrabi into 8 bite-sized pieces. Place the kohlrabi, vegetable stock and garlic in a saucepan. Simmer over medium-low heat until tender. Remove the kohlrabi from the stock and toss with the olive oil and season to taste with salt and pepper.

For the Endive:

- Cut the endive in half. Place the butter and endive in a preheated sauté pan, cut-side down. Caramelize the endive over medium heat for 3 minutes. Sprinkle with the sugar and continue to cook for 1 minute. Add the mirepoix, port wine, red wine and vegetable stock. Bring to a slow simmer and cover the pan with a tightly fitting lid. Braise the endive over low heat for 40 minutes, or until tender. Remove the endive from the liquid and season to taste with salt and pepper.

For the Roasted Mushrooms:

- Clean and cut the mushrooms into bite-sized pieces. Place the butter in a sauté pan set over medium-high heat. When melted, add the shallot and garlic. Once the shallot is translucent add the lobster mushrooms and cook for 1 minute. Add the white trumpet mushrooms and cook for 1 more minute. Finally add the cauliflower mushrooms, mushroom stock, sage, thyme and lemon juice. Sauté the mushrooms until they are tender and season to taste with salt and pepper.

For the Kalamata Olive Sauce:

- Place chopped kalamata olives and red wine in a saucepan over medium heat until reduced by 1/2. Add 1/4 cup hot meat stock reduction *(see side bar recipe)*. Strain through a fine-mesh sieve and set aside until needed.

To Finish and Serve:

- Place a piece of the rice cake *(see recipe on page 103)* on one side of each of four serving plates and place a piece of the endive over each rice cake. Spoon the kalamata olive sauce in a long line on the other side of the plates. Arrange the roasted mushrooms, pearl onions *(see recipe on page 103)* and kohlrabi in a free-form line over the kalamata olive sauce. Spoon the meat stock reduction and aged balsamic vinegar around the plate and sprinkle with the micro kohlrabi.

Meat Stock Reduction

1 each Spanish onion, chopped

1 each carrot, chopped

1 each stalk celery, chopped

1 tablespoon grapeseed oil

1 each small tomato, seeded and
chopped

1/2 cup red wine

1 quart veal stock

Place the onion, carrot and celery with the grapeseed oil in a medium saucepan and sauté over medium heat for 7 minutes, or until caramelized. Add the tomato and pour in the red wine to deglaze the pan. Cook until most of the wine has evaporated. Add the stock and simmer over low heat for 1 hour, or until reduced to 1 cup. Strain through a fine-mesh sieve. Set aside until ready to use.

Napoleon of Chocolate-Hazelnut Cream, Strawberries and Blueberries with White-Chocolate Gelée

Serves: 4

Crispy Phyllo Discs:

3 each large sheets fresh phyllo dough

3 tablespoons melted butter

Powdered sugar for dusting

Chocolate-Hazelnut Cream:

1 cup milk

1/4 each vanilla bean, scraped and pulp *(seeds)* reserved

1 tablespoon cornstarch

1/4 cup sugar

1 pinch salt

1 each egg

1-1/2 ounces chopped hazelnut chocolate

White-Chocolate Gelée:

1 each gelatin sheet, bloomed* *(may substitute 1 teaspoon powdered gelatin)*

1 cup heavy cream, heated

3-1/2 ounces chopped white chocolate

1 pinch salt

Blueberry Sauce:

1/2 cup blueberries

1/4 cup simple syrup *(to make 3/4 cup — boil 1/2 cup water and 1/4 cup sugar together for 1 minute)*

1 tablespoon water

Strawberry Sauce:

1/2 cup sliced strawberries

1 tablespoon sugar

Sauternes Reduction:

2 cups sauternes

1/4 cup sugar

1/2 each vanilla bean or 1 teaspoon vanilla extract

3/4 cup sliced strawberries

3/4 cup blueberries

Finish:

2 tablespoons mint leaves *(may substitute micro mint)*

1/4 cup chopped Hazelnut Praline**

For the Crispy Phyllo Discs:

- Preheat oven to 375 degrees. Lay flat a sheet of phyllo on a clean work surface. Lightly brush the phyllo with melted butter and dust with the powdered sugar. Place a second sheet of phyllo over the first sheet and repeat butter and sugar process. Lay a final sheet of phyllo over the second sheet and brush with butter. Cut the phyllo into twelve 2-inch circles and place the circles on an inverted sheet pan between 2 layers of parchment paper. Place a second inverted sheet pan over the phyllo discs and bake for 10 minutes or until golden brown. Remove from the sheet pan. Once cool, dust with powdered sugar.

For the Chocolate-Hazelnut Cream:

- In a small saucepan, bring milk and vanilla bean pulp to a boil. Whisk in the cornstarch until smooth. Whisk sugar and salt into the egg. Whisk a little of the hot milk mixture into the egg. Whisk the egg back into the hot milk in the saucepan. Return the mixture to the stove and cook over medium heat, stirring constantly, until the mixture coats the back of a spoon. Strain the hot mixture into a bowl holding the chocolate and mix until the chocolate is melted and fully incorporated. Refrigerate until needed.

For the White-Chocolate Gelée:

- Drain the gelatin from the blooming water and add to the hot cream. Pour the mixture over the chocolate and add the salt. Whisk together until smooth and refrigerate until ready to use.

For the Blueberry Sauce:

- Place the blueberries, simple syrup and water in a saucepan and simmer for 2 minutes. Purée in the blender until smooth and pass through a fine-mesh sieve. Set sauce aside.

For the Strawberry Sauce:

- Purée the strawberries and sugar in a food processor and pass through a fine-mesh sieve.

For the Sauternes Reduction:

- Place the sauternes, sugar and vanilla bean in a saucepan and simmer until reduced by half. Add the strawberries and blueberries and remove from the heat.

To Finish and Serve:

- In the center of each of four dessert plates, place a phyllo disc and layer with chocolate-hazelnut cream and some of the fruit from the sauternes reduction. Continue this process until you have 2 layers of cream and fruit, and finish each serving with a final phyllo disc. Spoon the blueberry and strawberry sauces around the plates. Place small dollops of the white-chocolate gelée around the plates and sprinkle with the hazelnut praline and mint leaves. Drizzle a touch of the liquid from the sauternes reduction around the plate if desired.

* To bloom (soften) gelatin, soak gelatin sheet or 1 teaspoon of powdered gelatin in 2 tablespoons of water.

** Available in candy shops and baking specialty stores.

Zucchini Slices

For the Mille-Feuille of Squashes, Roasted Eggplant, Heirloom Tomatoes with Swan Creek Farm Ricotta and Gazpacho Sorbet recipe. Page 91

Zucchini Slices:

1 each large zucchini, sliced 1/8-inch thick, reserve all trimmings

1/2 cup chopped carrot

1 cup chopped onion

1/2 cup chopped celery

3 sprigs thyme

1 sprig rosemary

Salt and Pepper to taste

For the Zucchini Slices:

- Place the zucchini trimmings, carrot, onion, celery, thyme and rosemary in a medium saucepan and cover with water. Bring to a simmer. Place the zucchini slices in a shallow pan and strain the hot liquid over the zucchini slices. Allow it to sit for 1 hour. Drain and pat the zucchini slices dry with a towel. Season the slices with salt and pepper.

Tomato Powder

For the Mille-Feuille of Squashes, Roasted Eggplant, Heirloom Tomatoes with Swan Creek Farm Ricotta and Gazpacho Sorbet recipe. Page 91

Tomato Powder:

1/2 cup finely chopped tomato concassé

For the Tomato Powder:

- Preheat oven to 175 degrees. Place the chopped tomato concassé on a Silpat® *(silicon baking sheet insert)* set on a sheet pan and bake for 10 hours or until completely dry. Cool to room temperature and grind in a spice grinder.

Gazpacho Sorbet

For the Mille-Feuille of Squashes, Roasted Eggplant, Heirloom Tomatoes with Swan Creek Farm Ricotta and Gazpacho Sorbet recipe. Page 91

Gazpacho Sorbet:

1 each red bell pepper, roasted and cleaned

4 teaspoons chopped basil

2 tablespoons tomato juice

2 teaspoons balsamic vinegar

2 tablespoons olive oil

Salt and pepper to taste

For the Gazpacho Sorbet:

- Finely chop the red bell pepper and toss together with the basil, tomato juice, balsamic vinegar and olive oil in a mixing bowl. Season to taste with salt and pepper. Reserve 8 teaspoons of the mixture for garnish. Purée the remaining mixture in the blender until smooth and pass through a fine-mesh sieve. Spin in an ice cream machine until frozen.

Preserved Ginger

For the Slow-Poached Breast of Squab with Napa Cabbage, Foie Gras and Spiced Squab Consommé recipe. Page 97

Preserved Ginger:

1 cup finely julienned fresh ginger

1-1/2 cup simple syrup *(1 cup water plus 1/2 cup sugar cooked over low heat until sugar is melted, then boiled for 1 minute)*

For the Preserved Ginger:

- Blanch the ginger in simmering water for 3 minutes. Strain and repeat the process 2 more times. Simmer the ginger in the simple syrup for 30 minutes. Remove from the heat and cool in the syrup. Refrigerate in the syrup until needed.

Rice Cake

For the Roasted White Trumpet Royale, Lobster and Cauliflower Mushrooms with Japanese Kumai Jasmine Rice Cake and

Kalamata Olive Sauce recipe. Page 99

Rice Cake:

2 tablespoons olive oil

1/4 cup minced shallot

2 cloves garlic, minced

1/2 cup Japanese Kumai
jasmine rice*

2 cups red wine

3 cups vegetable stock

1/2 cup grated Parmesan

Salt and pepper to taste

2 tablespoons grapeseed oil

For the Rice Cake:

- Sweat the shallot and garlic in the olive oil until translucent. Add the rice and coat the rice in the mixture. Slowly, over medium-low heat, begin to add the red wine and vegetable stock in 1/4-cup additions to the rice while constantly stirring *(like making a risotto)*. Once the liquid is absorbed, continue to add additional liquid until the rice is al dente. Fold in the Parmesan and season to taste with salt and pepper. Spread the cooked rice onto an 8-inch-square parchment-lined pan and refrigerate for 2 hours or until firm.

- Invert the pan onto a cutting board and cut the rice into four squares, trimming the sides clean. Just prior to serving, sauté the rice squares in a preheated sauté pan with the grapeseed oil until crispy.

* Available at Asian specialty markets

Pearl Onions

For the Roasted White Trumpet Royale, Lobster and Cauliflower Mushrooms with Japanese Kumai Jasmine Rice Cake and

Kalamata Olive Sauce recipe. Page 99

Pearl Onions:

8 each tiny pearl onions, peeled

1 tablespoon butter

2 teaspoons red wine vinegar

Salt and pepper to taste

For the Pearl Onions:

- Place the pearl onions and butter in a sauté pan and cook over medium heat until the onions are caramelized. Add the red wine vinegar and continue to cook for 2 minutes and season to taste with salt and pepper.

GARY DANKO

SAN FRANCISCO, CA

American Express Best Chef: California, 1995

In a business known for dynamic players, Chef Gary Danko stands out for his prodigious talents and energy. Danko has taught, consulted, studied, created and opened restaurants, and cooked his way from Vermont to California. Now he's very much at home at Restaurant Gary Danko in San Francisco.

The third oldest brother in a family of seven kids, Danko started multi-tasking early. "We lived in upstate New York where my dad was a contractor and he'd take my two older brothers on the job. I'd help my mom change diapers, clean house and cook."

The cooking part was a big deal. Danko's mother grew up on a farm in Louisiana where fresh food was prepared from scratch and feeding her family well was important to her. But, it was Dad who inadvertently opened the door to his son's future career.

Says Danko, "When I was 14 it was my turn to go to work with Dad, and I hated it. At the time he was remodeling a restaurant, and I pretty much disappeared into the kitchen. Dad lost a contractor and gained a chef."

He worked at the freshly renovated Village Inn throughout high school, but not to the exclusion of other activities. "I was the kind of kid who was totally into extracurricular activities; organizing events like prom and homecoming, building stage sets, editing the yearbook. I also expressed myself in every type of artistic media but eventually the restaurant became more and more important to me," says Danko.

Enrolling at the Culinary Institute of America, he spent his spare time out of class in what he calls "their cool old library." One book particularly caught his attention, *The Making of a Cook* by French culinary doyenne Madeleine Kamman.

Vermont, I foraged and found great breads and cheeses, free-range ducks, geese, turkeys and guinea hens."

In response, he began writing a different menu each night depending on what seasonal ingredients were available. Meanwhile, he continued tracking Kamman.

"I enrolled in a class she taught in a New York cooking school and made sure she got my menus and resumés. When she bought her own school in Glenn, New Hampshire, I tried to get in and couldn't. One student dropped out and I tried again. Finally I asked Madeleine what the problem was. Was it because I was a man? Turned out that Kamman had certain feelings about Culinary Institute of America training."

"Reading that really made it all come together for me, the art, the science, the creativity. In class we learned to make hollandaise but they never explained exactly what was going on in the pan, but Madeleine Kamman did."

After graduating, Danko moved to San Francisco where he cooked at lunchtime in a combination bookstore/bistro called Vanity Fair and waited tables at another restaurant in the evening. He helped the couple that owned Vanity Fair expand the business, but when they divorced, the enterprise fell apart.

Meanwhile, Madeleine Kamman kept writing books and Danko avidly devoured them, following her career and hoping someday to work with her. When he heard she had moved to Vermont, he headed there as well. Ironically, no sooner had he settled in as chef at Tucker Hill Inn in Waitsfield, Vermont, than he learned that Kamman had moved to France.

At Tucker Hill, Danko began honing his personal culinary style. "While I was living in California, I saw a big change in what was happening in restaurants. There had been a lot of fuddy-duddy steam table food but Chef Jeremiah Tower's influence started to be felt, and artisan products like Laura Chenel's cheese, Picard's escargot and locally grown produce became available. Then, when I got to

Danko's persistence won the day and Kamman accepted him as a student and eventually, a friend and peer. She suggested Danko send his resumé to Napa Valley's Beringer Vineyards which sponsors a food and wine program. They accepted him as an extern and in 1985, the winery hired him to head up the culinary center as executive chef. Then Beringer bought Chateau Souverain in Sonoma and appointed Danko executive chef of a restaurant there that was basically falling apart. In two years'

time, he turned it into a world-class dining destination and began receiving national attention for his cooking.

Says Danko, "It was such a great opportunity. The winery would send us out to different cities to do food and wine demonstrations. Twice I went to Tokyo for a month."

He also traveled to France with Kamman. "It was an amazing education. You take techniques from every culture and adapt them into your cooking."

By 1991, Danko was ready to move on and the newly opened San Francisco Ritz Carlton provided the opportunity. He worked in the three-meal restaurant while a succession of French chefs headed the dinner restaurant. Due to his grueling schedule Danko was ready to give his notice when the second French chef quit and he was given the position. "I knew the local products and purveyors and I knew what worked for me. I wanted people to walk into this overly fancy room and get a choice of three, four or five course meals with no surcharges, along with service that was friendly with no attitude and no upselling."

The food reflected Danko's exceptionally refined but straightforward style. He often comments that he never experiments on his guests and indeed his culinary creations are uncommonly accessible. "People like familiarity, not necessarily things that are cutting edge. I do high-quality food simply."

After winning the Beard award, Danko resolved to open his own restaurant. While making plans for it, he consulted with Draeger's Markets, a local gourmet food chain, when they opened the much-lauded Viognier restaurant in San Mateo.

Then came a fortuitously timed phone call from the owner of another local restaurant — one that he admired. "I had told him long before, if you ever want to sell, let me know. It was the perfect location and I loved the space, it just felt right," says Danko.

Danko jumped at the opportunity, remodeling the interior and putting together a formidable team of associates. "I brought in people I had worked with at the Ritz and opened to huge expectations. We knew we had to come out of the box perfectly or else...."

Restaurant Gary Danko comes as close to perfection as possible. It is warm and sophisticated with golden wood, soft lighting and masses of fresh flowers. Its stunning collection of contemporary paintings and drawings reflects Danko's lifelong interest in the arts. It provides a fitting background for the exceptional cuisine.

Danko doesn't rest on his considerable laurels. He has recently bought property in Yountville north of San Francisco that he intends to turn into a boutique farm that will supply the restaurant with produce and herbs. That will be a pleasure as well, since gardening is one of Danko's hobbies. He also enjoys antiquing and subscribes enthusiastically to shopping therapy.

"Another restaurant might be a possibility, but," he says, "there is enough drama in opening the doors of this place everyday."

He'd like to open a sophisticated Manhattan-style cocktail lounge. He feels San Francisco is sadly lacking in that type of gathering place. Then there is the pilot cooking school he plans to start. Clearly, Gary Danko is not slowing down any time soon.

Warm Mushroom Goat Cheese Tarts

Serves: 24 appetizer servings

Puff Pastry Rounds:

1/2 pound puff pastry,
   rolled 1/8-inch thick

Goat Cheese Mixture:

1/2 pound goat cheese,
   plain Montrachet-style

6 tablespoons grated
   Parmigiano-Reggiano

1/2 cup heavy cream or
   low-fat milk

Salt and pepper to taste

Wild Mushroom Ragout:

2 tablespoons butter or olive oil

1 pound mixed mushroom
   (shiitake, oyster, crimini),
   lightly chopped

2 cloves garlic, minced

1/4 cup finely chopped parsley

Salt and pepper to taste

- Start this recipe well in advance of serving, as all components should be made ahead of time. Final assembly and brief cooking should be done just prior to serving.

For the Puff Pastry Rounds:

- Preheat the oven to 350 degrees. Using a 1-1/2 inch round biscuit cutter, cut the puff pastry into rounds. Place the rounds on a parchment-lined sheet pan. Place another sheet of parchment paper on top of the puff pastry rounds. Place a second sheet pan on top of the parchment paper. Bake for 25 to 30 minutes. The baked rounds should be 1/4-inch thick, and crisp and flaky when snapped in half. Cool and store in a dry airtight container.

For the Goat Cheese Mixture:

- Combine the goat cheese, Parmigiano-Reggiano and cream. Mix until just combined. Season to taste with salt and pepper. Refrigerate until ready to assemble tarts.

For the Wild Mushroom Ragout:

- Melt the butter *(or heat the olive oil)* in a sauté pan. Sauté the mushrooms until they give off their juices. Salt lightly and cook until juices concentrate. Stir in garlic and parsley and cook for 30 seconds. Season with salt and pepper to taste. Cool and refrigerate until ready to assemble tarts.

To Finish and Serve:

- Spread each puff pastry round with 1 tablespoon of the goat cheese mixture. Press a tablespoon-sized portion of the mushroom ragout on top of the goat cheese. Place the rounds on a sheet pan and bake at 350 degrees until cheese melts, approximately 5 minutes. Serve hot.

Corn and Arugula Salad with Red Pepper Vinaigrette

Serves: 6

Corn:

3 each fresh ears of corn

Red Pepper-Tomato Vinaigrette:

2 each red peppers, grilled or
roasted, peeled and seeded*

1 each large tomato,
cored and diced

1 tablespoon tarragon vinegar

1/2 cup extra-virgin olive oil

2 teaspoons kosher salt

2 cloves garlic

Arugula Salad:

2 tablespoons tarragon vinegar

6 tablespoons extra-virgin
olive oil

Salt and pepper to taste

2 bunches arugula,
tough stems removed

6 tablespoons freshly grated
Parmigiano-Reggiano

Finish:

18 each olives
(*picholine, niçoise or other*)

1/2 pint cherry tomatoes

For the Corn:

- Pull back husks and remove corn silk. Push husks back around the corn. Place the corn on a grill over glowing embers and grill until lightly golden. Remove husks and any remaining silk, and cut corn from cob. Alternatively, corn may be husked and then blanched in boiling water for 4 minutes. Immediately remove corn from boiling water and plunge into ice water to stop cooking process. Cut from cob.

For the Red Pepper-Tomato Vinaigrette:

- In a blender, combine all of the ingredients and blend until well emulsified. Strain through a medium-mesh strainer. Adjust the seasonings to taste.

For the Arugula Salad:

- In a small bowl, whisk together the vinegar and olive oil and salt and pepper to taste.

- In a large mixing bowl, combine the corn, arugula and Parmigiano-Reggiano. Add the olive oil mixture and toss gently, coating the greens lightly.

To Finish and Serve:

- On each of six serving plates, place a puddle of red pepper-tomato vinaigrette around the base of the plate. Divide the salad evenly among the six plates. Garnish with olives and cherry tomatoes.

* To grill the peppers, place them over glowing embers and grill until charred and cooked through. Alternatively, peppers can be roasted in a 350 degree oven until they are engorged and the skins are blistered. Place in a paper bag or wrap in paper towels. Allow to cool before slipping off skins and removing seeds.

Zucchini Soup with Basil

Serves: 6

Zucchini Soup:

6 tablespoons olive oil

1 cup diced celery

1 cup finely minced onion

1 each bay leaf

1/2 teaspoon thyme

1-1/2 pounds zucchini,
cut into 1/2-inch chunks

3 cups chicken stock

10 each basil leaves, shredded

Salt and pepper to taste

Finish:

6 ounces fresh crab or lobster
meat, or smoked trout (*optional*)

For the Zucchini Soup:

- In a heavy soup pot over medium heat, heat the olive oil. Add the celery, onions, bay leaf and thyme, and cook until tender and sweet, about 20 minutes. Stir in the zucchini and the chicken stock, and cook until the zucchini is very tender, approximately 15 minutes. Remove and discard the bay leaf. Purée the soup in a blender or food processor. Strain through a medium-mesh sieve.

To Finish and Serve:

- Reheat the soup. Just before serving, purée the fresh basil leaves with a small quantity of the soup in a blender or food processor. Stir the mixture back into the warmed soup. Season to taste. Garnish with crab or lobster meat or smoked trout, if desired, before serving.

Open-Faced Smoked Chicken Ravioli

Serves: 8

Chicken:

1 **each** smoked chicken,
approximately 3-1/2 pounds

4 **cups** chicken stock, homemade
or low-salt canned

Sauce:

1/2 **cup** dry white wine, such as
Sauvignon Blanc or Chardonnay

1/2 **cup** chopped leeks

2 **each** bay leaves

2 **each** sprigs of thyme

1/2 **cup** heavy cream

12 **tablespoons** unsalted butter

Ricotta Mixture:

8 **ounces** Ricotta cheese, either
cow's or sheep's milk

1/2 **cup** grated
Parmigiano-Reggiano

1 **each** egg, lightly beaten

1 **tablespoon** chopped fresh basil

1 **tablespoon** chopped
flat-leaf parsley

1 **clove** garlic, minced

1/4 **teaspoon** salt

1/8 **teaspoon** ground pepper

1/2 **cup** heavy cream or cold
chicken stock

Pasta and Topping:

20 **sheets** fresh pasta, each
3-1/2 x 3-1/2 inches

1 **each** red pepper, roasted, seeded,
peeled and cut 1/2-inch dice

1 **each** zucchini, cut into 1/2-inch
dice, blanched in boiling water
for 1 minute and cooled

For the Chicken:

- Remove the skin and bones from the smoked chicken. Place the bones in a saucepan and cover with chicken stock. Simmer for 1 to 2 hours. This will give the sauce its smoky character. Strain the smoked chicken stock and skim off all fat. Cut the chicken meat into 2-inch strips and reserve.

For the Sauce:

- In a saucepan, combine the smoked chicken stock, wine, leeks, bay leaves and thyme. Bring to a simmer over low heat and cook slowly until reduced by 2/3. Add the heavy cream and return to a boil. Whisk in the 12 tablespoons of butter. Season to taste with salt and pepper. Strain through a fine-mesh strainer and discard the solids.

For the Ricotta Mixture:

- Combine all ingredients in a bowl and gently mix. Season with more salt and pepper to taste. Set aside until needed.

For the Pasta and Topping:

- Bring a large pot of water to a boil over high heat to cook the pasta. As the water is heating, in a 10-inch skillet, combine the smoked chicken sauce, chicken meat, the diced pepper and zucchini and heat gently. When the water is boiling, put the pasta sheets in the pot and cook until al dente, 30 to 60 seconds.

To Finish and Serve:

- Preheat oven to 350 degrees. On an ovenproof serving platter, layer the pasta, the smoked chicken sauce and the ricotta mixture, finishing with a layer of the chicken sauce on top. Bake for 10-20 minutes, until heated through.

Neat Stuff

Always striving to find ways to increase customer comfort, Gary Danko provides unusual monogrammed hooks to conveniently hang purses from the table, keeping the floor free of impediments and allowing easy access to the bags.

Stir-Fried Prawns with Sugar Snap Peas, Shaved Fennel and Fresh Mint

Serves: 6

Fennel Oil:

1 **ounce** dried fennel seeds

1 **teaspoon** water

1 **cup** extra-virgin olive oil

Prawns:

4 **tablespoons** Fennel Oil or extra-virgin olive oil

1 **head** fennel, sliced thin

2 **pounds** shrimp or prawns, peeled

1/2 **pound** sugar snap peas, topped and tailed

1 **teaspoon** grated or finely minced ginger

1 **teaspoon** minced garlic

2 **tablespoons** chopped mint

1 **pinch** red pepper flakes

Salt and pepper to taste

Finish:

Juice of one lime

For the Fennel Oil:

- Grind the fennel seeds to a fine powder in a blender or with a mortar and pestle. Place in a plastic container and stir in water and olive oil. Cover and refrigerate overnight or up to 7 days. Strain through cheesecloth or several layers of paper towels before using.

For the Prawns:

- In a 10-inch sauté pan or skillet, heat the fennel oil or extra-virgin olive oil over medium heat. Stir in the sliced fennel and cook until just tender, about 5 minutes. Stir in the shrimp or prawns and sugar snap peas, and cook until the shrimp or prawns turn opaque and the sugar snaps are crisp-tender. Stir in the ginger, garlic, mint, pepper flakes and salt and pepper to taste. Cook for 1 minute longer.

To Finish and Serve:

- Squeeze the fresh lime juice over all.

Lemon Drop Martini à la Gary Danko

1 part Meyer lemon juice

1 part simple syrup

1 part vanilla vodka
(Slice whole vanilla beans in half lengthwise and steep in vodka. Keep adding new vodka as needed.)

Shake over ice and strain into martini glasses.

GAY...
WINE AND TASTE

House Cured Salmon Caviar with Buckwh...

Iron Horse, Brut Classic, Green Valley, Sonom...

Pan Seared Gr... with Fennel Purée, Saffron and Ba...

Château la Canorgue, Viognier, Vaucluse, France...

Filet of Beef and Braised Short Ribs with

Endive Marmalade and Tangerine

Saint Julien, Clos du Marquis, Bordeaux, France 1996

A Selection of Farmhouse and Artisanal Cheeses

Amarone della Valpolicella, Classico, Le Salette, Veneto, Italy 1998

Warm Persimmon Pudding with Persimmon Sorbet

Walnut or Hazelnut Flourless Cake

Serves: 10

Cake:

8 each egg yolks

3/4 cup sugar

1 pinch salt

1 teaspoon vanilla extract

1-1/2 cups finely ground walnuts
   or hazelnuts

1 teaspoon baking powder

8 each egg whites

1/2 cup powdered sugar,
   or as needed

Chocolate Whipped Cream:

3/4 cup cocoa powder

3/4 cup sugar

2 cups heavy cream

Finish:

1 cup strawberry or apricot jam

For the Cake:

- Preheat oven to 350 degrees. Line a jelly-roll pan with parchment paper. Lightly brush the parchment with a thin coat of vegetable oil.

- In the bowl of an electric mixer with a whisk attachment, beat the egg yolks, sugar, salt and vanilla until thick ribbons form. Fold in the nuts and baking powder. In a separate bowl, beat the egg whites to soft peaks and fold into the egg yolks and sugar mixture. Spread evenly into jelly-roll pan.

- Bake until the cake bounces back when lightly touched, about 20 to 25 minutes. Let cool for 5 minutes. Turn the cake out onto a tea towel that has been dusted with powdered sugar. Sprinkle powdered sugar on top. Roll up loosely into a cylinder. Cool. Wrap with plastic wrap and keep refrigerated until ready to fill.

For the Chocolate Whipped Cream:

- Sift the cocoa and the sugar together. Combine with the cream and whip to soft peaks. *(This mixture whips up very quickly, so be careful not to over whip.)*

To Finish and Serve:

- Unroll the cake to fill it. Spread cake with a thin layer of jam of choice. Roll up firmly and frost with chocolate whipped cream and slice.

Artful Dining

Given the long and close relationship of San Francisco artist and gallery owner Marcel Sitcoske and restaurateur Gary Danko, it was natural for Danko to commission her to procure pieces to hang in his restaurant.

Artist Erin Parish is represented by two abstract works titled *Hover* and *Halcyon*.

Three pastels and a painting titled *Hydrangeas* are landscapes by Amagansett-based artist Robert Harm.

VLM, a painting by New York's Hunt Slonem, hangs in a secluded alcove of Restaurant Gary Danko.

LIDIA BASTIANICH
NEW YORK, NY

All-Clad Cookware Outstanding Chef, 2002

American Express Best Chef: New York, 1999

There are few distinctions between Lidia Matticchio Bastianich's professional and personal lives. Food crosses all boundaries.

Widely regarded as "The First Lady of Italian Cuisine," Bastianich says, "To Italians, food is more than survival and nourishment, they have magnified it into an art, and art adds to and delights our existence."

For almost 30 years, Bastianich has been sharing the art of Italian food and culture with an avid public through her restaurant empire, in cookbooks, via a food product line, on two television series and now by sponsoring food and wine tours of Italy.

That's an impressive resumé by any standard, but it is especially remarkable because Bastianich experienced considerable turmoil during her girlhood. After two years in a refugee camp, she and her family emigrated to America from Italy's Istrian peninsula when it became part of Yugoslavia in the aftermath of World War II.

The Matticchios settled in Queens and began building a new life. Her father worked for a car dealership and her mother found employment in a garment factory. Lidia attended school and helped out the family with a part-time job at Walken's Bakery, owned by actor Christopher Walken's family. Although she always gravitated to entry-level jobs in the industry, a career in food wasn't necessarily Bastianich's life plan.

"I didn't know that I would become so passionate about it. It took me a while to understand the foundation that the flavors of my childhood had given me," she says in retrospect.

Prior to the family's displacement, Bastianich had enjoyed what was in many ways an idyllic upbringing. Both Bastianich's paternal and maternal grandparents produced their own olive oil and wine, raised their own pigs and cured their own prosciutto. They distilled grappa and milled the wheat they grew. Every family had a garden, and people would barter for what they needed.

"When I was around 10 years old, my grandmother would cook for the laborers who came to town to work. I was involved in the excitement of the preparations. She would prepare a free-range chicken in sauce; there would be figs, bread and cheese. Then she'd wrap the food up in a clean

tablecloth and I would carry it to the men. Everybody ate from the same bowl. Those pristine, intense flavors were a benchmark for me, and my quest to communicate through food goes back to those flavors."

The after-effects of the war also meant some deprivations, and the respect and care given to what food they did have made a deep impression on the young Bastianich.

"In some restaurants the chef will just serve the chicken breast and it feeds one person. If the whole bird is used, it can feed 10. It's about balance of the earth."

Married at age 19 to her husband Felix, another Istrian immigrant, she and her spouse opened a restaurant in Queens three years later. By 24, she was the mother of Tanya and Joseph, working full time in the restaurant and soon to open a second one.

"We had a chef and I worked alongside him learning how to cook in a restaurant context," remembers Bastianich. "Meanwhile, I studied everything I could about food; the history, the cultural implications, nutrition and chemistry. We also regularly returned to Italy, and I became very involved with learning about traditional cuisine."

That was something she did by cultivating the housewives and the men who sold produce in the market.

Laughing, she recalls, "I was in Rome at the market in the Piazza Campo d' Fiori, and this guy had a huge pile of the most beautiful fennel. I asked him how to cook it and he said to me, 'Cooked fennel isn't worth a fig.' And he was right, of course, it is all about the crunch."

By the eighties, the Bastianichs decided the time was ripe to take a bite out of the Big Apple. They sold the restaurants in Queens and, in 1981, debuted Felidia, which proved to be her showcase restaurant.

At that point, Bastianich had thoroughly defined her culinary philosophy.

"I was mesmerized by the engineering of the four-star chefs and thought, 'Maybe I need to get into this.' But I couldn't do it. It just wasn't me. I come from a world that was real and the food I cook is an expression of that culture. It's the food my grandma cooked and that I eat every day. I knew that's what I should serve in the restaurant."

Felidia quickly attained iconic status. The menu featured dishes like pasutice all'istriana (delicate fresh pasta with shellfish sauce) and guazzetto (meats slow-cooked with sauce) that were new and exciting to jaded New York diners. Patrons also embraced the warmth and comfort of both the charming, intimate ambiance and the caring owners and staff. Unlike many restaurants "of the moment," Felidia is still going strong.

The reason? "The more I gain momentum, the more I retreat into simplicity. That is hard to achieve because there is nothing to hide behind."

In the ensuing years, the Bastianichs divorced, and the now-grown Tanya and Joseph eventually joined mom in the family business. Joseph, a former Wall Street stockbroker, is Lidia's

and they frequently cook together. Erminia is also a frequent guest on PBS's *Lidia's Italian-American Kitchen*. Bastianich recently completed her third cookbook based on the series.

Sailing is Bastianich's passion. Appropriately, her most memorable meal was after a day spent on the water foraging for sea urchins. She scraped them into a bowl, added olive oil, fresh pepper, a little chopped tomato, parsley and hot pasta. "Like eating the sea," she says.

partner in restaurants Felidia, Becco and Esca in Manhattan and Lidia's in Kansas City and Pittsburgh. With a doctorate in Renaissance art history, daughter Tanya is a natural to partner with her mom in Esperienze Italiane, a travel business that leads food wine, and culture-oriented tours of Italy.

Tanya and Joseph have presented Bastianich with five grandchildren, and she is a devoted, hands-on *nonna* who spends as much time as possible with the kids. Her spacious home in Queens overlooks Little Neck Bay, and the huge kitchen is the heart of the home. Bastianich's mother, Erminia, lives with her

Classical music, chess and travel are other free-time pursuits, and she also gives back to the community by raising funds for humanitarian causes, particularly UNICEF and UNIFEM. Her credo? "Maybe when you are blessed and have a bit more, you need to use what God has given you to help others."

A major factor in having "a bit more" is that Bastianich has never wavered from her core beliefs. "I'm completely tied to Italian culture. I'd never add an element to a dish on a whim. It is all based on diligent research, because after all, food tells the story of a people."

Sautéed Assorted Mushrooms with Buckwheat Polenta

Serves: 6

Mushrooms:

2 pounds assorted fresh
mushrooms, such as
chanterelles, bluefoot, hen
of the woods, cremini,
portobello, shiitake or porcini
(whole or large pieces look best)

4 tablespoons butter

2 tablespoons olive oil

5 cloves garlic, crushed

1 sprig rosemary

Salt and pepper to taste

2 tablespoons chopped
flat-leaf parsley

Buckwheat Polenta:

8 cups chicken or vegetable stock
(may substitute water)

2 each bay leaves, fresh or dried

1 tablespoon coarse salt,
or to taste

2 tablespoons extra-virgin
olive oil

2 cups buckwheat polenta
(may substitute regular polenta)

4 tablespoons unsalted butter

1 cup freshly grated
Parmigiano-Reggiano

Finish:

Extra-virgin olive oil

2 ounces Parmigiano-Reggiano,
shaved

For the Mushrooms:

- Clean the mushrooms, wash them under cold running water and drain well. Pat with paper towels to dry.

- In a skillet, combine the butter and oil. When hot, add the garlic and cook until golden. Add the mushrooms, rosemary, salt and pepper. Cover and simmer for 5 minutes. Uncover, toss and cook until the mushrooms are golden. Add the chopped parsley.

For the Buckwheat Polenta:

- Bring 4 cups of the stock or water to a boil in a large kettle, then lower the heat to very low and keep warm. Bring the remaining 4 cups of stock or water to a boil in a separate 3- to 4-quart heavy saucepan. Toss in the bay leaves and 1 tablespoon of salt, and then stir in the olive oil.

- Working with a small handful of the polenta at a time, let it fall through your fingers into the boiling seasoned water, stirring constantly with a wooden spoon. Pay special attention to the bottom edges of the pan as you stir; it is there that the polenta will stick and scorch first. It should take about 5 minutes to add all the polenta.

- When all the polenta is added, the mixture should be smooth and thick and begin to perk like a little volcano. Lower the heat so the polenta continues to perk slowly. Cook, stirring constantly, until it is smooth and shiny, about 5 minutes. If at any point while cooking the polenta it becomes too thick to stir easily, add some of the hot stock or water from the kettle — about 1/4 cup — to loosen the consistency a little. It is possible that you will not need to add all the hot stock or water in the kettle before the polenta is tender. The polenta is ready to serve at this point, or you can choose to cook it an extra minute or two, to intensify the flavor.

- Remove the pan from the heat, stir in the butter and cheese.

To Finish and Serve:

- In a deep bowl, mound the polenta, top with mushrooms, and sprinkle with some extra-virgin olive oil and Parmigiano-Reggiano shavings.

Lidia Bastianich's Beverage Recommendations

Sautéed Assorted
Mushrooms with
Buckwheat Polenta
Valentini Trebbiano
d'Abruzzo, 1993
page 123

Capon Soup with Passatelli
Gravner Ribolla Gialla, 1997
page 125

Spaghetti Squash
Salad with Gorgonzola
Damijan (Chardonnay,
Tocai, Malvasin), 1998
page 127

Seared Lamb Chops with Capers
and Jerusalem Artichokes
Moschioni Refosco, 1998
page 129

Palacinke
with Nutella
Vittorio Baratto
Calusa Passito, 1993
page 131

Palacinke with
Strawberries
Perrone Sourgal
Moscato d' Asti, 2001
page 131

Capon Soup with Passatelli

Serves: 6

Capon Stock:

1 each whole capon
(about 4 pounds — may substitute whole roaster chicken)

1 each large onion, halved

3 cups carrots, peeled and sliced into 1-inch rounds

3 stalks celery, cut crosswise into four pieces each

6 sprigs flat-leaf parsley

6 each whole black peppercorns

Salt to taste

Soup:

3 quarts Capon Stock
(see recipe above)

1 recipe Passatelli
(see side bar recipe)

3 cups spinach leaves, cleaned, washed and cut into a fine chiffonade

2 tablespoons truffle butter
(optional)

1/3 cup grated Parmigiano-Reggiano

Finish:

2 cups capon meat, shredded
(from Capon Stock preparation)

Freshly grated Parmigiano-Reggiano

For the Capon Stock:

- Wash the capon thoroughly under cold running water and drain well. Set the capon in a 12-quart stockpot filled with water and bring to a boil over high heat. Adjust the level of heat to medium and continue simmering for 1 hour, skimming off the surface foam and fat occasionally.

- Meanwhile, place the onion halves, with the sliced sides facing down, directly over an open flame and cook until the sliced surfaces are well browned, about 3 minutes. Move the onion halves with a pair of tongs as necessary to brown them evenly. Alternatively, the onion may be browned cut-sides down in a heavy skillet over medium heat.

- Add the onion and remaining ingredients except the salt to the pot. Bring to a boil again, skimming occasionally. Lower the heat until the liquid is "perking" — 1 or 2 large bubbles rise to the surface at a time. Cook, partially covered, for 3 hours. Add salt to taste.

- Strain the stock through a colander lined with a dampened kitchen towel or cheesecloth. Reserve the capon. If you want to use the stock immediately, you can remove much of the liquid fat floating on the surface by lightly dragging a folded paper towel over the surface. It will be easier to degrease the stock if you have time to chill it completely in the refrigerator; the fat will then rise to the surface and solidify and can easily be lifted off.

- When the capon is cool, remove the meat and shred it. Discard all skin and fat.

For the Soup:

- Bring capon stock to a boil. Add passatelli and cook for 5 minutes. Add spinach and cook an additional 3 minutes. Mix in truffle butter and Parmigiano-Reggiano.

To Finish and Serve:

- Place a small amount of shredded capon or chicken in each of six serving bowls. Ladle the soup over the chicken. The hot broth will warm the meat, which is simply a garnish for the soup. Finish each bowl with more freshly grated Parmigiano-Reggiano .

Passatelli

Serves: 6

Passatelli:

3 each eggs, whisked

1 cup breadcrumbs
(preferably from hard, dry bread)

2 tablespoons grated Parmigiano-Reggiano

Salt and white pepper to taste

Milk to moisten

For the Passatelli:

Combine all of the ingredients together and mix until you get a dough that is firm but malleable. Add a little of the milk if the dough is too tight or a little more breadcrumbs if too loose.

Press pieces of dough through a passatelli maker. The result looks like thick spaghetti that breaks in 1-inch pieces as it comes out of the passatelli press. *(There is also a passatelli instrument that looks like a 3-inch round colander with holes, attached to a handle-bar like piece.)* The dough is flattened about 1/2-inch thick on a hard surface, and the sieve is pressured into the dough. The passatelli emerge from the pressure through the holes in the sieve. Alternatively, the dough may be pressed through a large-bore colander or a German spaetzle maker or potato ricer. Set the passatelli on a sheet pan, covered with a dry cloth.

Spaghetti Squash Salad with Gorgonzola

Serves: 6

Salad:

4 heads Belgian endive

1 each spaghetti squash
(approximately 3 pounds)

5 tablespoons extra-virgin
olive oil

Salt and pepper to taste

2 each pears

1/4 cup toasted almonds

4 tablespoons white balsamic
vinegar

Finish:

10 ounces Gorgonzola
(not too ripe), cut into six slices,
or 18 small cubes

2 tablespoons aged balsamic
vinegar

For the Salad:

• Preheat the oven to 450 degrees.

• Cut 2 heads of the endive in half. Cut the squash in half, clean out the seeds, and season both the endive halves and the squash halves with 2 tablespoons of the olive oil, salt and pepper. Bake in the oven for 50 minutes. Let cool.

• Cut the rest of the endive in rounds. Scrape the cooled spaghetti squash out with a fork into a bowl. Peel and core the pears. Slice one of the pears very thinly and place in line with the base of each of six serving plates. Cut the other pear into matchstick sized pieces.

• Add the matchstick-cut pears, freshly cut endive rounds, and toasted almonds to the spaghetti squash in the bowl. Toss all well with the white balsamic vinegar and the remaining extra-virgin olive oil. Season to taste with salt and pepper.

To Finish and Serve:

• Top the slices of pear on each of the plates with several spears of the baked endive. Set the dressed spaghetti salad in the middle. Set a slice or arrange three small cubes of Gorgonzola on each plate and drizzle with the aged balsamic vinegar.

More Cooking with Lidia Bastianich

Lidia has published a
selection of cookbooks
available nationwide.

*Lidia's Italian-
American Kitchen
(Knopf 2001)*

*Lidia's Italian Table
(William Morrow & Co. 1998)*

*La Cucina di Lidia
(Doubleday 1990)*

Seared Lamb Chops with Capers and Jerusalem Artichokes

Serves: 4

Lamb Chops:

12 each "frenched" rib lamb chops* *(about 3 pounds)*

2 teaspoons extra-virgin olive oil

1 teaspoon salt

1 teaspoon freshly ground black pepper

Jerusalem Artichokes:

1 pound Jerusalem artichokes, peeled and cut into thick slices *(also called sunchokes)*

4 cloves garlic, sliced

4 tablespoons extra-virgin olive oil

6 each small artichokes, cleaned and cut in half

Salt and pepper to taste

4 tablespoons red wine vinegar

1/4 cup capers, washed and drained

1/4 cup golden raisins, soaked in water, drained and chopped

1 tablespoon chopped mint

Finish:

Mint sprig

For the Lamb Chops:

- Rub the chops with the olive oil, salt and pepper and let stand at room temperature for up to 2 hours, or refrigerate, covered, for up to 1 day.

- Heat a heavy griddle or large cast-iron pan over high heat. Add as many chops as will fit without touching. Cook the chops, turning them once, until well-browned outside and rosy pink in the center, about 3 minutes total. *(For more well-done chops, add 1 to 2 minutes to the cooking time.)* Repeat with the remaining chops, if necessary.

For the Jerusalem Artichokes:

- After artichokes have been cleaned, peeled and sliced, they should be soaked briefly in a bowl of water to which the juice of a lemon or 2 tablespoons of vinegar has been added to prevent discoloration. Drain and pat dry before sautéing.

- Sauté the Jerusalem artichokes and garlic in 2 tablespoons of the olive oil for 10 minutes. Add halved artichokes, season with salt and pepper to taste and cook slowly for an additional 20 minutes until tender. Add the vinegar and the remaining 2 tablespoons olive oil and simmer for a few minutes. Add the capers, raisins and mint and cook for 2 more minutes. Season to taste with salt and pepper.

To Finish and Serve:

- Serve the seared chops on top of the sautéed vegetables. Garnish with a sprig of mint.

*Ask the butcher to french the chops, or do it yourself: Cut the meat and fat away from each rib bone, starting at the point where the "eye" of meat meets the bone. Scrape the bone clean with the back side of a knife. There should be from 1-1/2 to 3 inches of bone protruding.

The Not-for-Profit Lidia Matticchio Bastianich Foundation

The foundation's goal is to benefit the indigent, abandoned, oppressed, neglected, ill or handicapped without regard to race or creed by promoting their health, welfare, happiness and academic and vocational training and development, and by otherwise assisting them in leading fulfilling lives. The foundation funds education programs at the elementary through post-graduate levels. Aid has been given to immigrants from war-torn Croatia, Albania, the former Yugoslavia, and other Eastern European countries to help in their integration into United States society by providing housing and educational and financial assistance. The foundation also promotes cultural activities and endeavors that preserve ethnic heritages. It supports programs and artistic efforts in music, the visual arts and the performance arts activities in general. Research in the field of medicine has been supported, bringing the latest medical technologies in the United States to doctors and medical personnel from other countries.

For more information or to make tax-free donations, please contact shelly@lidiasitaly.com.

Palacinke

Serves: 10

Crêpes:

2 each eggs

2 cups milk

1/2 **cup** club soda

1/4 **cup** sugar

1/4 **teaspoon** salt

1 tablespoon dark rum

1 teaspoon vanilla extract

2 cups flour

3 tablespoons olive oil

Grated zest from one lemon

Grated zest from one orange

Vegetable oil, for frying as needed

Finish:

Strawberries marinated in Grand
  Marnier *(optional)*

Nutella or bittersweet chocolate
  (optional)

Ricotta and honey *(optional)*

Whipped cream *(optional)*

For the Crêpes:

- In a bowl, whisk the eggs. Add the milk, club soda, sugar, salt, rum and vanilla and blend well until the sugar has dissolved. Gradually sift in the flour to form a batter, then stir in the olive oil. The consistency should be that of melted ice cream. If there are any lumps in the batter, strain it through a colander. Add the citrus zests.

- In a 6- to 7-inch crêpe pan or small non-stick skillet, heat 1 tablespoon of vegetable oil over moderately high flame, pouring off the excess. Pour a small amount of batter into the oiled pan and tilt and swirl it to distribute batter as thinly and evenly as possible. The secret is to flex your wrist as you tilt the pan.

- Return the pan to the heat, reduce the flame to moderate, and cook the crêpe until lightly browned, 30-40 seconds. Flip it carefully with a silicone or other flexible spatula and cook the second side until brown spots appear. Remove from the pan to a warmed platter and repeat the process with the remaining batter, re-oiling the pan only as necessary. Stack the finished crepes and keep warm under a mixing bowl.

To Finish and Serve:

- The finished crêpes are best served warm. They can be sprinkled with sugar or spread with marmalade, then folded into quarters, and topped with strawberries marinated in Grand Marnier, or they can be sprinkled with confectioners' sugar and served hot with a spoonful of whipped cream. For a chocolate finish, spread 1 tablespoon of Nutella or melted bittersweet chocolate on each of the warm crêpes, top with toasted walnuts, and then fold into quarters and top with whipped cream. Finish with a drizzle of warm melted chocolate.

- Simplest of all — blend some ricotta cheese with honey and spread on a hot palacinke. Fold in quarters, top with whipped cream and garnish with a small piece of honeycomb.

KEN ORINGER

BOSTON, MA

American Express Best Chef: Northeast, 2001

Asked what they want to be when they grow up, many boys answer, "a fireman, putting out blazes." Not Ken Oringer — the future chef/owner of Boston's Clio restaurant was far more interested in stoking kitchen fires.

"Growing up in Paramus, New Jersey, we were close to New York, and since my parents were interested in food my brother, sisters and I were exposed to a wide variety of different cuisine — nothing like foie gras, but certainly Chinese and Italian," he says.

Oringer's best friend's family owned a restaurant, and while the other kids were outside playing, the two buddies would be preparing pastries and consommé. By the time he was 12, Oringer had devoured every cookbook he could get his hands on (he's still an omnivorous reader) and watched every available episode of Julia Child's *The French Chef* and *The Galloping Gourmet* on TV. Since both his parents worked, Oringer happily assumed dinner-making duties.

"They always encouraged me to pursue my dream," he says, "but my dad wanted me to go to business school so I'd have a firm grounding when the day came that I'd have my own restaurant."

While pursuing a degree in hotel and restaurant management at Bryant College, Oringer worked in restaurants washing dishes, prepping and making sandwiches. "I remember cracking 500 eggs one day and loving every minute of it," he laughs.

Oringer's first semester at the college wasn't nearly as engaging. He wanted to cook, not sit in a classroom. Oringer quickly decided, though, that putting in the time was a necessary career requirement. Buckling down, he made the dean's list every semester thereafter.

"My experience at Bryant taught me how to study, to be serious about what I was doing. I learned to take advantage of every opportunity

Chef de cuisine at Silks in San Francisco's Mandarin Oriental Hotel was what Oringer calls "the big job." It offered him an unprecedented opportunity to explore Asian cooking and find ways to meld it with contemporary French styles. "I was like a kid in a candy store; all the ingredients were right there," recalls Oringer. "I experimented like crazy and at the same time I was also learning new kinds of food and wine pairings from vintners in Napa and Sonoma."

The national food press began to pay attention to the youthful chef as he honed his skills. "I've always looked for the 'WOW!' effect, the things that will separate my food from the pack — the unusual ingredients, offbeat spices and seasonings, unexpected combinations."

Within that willingness to experiment, Oringer pays strict attention to classic combinations and then uses them as a jumping-off point.

As an example, "I love Japanese food for its cleanliness, purity and Zen-like feel," explains Oringer. "But why be stuck in tradition? Why not take it a step further? Why can't a Japanese dish include olive oil, or horseradish instead of

that came my way, like helping Jacques Pépin do a cooking demo. He then became one of my mentors."

As mentors go, Oringer has had phenomenal luck. After graduating, he went to work for David Burke at River Cafe, which at the time was *the* restaurant in Manhattan. He says, "David taught me not to be afraid to try anything, that no combinations were too crazy as long as they made culinary sense."

His next gig was under Chef Jean George Vongerichten in Boston who soon promoted Oringer to sous chef. "Jean George was doing something entirely different, using exotic spices, exciting ingredients, infused oils. I could see from what he was doing that French cuisine wasn't static, that it could be taken in different directions."

wasabi? As long as it makes sense together, why not take it as far as your imagination will go?"

Clio, his small, glamorous restaurant (think leopard print carpet, masses of fresh flowers and warm amber lighting) in the charmingly European-feeling Eliot Hotel located in Boston's Back Bay, is the proving ground for Oringer's imagination.

His culinary creations are dazzlingly inventive but always based on consistency of flavor and texture. The dishes are also meticulously appropriate to the season. Diners have the option of choosing from a tasting menu or ordering from the regular menu — although there is nothing "regular" about it. Examples might include quivering pink sea urchin and slices of hamachi tuna garnished with onion seeds and minuscule cilantro leaves served in the spiky shell, and vividly flavored, slow-cooked wild Scottish salmon with celery root, maitake mushrooms and black truffle vinaigrette. It's all about bold, distinctive flavors and delicacy of presentation.

Continuing to explore relationships between cultures and flavors, Oringer turned the small lounge adjacent to Clio's dining room into a one-of-a-kind sashimi bar that features flights of fancy such as foie gras and lobster with dashi and honshimiji mushrooms, or toro tartare garnished with osetra caviar, miso mustard sauce and freshly made wasabi.

If this sounds a long way from Oringer's suburban roots, it's not entirely. One of the seminal experiences of his childhood was peering into the kitchen of a New York restaurant from a window next to the sidewalk and avidly watching the crew at work. When the build-out was done on Clio, he made sure there was a similar window. He says, "I want people to appreciate the drama and know there are no secrets."

Although he admits to a virtually non-stop work schedule, Oringer travels every chance he gets, and the more distant the destination, the better. Asia is a magnet for him with Thailand perhaps his favorite country. "You can eat *anywhere* there, anywhere; in the market, on the street, restaurants large or small and you're going to get something that is unbelievable," he says.

When he is home he rarely cooks for himself. If he does, he prefers simple fare; BLT's or grilled cheese accompanied by a good bottle of wine. His comfort foods of choice are Sabrett's® hot dogs with onions and mustard, White Castle® hamburgers and microwave burritos.

Oringer is currently writing a cookbook, but says it's laborious since he cooks on instinct and has few written recipes. Nonetheless, it's a goal and he is an intensely goal-oriented person. His final word on that subject, "I want to continue to be motivated and keep pushing myself to excel."

Ragout of Calamari

Serves: 4

Carrot Emulsion:
2/3 **cup** carrot juice
1/3 **teaspoon** ground cardamom
1/8 **teaspoon** ground coriander
1/8 **teaspoon** ground cinnamon
Pinch ground cayenne pepper
Salt to taste
2 **tablespoons** butter

Calamari:
2 **tablespoons** canola oil
1 **pound** calamari, tubes only,
   sliced thin
Salt to taste
1 **tablespoon** argan oil*
1 **tablespoon** chopped chives

Finish:
12 **each** nasturtium leaves
12 **each** nasturtium flowers

For the Carrot Emulsion:

- Combine all ingredients except the butter in a saucepan and cook over medium heat until reduced by 1/3. Whisk in the butter to finish the sauce.

For the Calamari:

- Heat the canola oil in a sauté pan. Add the calamari and season with salt. Sauté quickly, being careful not to overcook. Remove from heat and add the argan oil and the chives.

To Finish and Serve:

- Drizzle each of four serving plates with the carrot emulsion. Place a mound of nasturium leaves on each plate. Top each mound with a scoop of the calamari mixture. Garnish with the nasturtium flowers.

* Available at health food stores

Tomato Water Martini

Oringer serves this refreshing beverage as a non-alcoholic apéritif, but those inclined can add a jigger of premium vodka.

Tomato Water Martini:
5 **each** vine-ripe tomatoes
3/4 **teaspoon** salt

Finish:
Pickled green tomato slices *(optional)*
Caper berries *(optional)*
Opal basil leaves *(optional)*
Basil oil *(optional)*

For the Tomato Water Martini:

Purée the tomatoes in a food processor. Line a strainer with a triple layer of cheesecloth, pour in the purée and let drip into a bowl overnight. Season with salt. Chill.

Divide tomato water into four martini glasses and garnish each one with a pickled green tomato slice, halved caper berry and opal basil leaf along with a drop of basil oil. *(Use a store-bought brand such as Boyajian or make your own by blending a cup of basil leaves with a cup of good-quality olive oil and straining into a clean container.)*

Finish:

Oringer also adds a bit of peeled, seeded and finely diced red and yellow tomato as well as jicama to float in the liquid.

Salad of Roasted Red, Golden and Candy Striped Beets with Fresh Horseradish and Heirloom Apples

Serves: 8

Roasted Beets:

4 each large red beets*

4 each large golden beets*

4 each large Chioggia beets*
  (candy cane beets)

2 tablespoons canola oil

Salt and pepper to taste

5 each thyme sprigs

6 each cloves

Apple Syrup:

1 cup apple juice

Beet Syrup:

2 cups sugar

2 cups water

1 each large red beet, grated

1/4 cup vinegar

Salt and pepper to taste

Neutral Vinaigrette:

1/4 cup freshly squeezed
  lemon juice

3/4 cup grapeseed oil

Salt and pepper to taste

Finish:

1 recipe ravigote sauce
  (see side bar)

2 tablespoons freshly grated
  horseradish

1/4 cup julienned beets

1/4 cup julienned green apples

2 bunches micro beet greens
  (may substitute sprouts)

2 bunches micro apple mint
  greens *(may substitute sprouts)*

For the Roasted Beets:

- Preheat oven to 350 degrees. Wash the beets thoroughly under cold water. Toss with canola oil, salt and pepper. Wrap the beets in heavy-duty aluminum foil with the thyme and cloves. Roast until cooked through, about 1-1/2 hours. Open foil packet and let the beets sit and cool, then peel *(use gloves so your hands do not get stained)*. Cut the beets into desired shape and cool until needed.

For the Apple Syrup:

- Cook the apple juice over low to medium heat until reduced by half and syrupy in consistency. Cool.

For the Beet Syrup:

- Combine the sugar and water and heat until all the sugar is dissolved. Add the grated beet and cook until syrupy and reduced by half. Strain, season with vinegar and salt and pepper to taste and cool.

For the Neutral Vinaigrette:

- Combine all of the ingredients and mix well. Season to taste.

To Finish and Serve:

- Toss the golden roasted beets with 2 tablespoons of the neutral vinaigrette, salt and pepper. Toss the red roasted beets with 2 tablespoons of the apple syrup, salt and pepper. Arrange beets in bundles on serving platter. Add a generous dollop of the ravigote sauce to each beet bundle. Top each bundle with a bit of the grated horseradish. Arrange the beet and green apple juliennes on the platter around the beets, and then top with the micro greens. Draw a simple design on the plate with the apple and beet syrups.

* Any combination of red and golden beets may be used.

Ravigote Sauce

Makes: 1-1/4 cups

Ravigote Sauce:

2 each egg yolks

1 tablespoon lemon juice

2 teaspoons Dijon mustard

1 teaspoon minced garlic

6-8 ounces canola oil

Finely chopped fresh
  tarragon to taste

Finely chopped cornichons to taste

Finely chopped capers to taste

Salt and pepper to taste

For the Ravigote Sauce:

Combine the egg yolks, lemon juice, mustard and garlic in a food processor. With motor running, add the oil in a thin stream until a complete emulsification is achieved. Add the tarragon, cornichons and capers and mix thoroughly. Season with salt and pepper and chill.

Swordfish au Poivre with Parsnip Purée and Red Wine Braised Shallots

Serves: 4

Parsnip Purée:

1 pound parsnips

2 tablespoons butter

Salt and pepper to taste

Red Wine Braised Shallots:

12 each shallots, peeled

1 cup red wine

1 teaspoon honey

Salt to taste

Swordfish au Poivre:

4 each swordfish steaks, 6 ounces each, cut into blocks 2 inches thick by 3 inches wide

2 teaspoons coarsely cracked black peppercorns

Salt to taste

2 teaspoons canola oil

Finish:

Chervil leaves as needed

For the Parsnip Purée:

- Peel the parsnips. Place in a saucepan with enough water to fully cover. Cook on high heat until tender. Drain. Purée in a food processor with the butter. Season to taste with salt and pepper. Set aside until ready to assemble dish.

For the Red Wine Braised Shallots:

- Place the shallots and the red wine in a heavy saucepan. Add the honey and cook on medium heat until syrupy, approximately 20 minutes. Set aside until ready to assemble dish.

For the Swordfish au Poivre:

- Preheat oven to 400 degrees. Coat the swordfish pieces with cracked pepper and salt on both sides. Heat the canola oil in a sauté pan and cook until the swordfish is golden brown and crusty on one side. Remove swordfish from pan and place, cooked-side down, on a baking sheet. Finish cooking in preheated oven until the fish is just cooked, approximately 8 minutes.

To Finish and Serve:

- Spoon the parsnip purée onto each of four serving plates. Place the swordfish on top of the purée on each plate. Glaze each piece of swordfish with the red wine braised shallots. Garnish with chervil leaves.

Ken Oringer's Beverage Recommendations

Ragout of Calamari

Syrah

page 137

Salad of Roasted Red, Golden and Candy Striped Beets with Fresh Horseradish and Heirloom Apples

Sauvignon Blanc

page 139

Swordfish au Poivre with Parsnip Purée and Red Wine Braised Shallots

Cabernet

page 141

Aromatic Glazed Short Ribs

Syrah

page 143

Chicory Flavored Eggnog

Demi-sec Champagne

page 143

Hot Chocolate Fondant with Coconut Sorbet and Hazelnut Nougatine

Banyuls

page 145

Aromatic Glazed Short Ribs

Serves: 4

Roasted Bones:

5 pounds short rib bones

Short Ribs:

4 pounds short ribs of beef

Salt and pepper to taste

5 tablespoons olive oil

3 each carrots, roughly chopped

3 each celery stalks, roughly chopped

2 each onions, roughly chopped

1/2 cup port

1 cup red wine

1 tablespoon ground coriander

1/2 tablespoon fennel seed

4 each cinnamon sticks

1 each star anise

2 each bay leaves

1/2 tablespoon black peppercorns

1 each 1/4-inch piece fresh ginger

6 each thyme sprigs

5 each parsley sprigs

1/2 teaspoon lavender

6 cloves garlic

2 each juniper berries

4 cups chicken stock

For the Roasted Bones:

- Preheat oven to 450 degrees. Place the bones in a heavy roasting pan and roast for about 20 to 30 minutes, or until dark golden brown.

For the Short Ribs:

- Season ribs with salt and pepper. Heat oil in large stockpot and sear ribs until well browned. Add carrots, celery and onions and brown slightly. Add roasted bones, then deglaze the pan with port followed by the wine. Add all remaining ingredients, plus enough chicken stock to cover everything. Cover pot with foil and simmer until the ribs are fork tender, approximately 2 hours. Remove ribs from pot and set aside. Strain liquid through a sieve. Degrease liquid and then reduce over medium-high heat until it reaches a sauce-like consistency.

To Finish and Serve:

- Dip ribs in sauce to glaze and serve immediately.

Chicory-Flavored Eggnog

Serves: 2

Eggnog:

1-1/2 tablespoons chicory extract*

1 cup milk

3 tablespoons cream

2 each eggs

4 tablespoons sugar

For the Eggnog:

In a saucepan, combine the chicory extract, milk and cream and bring to a simmer over medium heat. Saw the egg tops off very carefully with a serrated knife. Keep the large portion of the shell to use later. Separate the eggs and discard the whites or save for another use. Whisk together the egg yolks and the sugar. Whisk the milk mixture into the yolk a little at a time. Strain through a fine-mesh strainer and allow it to chill thoroughly in the refrigerator. Once chilled, froth up the eggnog using a handheld or immersion blender.

Finish:

Pour the eggnog into 2 egg shells. Serve immediately.

* Available at health food stores

Hot Chocolate Fondant with Coconut Sorbet and Hazelnut Nougatine

Serves: 8

Hot Chocolate Fondant:

10 ounces chopped high-quality semisweet chocolate

6 ounces chopped high-quality bittersweet chocolate

1 pound unsalted butter

7/8 cup sugar

Pinch kosher salt

8 each eggs

8 each egg yolks

Chocolate Sauce:

5-1/2 ounces finely chopped semisweet chocolate

1/2 cup plus 1 tablespoon heavy cream

4 tablespoons glucose, corn syrup or fructose*

1 scant tablespoon water

Pinch kosher salt

Hazelnut Nougatine:

1-7/8 cups toasted hazelnuts

7/8 cup sugar

1-1/2 tablespoons glucose, corn syrup or fructose*

1 tablespoon water

Chocolate Caramel:

3 ounces cocoa paste, unsweetened chocolate

7/8 cup sugar

7/8 cup glucose *(may substitute light corn syrup or fructose)*

Coconut Sorbet:

Pinch stabilizer such as gelatin

1 tablespoon sugar

1-1/2 tablespoons powdered glucose or powdered fructose

4 tablespoons water

7/8 cup coconut purée**

Kosher salt to taste

Finish:

Non-stick cooking spray *(such as Pam)*

For the Hot Chocolate Fondant:

- In a double boiler, melt both chocolates together with the butter. In a separate bowl, whisk together the sugar, salt, eggs and egg yolks until just combined. Using a whisk, carefully combine the chocolate and egg mixtures. Set batter aside in the refrigerator.

For the Chocolate Sauce:

- Place the chocolate in a stainless steel bowl. In a saucepan, combine the cream, glucose, water and salt. Bring to a boil and pour over the chocolate. Let rest for 1 minute and combine thoroughly with a wooden spoon.

For the Hazelnut Nougatine:

- Finely chop the hazelnuts. In a heavy-bottomed saucepan, combine the sugar, glucose and water. Stir to combine and boil to a temperature of 320 to 338 degrees *(use a candy thermometer)*. Add the hazelnuts and mix with a wooden spoon. Pour hot mixture onto a non-stick surface. Allow to cool.

For the Chocolate Caramel:

- Finely chop the cocoa paste. In a heavy-bottomed saucepan, combine the sugar and glucose with just enough water to moisten the two. Heat the mixture to a temperature of 320 to 338 degrees. Remove from the heat and add the cocoa paste. Let rest for 1 minute. Using a wooden spoon, mix thoroughly and pour mixture onto a non-stick surface. Allow to cool.

For the Coconut Sorbet:

- In a bowl, combine the stabilizer, sugar and glucose powder and mix thoroughly. In a saucepan, combine the sugar mixture and water and bring to a boil. Once it reaches a boil transfer to a blender with the coconut purée and blend. Pass through a fine-mesh strainer and season to taste with salt. Freeze in an ice cream machine according to the manufacturer's directions.

To Finish and Serve:

- Finely chop the hazelnut nougatine. Cover the bottoms of eight 4-inch by 2-inch deep ring molds with aluminum foil and spray with non-stick spray. Fill each mold halfway with the fondant batter and place on a sheet tray. Bake at 375 degrees for 10 to 12 minutes. Remove from the oven and allow to rest.

- Decorate each of eight dessert plates with some of the chocolate sauce. Place two mounds of hazelnut nougatine on each plate. Using a small offset spatula, release the hot chocolate fondant from the sides of each mold and carefully place one fondant on one of the two mounds of hazelnut nougatine on each plate. Place a scoop of coconut sorbet on top of the other mound of hazelnut nougatine on each plate and serve immediately.

* Available at health food stores
** Available at Asian specialty markets

ALESSANDRO STRATTA

LAS VEGAS, NV

American Express Best Chef: Southwest, 1998

He spent his childhood traveling the globe, but now as executive chef of Renoir at The Mirage in Las Vegas, the world comes to Alessandro Stratta.

Stratta is fifth generation in a family of hoteliers. His great-grandfather owned a hunting lodge in the Piedmont region of Northern Italy at the foot of the Alps. It became a favorite haunt of Italian royalty, including the king and members of the House of Savoy; but everything changed with the onset of World War I, and the family moved to Colombia where Stratta's grandfather had a hotel in Bogota.

When the war ended the family returned to Italy. Stratta's father got a soccer scholarship to Cornell University. He married after graduation, and Alessandro and his two older sisters were born in the United States.

From the time Stratta was a baby, his family was on the move — from Pakistan to Karachi, Malaysia to Indonesia and then to Singapore. In 1970, when Stratta was six years old, his father opened The Princess Hotel in Acapulco, and the family remained in Mexico until he was ten.

Stratta laughs when he recalls that they dined almost exclusively in the house restaurants or ordered from room service. "We went through a lot of club sandwiches," he says.

However, there were other culinary influences at work. Stratta learned to appreciate the robust straight-forward food of Mexico. When his French-descent mother did cook, it tended to be elaborate meals much different than the simple room service fare. Hailing from Italy, his father's tastes ran to food from his birthplace.

The next post was Rome's Excelsior Hotel where the Strattas stayed for two years. In many ways it was an exciting and broadening lifestyle but there were drawbacks to this exotically nomadic childhood. Says Stratta, "You never feel stable. Each place was so different and living in a hotel you really don't become part of a community. I actually had very little formal schooling." — This from a man who speaks fluent French, Italian, Spanish and English.

Then it was back to the states where Stratta senior took over as CEO of a hotel company, and for a while the family stayed put in Connecticut. "It was literally the first time I ever lived in a house," says Stratta.

The Strattas were in California by the time Alessandro entered high school. "I needed a job to support my motorcycle habit, so I went to work at a steak house as a dishwasher. I felt really comfortable in the environment and my boss moved me up to onion ring guy."

He enrolled at St. Regis College in Denver intending to get a degree in business administration, but ended up doing more skiing than studying. Deciding he needed a change of scene, he returned to Los Angeles and took a job first at the Westlake Plaza as a banquet cook and then as a sauté cook at The Beverly Hills Hotel. "Old standards like souffléed potatoes, Dover sole and hollandaise, that was fine dining," he recalls.

At that point he knew he enjoyed the work, was determined to succeed and was chalking up great references in the process. His dad encouraged Alessandro to seriously pursue a career in cooking if that was what he wanted to do. He graduated with honors from the California Culinary Academy.

Initially, Stratta wanted to be a pastry chef and secured the enviable post of Jim Dodge's assistant at

The Stanford Court Hotel in San Francisco, but once again, the opportunity to travel knocked. An old friend of Stratta's dad offered a chance at a two-month apprenticeship at Hotel de Paris in Monte Carlo.

"Monaco really opened my eyes. I had done well in school and I thought that I was pretty good, but there I started to see that European devotion to the details, the discipline and passion these people brought to cooking. I got completely hooked. They couldn't get over the crazy American. We worked from 7 AM to 3 PM and then broke until the 6 PM to midnight shift, but I worked straight through just trying to stay ahead."

When the apprenticeship ended, Stratta grabbed the chance to fill in for an injured cook at Alain Ducasse's Michelin three-star restaurant Louis XV. Ducasse was so impressed with his work, Stratta stayed for two years.

"At the time Ducasse was not a big name. He was doing something new — combining French and Italian influences — and that's exactly what I loved and felt most comfortable with."

It also perfectly mirrored his Italian-French heritage. On his own, Stratta began studying food history, a passion that persists.

With the assistance of Ducasse, Stratta landed a job with Daniel Boulud at Le Cirque in Manhattan where he spent another two years and began to formulate his culinary philosophy. "I saw all this complex, confused food being done elsewhere and compared it to a simple lobster soup or perfectly braised carrot and realized minimalistic cooking techniques that make the ingredients just pop was what I'd always searched for."

By age 25, Stratta became executive chef at Mary Elaine's at The Phoenician Resort in Scottsdale, Arizona. With his clean, focused balance of French and Italian techniques and his insistence on superior-quality seasonal ingredients, he turned it into one of the top restaurants in the country.

When the call came from Steve Wynn at the Mirage in Las Vegas, Stratta was ready. He spent over a year putting the restaurant together, working with the designer and gathering a stellar crew, most of whom had worked with him at Mary Elaine's.

Renoir is named, of course, after the French artist whose works, along with those of other impressionists, hang in the dining room. It is decorated in a rich layering of lemon, pistachio and coral print fabrics. Huge mirrors reflect the stunning artwork, massive floral arrangements and immaculately set tables. The lush décor provides a picture perfect setting for restrained yet voluptuous creations such as a warm salad of duck confit with crisp potatoes, and aged balsamic vinegar and potato crusted Dover Sole with red wine, wild mushrooms and Serrano ham.

Explains Stratta, "My dishes are exactly as they are described on the menu. I continue to refine and define, to distill and simplify."

Not that simplification comes easy. Says Stratta, "Each day I check product, make sure we have enough and that it is of the highest quality. I might write a couple recipes and then I go into the pasta room and make pasta for five hours at a time." And five nights a week he cooks and supervises.

When he's not in the kitchen, Stratta, his wife Laura, who he met at The Phoenician, and their two dogs, enjoy taking long hikes. They bike as well, and each year he travels to some destination in France or Italy with a group of fellow chefs that includes Roberto Donna and Sanford D'Amato. In his rare spare moments, Stratta plays the guitar to relax.

He wants to get to work on a cookbook soon, but most important to him is striving for balance in his daily life and as part of that says Stratta, "I really want to help develop other people, turn cooks into chefs because great chefs make a difference in quality of life." Stratta's customers can testify to that. His travels and dedication to his art have certainly made him one of the great American chefs.

Asparagus Cannelloni with Morel Mushrooms

Serves: 4

Pasta Dough:
(makes 1 kilo)
10 each large eggs
3-1/3 cups all-purpose flour
3-1/3 cups fine semolina flour
2 tablespoons extra-virgin
 olive oil
1 teaspoon fine sea salt
1 to 2 tablespoons water,
 as needed

Cannelloni:
16 each large, fresh, firm
 asparagus spears
8 each squares of pasta
 (see above recipe)
1 cup finely grated
 Parmesan cheese
4 tablespoons melted butter

Additional Items:

Morel Mushrooms
Recipe on page 160

For the Pasta Dough:

- Place all of the ingredients except for the water in a mixer fitted with a paddle or dough hook. Mix at a low speed until dough begins to form. Check as the dough is forming if it is too dry or too wet. If the dough is too dry, add water a little at a time. If it is too wet, add extra all-purpose flour a little at a time. Once the dough begins to come together, remove from the bowl and knead with your hands until the dough forms into a ball. Wrap the dough in plastic wrap and refrigerate for 2 hours.

- Divide the dough into four equal parts. Using a pasta machine, roll out the dough as thin as possible into smooth sheets. Cut the sheets into 3- x 2-inch squares and set aside. This recipe calls for two squares per portion, or eight squares total. Reserve the eight squares on a floured piece of parchment paper. Remaining pasta may be reserved for another use.

For the Cannelloni:

- Peel each asparagus spear with a paring knife, from just below the tip down to the stem end. Trim each spear so that it is approximately 3-1/2-inches long and discard the ends. Bring a large pot of salted water to boil. Add the asparagus spears and cook for 3 minutes. Remove the asparagus from the water and immediately plunge it into an ice water bath. Once cooled, remove from the water and place on a clean towel to drain.

- Blanch the eight squares of pasta in boiling salted water for 30 to 40 seconds *(or until the pasta is thoroughly cooked)* and cool in an ice water bath. Remove the squares of pasta from the water and dry them by placing them over the edge of a sheet pan or baking dish *(just like hanging sheets on a clothesline to dry)* for 5 minutes. Place a clean sheet or towel over a flat surface and sprinkle the pasta squares liberally with half of the cheese. Place the squares of cooked and dried pasta on the sheet pan. Place 2 asparagus spears, side by side, on one end of the pasta. Using the dull side of a paring knife, gently roll the pasta tightly around both asparagus stalks. Repeat with the remaining pasta and asparagus. Once the cannelloni are complete, cut and trim the "bottom end" of each piece so that all of the cannelloni are the same size. Place the cannelloni in pairs on a buttered sheet pan or cookie tray. Brush the top portion of the dough liberally with the melted butter and add the remaining grated cheese to cover the pasta. Refrigerate until needed. For best results, use the cannelloni the same day as it is made.

To Finish and Serve:

- Preheat the broiler. Place the sheet pan of cannelloni under the preheated broiler for 3 minutes, or until the pasta is lightly browned and the asparagus is warm. Remove the cannelloni from the baking sheet with a spatula and place two in the center of each of four warmed serving plates. Arrange the mushrooms around the asparagus and spoon the juices around the plates. Serve hot.

Cream of Maui Onion Soup with Gruyère Crouton and Pancetta

Serves: 4

Maui Onion Soup:

2 tablespoons butter

1-1/2 pounds Maui onions

1-1/2 teaspoons thyme

1 tablespoon sugar

2 quarts rich chicken stock

1 quart heavy cream

Salt and pepper to taste

Gruyère Croutons:

4 slices white country-style bread, crusts removed

1 tablespoon olive oil

1/4 teaspoon garlic purée

1 cup grated Gruyère cheese

Pancetta Chips:

4 each very thin slices pancetta

Finish:

1/4 cup heavy cream, whisked until frothy

4 teaspoons chopped chives

1/2 cup frisée salad mix

For the Maui Onion Soup:

- Heat a large, heavy saucepot over low heat and melt the butter. Slice the onions and sweat in butter for 15 minutes, until translucent. Add the thyme and sugar. Cook until lightly caramelized. Add the chicken stock and simmer for 1-1/2 hours, reducing to 1-1/2 quarts. Add the heavy cream. Simmer for an additional half hour and season to taste with salt and pepper. In a blender, blend the soup well and strain. Keep hot until needed.

For the Gruyère Croutons:

- Preheat oven to 400 degrees. Cut each slice of bread into a 2-inch or 3-inch square, or use a decorative cookie cutter. Combine the oil and garlic purée and rub the bread shapes with the mixture. Bake until golden brown. Preheat broiler. Top each piece of bread with a generous amount of cheese and broil until melted, approximately 30 seconds.

For the Pancetta Chips:

- Preheat oven to 300 degrees. Place the pancetta slices on a foil-lined baking sheet. Bake for 20 to 25 minutes, or until crisp.

To Finish and Serve:

- Place a Gruyère crouton in each of four soup bowls. Ladle hot Maui onion soup over each crouton. Top each bowl with a teaspoon of the frothed heavy cream and 1 teaspoon of chopped chives. Place the frisée and the pancetta chips as a garnish in a side dish for each bowl.

Alessandro Stratta's Beverage Recommendations

Asparagus Cannelloni with Morel Mushrooms
Château Carbonnieux, Bordeaux, France, Sauvignon Blanc/Semillon, 1999
page 151

Cream of Maui Onion Soup with Gruyère Crouton and Pancetta
Frankland Estate 'Isolation Ridge,' Western Australia, Chardonnay, 2000
page 153

Quail Salad with Caramelized Onions, Oven-Dried Tomatoes and Pancetta
Bethel Heights Vineyard, Willamette Valley, Oregon, Pinot Noir, 2000.
page 155

Santa Barbara Prawns with Sweet Curry, Green Apples and Carrot-Ginger Sauce
Domaine Laroche, 'Saint Martin,' Chablis, France, Chardonnay, 2000
page 157

Lemon Meringue Tart
Domaine de Durban, 'Beaumes-de-Venise,' Rhône Valley, France, Muscat, 1997
page 159

Quail Salad with Caramelized Onions, Oven-Dried Tomatoes and Pancetta

Serves: 4

Quail:

4 **each** fresh quail,
   7 to 8 ounces each*

1/4 **cup** extra-virgin olive oil

1 **head** garlic, peeled and
   separated into cloves

1 **tablespoon** rosemary leaves

1 **tablespoon** freshly ground
   black pepper

Salt and pepper to taste

Caramelized Onions:

1/2 **each** Maui onion, cut in half
   lengthwise *(may substitute
   other sweet onion)*

1 **teaspoon** olive oil

Salt and pepper to taste

1 **tablespoon** chicken stock

Oven-Dried Tomatoes:

8 **each** firm Roma or plum
   tomatoes *(any small ripe and
   sweet tomato may be used)*

1/2 **teaspoon** kosher salt

1/2 **teaspoon** freshly cracked
   black pepper

1 **teaspoon** vinegar *(any kind)*

2 **tablespoons** olive oil

Pancetta Lardons:

1/2 **cup** 2- x 1/4-inch
   strips pancetta

Vinaigrette:

1/4 **cup** chicken stock

1/4 **cup** aged sherry vinegar

1/4 **cup** pancetta fat

3 **cups** extra-virgin olive oil

Salt and pepper to taste

Additional Items:

Foccacia Croutons:
Recipe on page 160

Farce à Crouton:
Recipe on page 160

Finish:

4 **cups** baby frisée lettuce or
   spinach

For the Quail:

- Clean and trim the quail. Quarter each quail into two breast-wing sections and two leg-thigh sections. Debone the thighs. *(Each quail is being cut into 4 pieces.)* Combine the oil with the remaining ingredients and add the quail pieces and refrigerate for 24 hours.

- Preheat oven to 500 degrees. Remove the quail from the marinade. Season with salt and pepper. Place the quail skin-side down in a preheated sauté pan over medium heat and sear on all sides. Remove the quail from the pan and place in an oven-proof baking dish in the preheated oven. Roast for 3 minutes.

For the Caramelized Onions:

- Cut the onion into 1/8-inch thick slices. Heat the oil in a heavy sauté pan over medium heat. Add the onions. Brown the onions well on both sides and season with salt and pepper. Add the chicken stock and simmer, cooking until reduced by 1/2 and stock coats the onion completely. Reserve at room temperature until needed.

For the Oven-Dried Tomatoes:

- Preheat the oven to 300 degrees. Core the tomatoes and cut each in half lengthwise. Sprinkle with salt and pepper. Place the tomatoes in rows in a greased shallow baking dish. Bake the tomatoes for 1-1/2 to 2 hours, or until shriveled but not dried out. When done, remove from oven and sprinkle the vinegar and oil over the tomatoes.

For the Pancetta Lardons:

- Heat 1/2 cup pancetta over low heat to melt out 1/4 cup fat. Remove pancetta pieces from fat and set aside. Let fat cool.

For the Vinaigrette:

- Warm the chicken stock in a small pan. Pour the warm stock and vinegar into a blender and blend at high speed until thoroughly mixed. Slowly incorporate the pancetta fat and the olive oil by pouring them in a slow and steady stream with the blender set on low. Mix until smooth and emulsified. Season with salt and pepper to taste. Keep at room temperature until ready to use.

To Finish and Serve:

- Spoon about 1 tablespoon of the farce à crouton *(see recipe on page 160)* mixture onto each of the focaccia croutons *(see recipe on page 160)* and broil until just glazed. Arrange the leaves of frisée or spinach in the center of a round serving plate and place the caramelized onions, oven-dried tomatoes and pancetta lardons on top of the frisée or spinach. Arrange the quail and the focaccia croutons *(see recipe on page 160)* on the frisée and drizzle with the vinaigrette. Serve warm.

*Fresh quail may be substituted with partially deboned split quail found in the freezer section of most grocery stores.

Santa Barbara Prawns with Sweet Curry, Green Apples and Carrot-Ginger Sauce

Serves: 4

Carrot-Ginger Base:

1 tablespoon olive oil

2 each carrots, chopped

1 cup chopped shallots

1/2 cup chopped fresh ginger

1 tablespoon lavender honey
(may substitute regular honey)

1 cup dry white wine

2 quarts chicken stock

Carrot Ginger Sauce:

1 quart fresh carrot juice
(from about 20 carrots)

1/2 cup carrot-ginger base
(see above)

2 cups extra-virgin olive oil

Salt and pepper to taste

Parsley Purée:

1/4 cup parsley leaves

1 tablespoon water

Yuzu Vinaigrette:

1 tablespoon yuzu juice*

1 tablespoon olive oil

Apple:

1 each Fuji apple

Prawns:

12 each large Santa Barbara
prawns, peeled, deveined
and heads removed

Salt and pepper to taste

1 cup all-purpose flour

1 teaspoon olive oil

1 tablespoon butter

1/2 teaspoon garlic purée *(in oil)*

1/4 cup chicken stock

1 teaspoon minced chives

Additional Items:

Curry Sauce:
Recipe on page 161

Mango Relish:
Recipe on page 161

Apple Chips:
Recipe on page 161

For the Carrot-Ginger Base:

- In a medium-sized saucepan, heat the olive oil over low heat. Add chopped carrots, shallots, ginger and honey. Sweat the vegetables for 4 or 5 minutes by placing a tight lid over the pot. This will soften the vegetables without browning them. Add the wine and cook, stirring, until all liquid has evaporated. Add the chicken stock and simmer until the total volume equals 1 cup. Strain the mixture through a fine strainer and chill until needed.

For the Carrot-Ginger Sauce:

- Heat the carrot juice in a saucepan over medium heat. Cook until the carrot juice has been reduced to 1 cup. Refrigerate until chilled. Place the carrot-ginger base in a blender with the reduced carrot juice and blend on high speed to create an emulsion. Continue blending, adding the oil slowly to thicken. Season to taste with salt and pepper, then strain through a fine strainer. Reserve at room temperature until needed.

For the Parsley Purée:

- Purée the parsley leaves with the water in a blender. Set aside.

For the Yuzu Vinaigrette:

- Whisk the yuzu juice with the 1 tablespoon of olive oil. Set aside.

For the Apple:

- Julienne the apple and toss with the parsley purée and yuzu vinaigrette. Set aside until ready to assemble dish.

For the Prawns:

- Season the prawns with salt and pepper, then lightly dredge them in the flour, patting off any excess. Heat the oil in a sauté pan over medium-high heat and sear the prawns. Add the butter and garlic purée, cooking the garlic thoroughly. Deglaze with the chicken stock, reduce to a glaze and add the chives. Reserve until needed.

To Finish and Serve:

- Arrange the apple mixture on an oval platter. Arrange the warm prawns on top of the apple mixture. Make a line of both the curry *(see recipe on page 161)* and the carrot-ginger sauces on the plate. Garnish with the mango relish *(see recipe on page 161)* and the apple chips *(see recipe on page 161)*. Serve hot.

* Available at Asian specialty markets

Lemon Meringue Tart

Serves: 6

Lemon Curd:

3 each whole eggs

3 each egg yolks

1-1/2 cups granulated sugar

1-1/2 cups fresh lemon juice

1/2 cup unsalted butter
(cold, cut into small cubes)

Lemon Soufflé:

2 each eggs
(yolks and whites separated)

1/4 cup fresh lemon juice

3/4 teaspoon freshly grated
lemon zest

2 tablespoons sugar

1/2 teaspoon cornstarch

Pie Crust:

1/2 cup granulated sugar

1 cup butter

1 each egg

3-1/2 cups cake flour

Vanilla Sauce:

1 cup sugar

1/2 cup water

4 each vanilla beans, split and
seeds removed

For the Lemon Curd:

- In a bowl, combine the eggs, yolks and sugar. Whisk until smooth. Add the lemon juice and whisk briskly. Place the bowl over a double boiler and whisk over the heat until mixture begins to thicken. Remove from heat and add the diced cold butter, whisking in a little at a time until fully incorporated. Strain through a fine strainer. Let cool in the refrigerator for at least 2 hours.

For the Lemon Soufflé:

- In a mixing bowl, combine the egg yolks, lemon juice, lemon zest and 1 tablespoon of the sugar. Whisk until smooth. Whisk in the cornstarch in a slow steady stream until smooth, avoiding lumps. In a separate bowl, whip the egg whites with the remaining 1 tablespoon of sugar until soft peaks are formed. Gently fold 1/2 cup of the egg yolk/lemon mixture into the egg white mixture. Discard any excess egg yolk mixture.

For the Pie Crust:

- Place the sugar and butter in the bowl of a kitchen mixer fitted with a paddle attachment. Mix together. Add the egg and blend well. Add the flour and mix on the lowest speed until well blended. Chill to firm the dough before use.

For the Vanilla Sauce:

- Combine the water, sugar and vanilla beans and simmer for 20 minutes. Allow to cool, remove the vanilla beans and discard. Serve at room temperature.

To Finish and Serve:

- Preheat the oven to 450 degrees. Roll out the pie dough 1/4 inch thick. Line six 3-inch-diameter, 1-inch-high tart pans with removable bottoms with the pie dough. Pre-bake for approximately 8 minutes and let cool. Line the bottom of the cooled, pre-baked tart with a thin layer of the lemon curd mixture and set aside. Place the lemon soufflé meringue mixture in a piping bag fitted with a tip of your choice and pipe the meringue into the tart directly over the curd. Pipe out until the meringue is 2-1/2 inches thick. Bake in the oven for 6 to 8 minutes, or until lightly browned. The center should still be cold, and the meringue hot.

- Pour the cooled vanilla sauce on the side of the lemon meringue tart in a decorative pattern and serve immediately.

Morel Mushrooms

For the Asparagus Cannelloni with Morel Mushrooms recipe. Page 151

Mushrooms:

1 pound fresh morels
*(may substitute wild mushrooms
such as shiitakes or crimini)*

4 tablespoons butter

Salt and pepper to taste

1/4 cup rich chicken stock

1 tablespoon chopped chives

For the Mushrooms:

- Rinse the mushrooms under cold running water, drain and towel dry. Cut them in half lengthwise and reserve at room temperature. Heat a heavy sauté pan over high heat until the pan is very hot. Add 1/2 of the butter and place the mushrooms in the pan. Sauté about 2 minutes and season to taste with salt and pepper. Add the chicken stock and simmer on high, covered, for 3 to 4 minutes. Once the mushrooms are tender, remove the cover and allow the liquid to evaporate by 1/2. Add the remaining butter and chives and keep warm.

Foccacia Croutons

For the Quail Salad with Caramelized Onions, Oven-Dried Tomatoes and Pancetta recipe. Page 155

Foccacia Croutons:

8 each foccacia bread pieces,
each 2-inches x 3-inches

2 cloves garlic, peeled

For the Foccacia Croutons:

- Preheat oven to 300 degrees. Bake the focaccia pieces on a baking sheet in the oven for 30 minutes, or until dry and crisp. Halve the cloves of garlic and rub cut surface of garlic over each piece of focaccia.

Farce à Crouton

For the Quail Salad with Caramelized Onions, Oven-Dried Tomatoes and Pancetta recipe. Page 155

Farce à Crouton:

1 tablespoon olive oil

1/2 pound chicken livers

1/4 pound fresh foie gras
(may substitute pâté)

2 tablespoons brandy

2 tablespoons
cold butter

Salt and pepper to taste

1/4 cup sultana
(golden) raisins
soaked in sherry
vinegar then drained

For the Farce à Crouton:

- Heat a heavy sauté pan over high heat and add the oil. Sear the chicken livers until golden brown and medium rare. Remove the livers from pan and place on a warm plate. Sear the foie gras in the pan until golden brown and medium rare. Deglaze the pan with the brandy and flame *(the brandy will ignite with a gas stove; if you are using an electric stove you will need to use a long match to ignite)*. Combine the warm livers and the foie gras mixture from the pan in a bowl. Add the cold butter and season to taste with salt and pepper. Let mixture cool. Once cooled, blend in a food processor or blender until smooth. Pass through a fine-mesh sieve and add the raisins. Refrigerate until needed.

Curry Sauce

For the Santa Barbara Prawns with Sweet Curry, Green Apples and Carrot-Ginger Sauce recipe. Page 157

Curry Sauce:

1 cup plus 1 teaspoon
   extra-virgin olive oil

2 tablespoons shallots, minced

1/2 head garlic

2 tablespoons minced
   fresh ginger

2 tablespoons madras
   curry powder

1 teaspoon turmeric

2 cups chicken stock

1 cup white wine

2 tablespoons passion fruit purée
   (may substitute mango purée)

1 tablespoon sugar

1 tablespoon lime juice

2 tablespoons Dijon mustard

1 each egg yolk

Salt and pepper to taste

For the Curry Sauce:

- Heat the 1 teaspoon of olive oil in a heavy saucepan and add the minced shallots, garlic and ginger. Cook until lightly caramelized. Season to taste and then add the curry powder and turmeric. Deglaze the pan with the stock and white wine and cook until reduced by 1/2. Strain through a fine-mesh sieve and chill. Place the chilled reduction in a blender. Add the passion fruit purée, sugar, lime juice, mustard and egg yolk and blend until creamy. With the motor running, pour the olive oil into the blender in a slow steady stream. Season to taste with salt and pepper and dilute with lime juice or water until desired consistency is reached, which should be slightly thicker than heavy cream. Reserve at room temperature until needed.

Mango Relish

For the Santa Barbara Prawns with Sweet Curry, Green Apples and Carrot-ginger Sauce recipe. Page 157

Mango Relish:

1 each mango, diced

1 each red jalapeño chile, diced

16 each lime segments

1 tablespoon micro cilantro
   *(may substitute regular
   chopped cilantro)*

8 tablespoons extra-virgin
   olive oil

2 tablespoons lime juice

Salt and pepper to taste

For the Mango Relish:

- Mix all ingredients together in a bowl. Refrigerate until ready to use.

Apple Chips

For the Santa Barbara Prawns with Sweet Curry, Green Apples and Carrot-Ginger Sauce recipe. Page 157

Apple Chips:

1 each Fuji apple

1 cup water

1 cup sugar

1 teaspoon fleur de sel
   (may substitute kosher salt)

1 teaspoon curry powder

1 teaspoon black sesame seeds

1 tablespoon crushed red pepper

For the Apple Chips:

- Preheat the oven to 175 degrees. Combine the sugar and the water in a saucepan. Over medium heat, stir until the sugar dissolves fully, and then boil for 3 minutes. Slice the apple into 1/8-inch-thick slices and brush with the syrup. Combine the remaining ingredients and dust the slices with them. Place the slices on a sheet pan lined with a silpat®, or use a non-stick or Teflon baking sheet, and bake until lightly colored. Turn apple slices over and continue to cook until apple slices are dried out. Place the dried apples on a chilled stainless surface until crisp. Reserve in an airtight container until needed.

ROBERT KINKEAD

WASHINGTON, DC

American Express Best Chef: Mid-Atlantic, 1995

One could argue that seafood was Bob Kinkead's destiny. Born in Wellesley, Massachusetts, he and his nine brothers and sisters vacationed each year at the Cape Cod shore where his parents had a second home. That early exposure to clambakes and lobster boils was followed by his first summer job, washing dishes in a family-style restaurant.

The next year he started doing prep work, and though he subsequently studied for a degree in psychology and made forays into disk jockeying in nightclubs and selling insurance, the future was clear. Says Kinkead, "It seems to be universal in this business — once you get bit by the bug, you're in it for life."

Working his way up the culinary ladder, he decided that, "If I like doing this, I'd better get good at it."

He got so good he landed at the helm of the kitchen at Chillingsworth in Brewster, arguably, the best and best-known restaurant on Cape Cod. There, Kinkead met his future wife, Dianne, who was waitressing while attending graduate school.

Kinkead moved on to become head chef (and later partner) of Twenty-One Federal in Nantucket and then to open Twenty-One Federal in Washington, a move that made him a major player on the American culinary stage.

During the years of learning his craft, Kinkead says he had no real mentors along the way and that has strongly influenced the way he works with his own staff. He says straightforwardly, "I'm a good cook, but never learned to be a good teacher. So I hire good teachers and if people want to learn from them, they can."

Working in one of Kinkead's two restaurants — flagship Kinkead's on Pennsylvania Avenue's historic Red Lion Row or his newest venture,

Colvin Run Tavern in Vienna, Virginia — means first learning Kinkead's rigorous culinary philosophy. "My cooking style is fairly conservative," he explains. "It is based on classic flavor combinations. If there are Mexican, Italian or Asian influences in a dish, I make sure they are authentic to the cuisine."

That insures dishes containing sea urchin, sea cucumber, jellyfish, calves liver and pig trotters are unlikely to ever show up on one of his menus.

In the way of favorites, his longstanding appreciation for excellent quality fresh seafood and skill in preparing it came together smoothly in 1993 with what Kinkead describes as "a screaming need for a top quality seafood restaurant in D.C.". He met that need with a spacious two-story building that offers pretty much something for anybody looking for a great meal in attractive surroundings. Downstairs is casual with a comfortable lounge and raw bar. On the second floor, an exhibition kitchen dominates the dining room. Aquatic-themed art and sculpture pulls the look together.

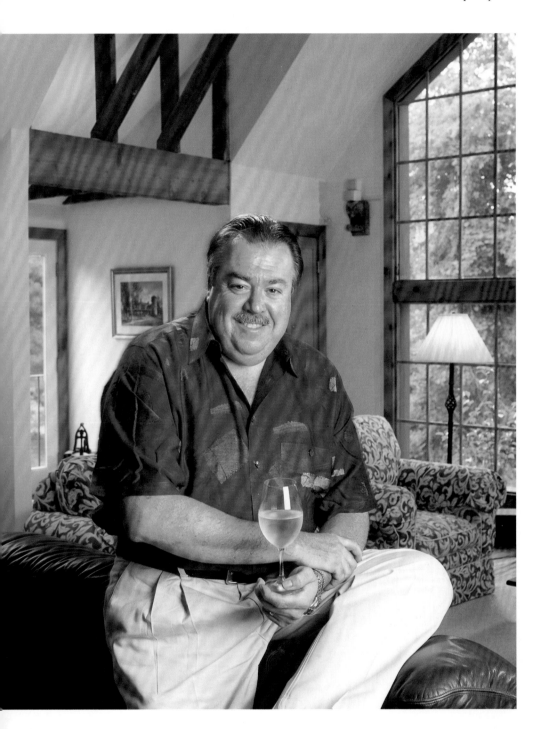

The menu changes daily, dazzling diners with creations like grilled swordfish with a tomato, caper, garlic broth and broccolini, a chick pea patty and black olive tapanade or sautéed flounder with hush puppies, crayfish, tasso ham and baby artichokes. Nor does Kinkead forget the charms of simpler fare, featuring fried clams with French fries and coleslaw, a traditional Maine lobster roll, and, of course, New England clam chowder. Kinkead purchases most of the seafood served in the restaurants locally but he also draws from suppliers all over the country.

Kinkead's dessert lists reflect what he describes as his "ferocious" sweet tooth. He and his pastry chef collaborate on such sumptuous creations as berry upside-down cake with apricot sauce accompanied by lavender ice cream, pecan-crusted carrot cake with nutmeg ice cream and butterscotch sauce, chocolate, caramel and hazelnut tart and milk chocolate mousse with caramelized pears.

No matter what the dish, it is based on Kinkead's favorite ingredients and flavors. "I put things on the menu that I like to eat. I don't believe a chef can really produce something good using food he doesn't like."

While he relishes the creative and administrative side of running the restaurants, he isn't shy about admitting that except for trying out new ideas in his home kitchen, he is "over the cooking part."

Maybe one of the reasons cooking at home is so appealing is because the house he and Dianne share is a stunning, renovated 60-year-old dairy barn complete with silo. It sprawls over two floors with a massive great room on the second level along with a roomy kitchen and adjoining wooden deck. Situated in suburban Virginia, the property has its own Revolutionary War-era cemetery, but as of yet no ghosts have been spotted. Kinkead admits, however, it was somewhat spooky moving into the place on Halloween.

Though Kinkead's own culinary style is characterized by a cool, logically structured sensibility, his favorite cuisine is the vibrant, spicy food of Mexico. When he is cooking for fun, if he can get the ingredients, that is what he will prepare. Steak, pasta and hot dogs "his way" (with chili meat sauce, Weber's™ mustard, diced raw onions with celery salt on a Martin's potato roll) are his comfort foods of choice.

Though he is a straight talking Yankee and can come across as gruff, wife Dianne says Kinkead is a pussycat. "As the oldest of ten he's used to taking care of people. It isn't at all unusual for him to do something like covering funeral expenses for a member of a Salvadoran dishwasher's family."

It's not surprising then, to learn that outside the restaurant, his primary interest is his three grandchildren. They live in the Marches region of Italy with their parents, giving the Kinkead's an excuse to travel, along with dining out, another favorite leisure time activity.

After having earned virtually every award and accolade his industry has to offer, Kinkead has turned his considerable attention to an important segment of that industry and one close to his heart. Five years ago he co-founded an organization called CIRA, Council of Independent Restaurants of America. There are chapters in Milwaukee, Minneapolis, Kansas City, Indianapolis, Chicago, Denver and Tucson. Kinkead, who is a founding member and past president, hopes to help the organization grow to national prominence.

"This is something that is extremely important for the future of American food," says Kinkead. CIRA members believe that in the battle for a share of the restaurant market, large chains have an enormous advantage: the money to acquire prime real estate, the marketing dollars to buy huge amounts of publicity and advertising, and the ability to sustain losses for a longer time, all to the detriment of the "little guys." The ultimate result, says Kinkead, could be the same 30 or 40 restaurants dominating every city in America.

Sesame-Seared Tuna with Seaweed Salad, Pickled Ginger, Wasabi and Fried Wonton

Serves: 10-12 (makes 36 pieces)

Tuna:

2 pounds sushi-grade tuna, trimmed and cut into "logs" 1-1/2 to 2 inches in diameter*

2/3 cup soy sauce

1 cup sesame seeds *(black and white)*

1/3 cup vegetable oil

Wontons:

Peanut oil for frying

36 each 2-inch-square wonton skins *(about 1 package)*

Seaweed Salad:

2 cups seaweed salad** *(prepared)*

1 medium cucumber, peeled, seeded and cut into fine julienne

1 large carrot, cut into fine julienne

3/4 cup pickled ginger, cut into fine julienne, with juice

1/3 cup soy sauce

1/4 cup rice wine vinegar

2 teaspoons sesame oil

1 bunch scallions, sliced thinly on the bias

1 teaspoon cracked toasted coriander seeds

Finish:

3 ounces prepared wasabi *(placed in pastry bag fitted with a fine tip)*

1 pint radish sprouts

For the Tuna:

- Marinate the tuna at room temperature in the soy sauce for approximately 45 minutes. Remove from marinade and let stand until mostly dry. Roll the tuna in the sesame seeds. Refrigerate.

- Heat oil in a sauce pan over medium heat and sear the tuna until sesame seeds are lightly browned and tuna is still raw in the center. Let cool and slice into 1/4-inch-thick medallions.

For the Wontons:

- Heat peanut oil to 350 degrees and deep-fry the wontons *(flat)* until crisp. Drain on paper towels.

For the Seaweed Salad:

- Toss the prepared seaweed salad with the cucumber, carrot, ginger and juice, soy sauce, vinegar, sesame oil, scallions and cracked coriander seeds. Let sit for 10 minutes. Drain.

To Finish and Serve:

- Place approximately 1 ounce of seaweed salad on each of the wontons, top with a slice of the tuna, and garnish with piped wasabi and radish sprouts.

* Fish can be prepared in this manner by most fresh fish merchants upon request.

** Can be purchased at many fish markets and most supermarkets that sell prepared sushi.

Kinkead Cooking Tip

"Match your cooking method to the fish. Sauté delicate fish in peanut oil, which tolerates heat and fast cooking. That also works for tuna and swordfish, which are best served rare. Firm fish like grouper should be roasted and any fish can be poached in seasoned liquid."

Red and Yellow Tomato Salad with Lentils, Basil and Goat Cheese

Serves: 8

Tomato Salad:

4 **each** ripe red tomatoes, large

4 **each** ripe yellow
tomatoes, large

1/4 **cup** extra-virgin olive oil

2 **tablespoons** red wine vinegar

2 **cloves** garlic, minced

6 **leaves** basil, chiffonade

1 **each** red onion,
sliced finely

1 **pinch** sugar

1 **pinch** salt

1 **pinch** pepper

Lentil Salad:

1 **cup** red lentils *(Indian)*, dried

1 **cup** green lentils, dried

1/2 **cup** finely chopped celery

1/2 **cup** finely chopped onion

1/2 **cup** finely chopped carrots

2 **cloves** garlic, minced

1/4 **cup** extra-virgin olive oil

1/4 **cup** red wine vinegar

Salt and pepper to taste

Goat Cheese:

1/3 **cup** toasted walnuts,
finely chopped

12-**ounce log** goat cheese

Finish:

6 **leaves** basil, chiffonade

8 **each** fresh basil sprigs

For the Tomato Salad:

- Bring 1 gallon of salted water to a boil in a large pot. Score one end of each tomato lightly with a knife and plunge them in the boiling water for approximately 30 to 45 seconds each. Refresh tomatoes immediately in an ice water bath. When cool, peel the tomatoes.

- Core and slice the peeled tomatoes and combine with the olive oil, vinegar, garlic, basil and red onion. Add the sugar, salt and pepper. Let marinate for 30 minutes.

For the Lentil Salad:

- Take 4 cups of the boiling water from the tomatoes and pour over the red lentils in a separate pan. Simmer over very low heat for 10 minutes, checking frequently to avoid overcooking. Drain red lentils and set aside.

- Bring 4 cups of salted water to a boil in a separate pan and add the green lentils. Cook over medium heat for 10 minutes. Do not over cook. Drain the green lentils.

- Combine the red and green lentils in a mixing bowl. Add the celery, onion, carrots, garlic, olive oil and vinegar. Season to taste with salt and pepper.

For the Goat Cheese:

- Spread the toasted walnuts on a large piece of plastic wrap. Place the goat cheese in the center of the plastic wrap, rolling the plastic wrap with the nuts around the cheese log. Chill the wrapped log for 30 minutes.

- Using a knife dipped in hot water and dried between each slice, slice the goat cheese into eight rounds of equal size, removing plastic wrap from each slice. Heat oven to 375 degrees and place goat cheese slices on a cookie sheet. Warm slices in oven for 2 to 3 minutes.

To Finish and Serve:

- Divide the lentil salad among each of eight chilled serving plates and top with alternating red and yellow tomato slices in overlapping circles. Top each serving with a round of warm goat cheese and the basil. Garnish each plate with a basil sprig, if desired.

Nantucket Bay Scallops and Cod Cheeks with Garlic, Parsley and Sunchoke Gratin

Serves: 8 as an appetizer, 4 as a main course

Scallops and Cod Cheeks:

1 pound Nantucket bay scallops

16 each cod cheeks
(may substitute 1/2-inch cubes of cod or halibut)

1 recipe creamy sunchoke gratin
(see recipe below)

8 sheets phyllo dough

2 tablespoons melted butter

Sea salt and ground black pepper to taste

All-purpose flour for dredging

1 each large egg, whisked with 1/4 cup milk *(egg wash)*

2 tablespoons butter

4 tablespoons olive oil

4 cloves garlic, minced

Lemon-Parsley Butter Sauce:

1/4 cup white wine, preferably Sauvignon Blanc

3 tablespoons lemon juice

2 tablespoons butter

1 cup coarsely chopped flat-leaf parsley

Salt and pepper to taste

For the Scallops and Cod Cheeks:

- Clean connector muscles from the Nantucket scallops. Trim the cod cheeks of exterior sinew, if necessary.

- Prepare sunchoke gratin per recipe below.

- Preheat oven to 375 degrees. Lay out one layer of phyllo dough and brush with melted butter. Place a second layer of dough on top of the first and brush with butter again. Cut into 6-inch squares and place each square in a greased muffin tin. Repeat until you have eight lined cups. Fill the phyllo dough "cups" with rounds of Sunchoke Gratin that have been cut out with a round pastry cutter the approximate size of the muffin cups. Bake until the phyllo is brown and crisp.

- Season the scallops and cod cheeks with salt and pepper. Dredge the cod in the flour and then in the egg wash. In a sauté pan over medium-high heat, add 1 tablespoon of the butter and 2 tablespoons of olive oil. Place the cod cheeks in the pan and sauté on one side for approximately 2 minutes until brown. Turn the cod over and repeat cooking for 2 minutes. Remove from the pan and empty out the butter/oil mixture. Wipe the pan clean. Place another 1 tablespoon of butter and 2 tablespoons of olive oil in the pan and sauté the scallops and garlic over medium heat for about 1 minute. Do not overcook. Remove and keep warm.

For the Lemon-Parsley Butter Sauce:

- Deglaze the pan with the white wine and cook over medium heat until reduced by 1/2. Add the lemon juice and butter. Cook, stirring constantly, until sauce is the consistency of heavy cream. Do not allow the sauce to come to a boil. Add the chopped parsley and season with salt and pepper to taste.

To Finish and Serve:

- Place one phyllo cup with sunchoke gratin in the center of each of eight plates *(put two on each plate if serving as a main course)*. Divide the scallops and cod cheeks among the plates and top with the lemon-parsley butter sauce.

Creamy Sunchoke Gratin

Sunchoke Gratin:

18 each large sunchokes
(Jerusalem artichokes), scrubbed
(approximately 6 cups sliced)

1 each lemon, juiced

2 tablespoons butter

3 cloves garlic, minced

Salt and pepper

1 cup shredded Gruyère cheese

1/4 cup shredded Parmesan cheese

1/4 cup crème fraîche *(or sour cream, if not available)*

1 cup heavy cream

For the Sunchoke Gratin:

- Scrub and peel the sunchokes and slice into 1/8 inch slices *(a mandoline is best for this purpose)*. Place in a bowl of water to which the lemon juice has been added.

- Preheat the oven to 375 degrees. Butter a ceramic casserole dish, or individual casserole dishes, and sprinkle a little minced garlic over the bottom of the dish*(es)*. Top with a single overlapping layer of the sliced sunchokes, salt and pepper, 1/4 cup of the Gruyère cheese, 1/3 of the Parmesan and minced garlic. Repeat for 2 more layers. Whip together the crème fraîche and the heavy cream and pour over the sunchokes. Top with the remaining Gruyère. Bake for approximately 30 minutes. If the gratin is too dry, add a little milk or cream.

Grill Roasted Prime-Aged Sirloin with Garlic-Scallion Potato Cake

Serves: 6

Sirloin:

1 **each** aged prime sirloin*,
about 4-1/2 pounds

Olive oil

Salt to taste

1/2 **cup** fresh coarsely ground
black pepper

3 **cloves** garlic, minced

Potato Cake:

3 **pounds** Idaho russet potatoes

1/2 **cup** bacon or duck fat
(or butter)

1/2 **cup** olive oil

6 **cloves** garlic, minced

4 **each** scallions, chopped

Salt and pepper to taste

Finish:

Béarnaise sauce *(optional)*

For the Sirloin:

- Rub the sirloin with olive oil, salt, cracked black pepper and minced garlic. Let rest for an hour. Heat a grill *(preferably wood or charcoal fired)* to very hot, but leave one side cool.

- Place the sirloin on the hot side of the grill, fat-side down. Watch closely to avoid flare-ups. Grill about 6 minutes on the first side and turn. Cook for 4 minutes more and move to the cool side of the grill. Cover the grill and let the sirloin rest there about 10 minutes. The meat will be rare. Cook sirloin longer if more doneness is desired. Remove the meat from grill and keep warm. A kitchen thermometer is a handy tool here.

For the Potato Cake:

- Preheat the oven to 375 degrees. Wash the potatoes and cook them whole in a pot of salted boiling water. When just tender, drain and peel the potatoes. Chop coarsely.

- Heat a cast-iron pan over medium-high heat and add the fat or butter and olive oil. Add in a layer of the potatoes and sprinkle with some chopped garlic, scallions and salt and pepper. Repeat until all the potatoes, garlic and most of the scallions are gone *(save some scallions to top the cake with after cooking)*. Cook until very well-browned on the bottom side. Invert the potato cake onto a plate and slide it back into the pan with the browned side up. Cook until bottom side is also well-browned.

- Place in the oven and bake for 12 minutes. Slide the potato cake out onto a serving plate and garnish with scallions *(and more chopped garlic of you like)*.

To Finish and Serve:

- Slice the sirloin and serve with wedges of the potato cake. If desired, pass béarnaise sauce on the side.

* Aged prime sirloin is very expensive, but worth the cost. Try to get the rib end, not the sirloin butt end. Trim some of the fat cap but not all. Score the top fat cap with crisscross cuts about 1/2-inch deep.

Kinkead Factoids

Always in his home refrigerator — soda, wine and lots and lots of unusual condiments, but generally not really much to eat.

Favorite beverages — diet root beer and Moxie®, Tanqueray® martinis (shaken to death), Scotch and Pinot Noirs with some age.

Worst cooking experience — cooking brunch to order for 800 people with the help of one prep person in Newport, Rhode Island, when the tall ships set sail in 1976.

Lobster Stew with Spring Vegetables, Chervil and Cauliflower Flan

Serves: 6

Lobster Stew:

3 each 2-pound lobsters *(may substitute 6 each, 1-pound lobsters)*

6 tablespoons butter

2 cups combination of finely chopped onions, celery, and carrots

1/4 cup cognac or brandy

1 cup cream sherry

1 tablespoon chervil leaves, save stems

4 cups heavy cream

4 cups milk

1 recipe cauliflower flans *(see recipe below)*

1 cup quartered mushrooms

1 cup diced and blanched carrots

1 cup diced celery *(white inner stalks only)*

1 cup chopped leeks, washed

12 each new onions or scallions *(white parts only, reserve greens for another use)*

1 cup haricot verts, cut into 1-inch lengths and blanched

1 cup shelled fava beans, blanched and peeled

Sea salt

Fresh cracked pepper

Finish:

1/2 bunch chervil leaves

For the Lobster Stew:

- In a stockpot, bring 1-1/2 gallons of salted water to a boil. Cook the lobsters for 3 minutes or so and remove and run under cold water. Cut tails and claws from the body. Cut tails in half and remove tail meat. Crack claws and remove meat. Set the tail and claw meat aside *(they still will be half raw)*.

- Remove all of the meat from the bodies, including the trimmings and the liver. Remove as much knuckle meat as possible from the legs. Break up the shells.

- Place the body meat, trimmings, knuckle meat and shells *(not the liver)* in a saucepan. Add 3 tablespoons of the butter and the combination of finely chopped onions, celery and carrots and cook for about 15 minutes over medium heat. Add the cognac, sherry, lobster liver, chervil stems, heavy cream, and milk and bring to a light boil. Simmer for about an hour. Strain and reserve liquid.

- Prepare cauliflower flans according to recipe below.

- In a sauté pan, melt 1 tablespoon of butter and brown the mushroom quarters on all sides.

- In a small broad, shallow-sided oven-proof pot *(brassier)*, melt 2 tablespoons of butter. Add the carrots, celery and leeks and sauté until soft. Add the new onion and cook for 2 more minutes. Add the haricot verts, favas and the reserved lobster meat and sauté for 2 additional minutes. Remove the lobster meat from the pan. Add the lobster cream and sautéed mushroom quarters and bring to a boil. Reduce heat and return the lobster meat to the pan. Adjust seasonings to taste. Keep warm.

To Finish and Serve:

- Place a cauliflower flan in the center of each of six large soup or pasta bowls. Divide the lobster meat evenly between the six bowls and ladle on the stew. Garnish with chervil leaves.

Cauliflower Flans

Makes approximately 6 2-1/2 ounce flans

Cauliflower Flans:

1/4 head cauliflower, cut into flowerets *(1 cup)*

1/2 cup heavy cream

1/2 cup milk

1 clove garlic, peeled

Salt and pepper to taste

2 large eggs

2 large egg yolks

1/8 cup freshly grated Parmigiano-Reggiano cheese

Vegetable cooking spray *(such as Pam)*

For the Cauliflower Flans:

- In a non-corrosive saucepan over high heat, bring cauliflower, cream, milk, garlic, salt and pepper to a boil. Cook until cauliflower is very tender. Remove from heat and let cool. Purée in a blender with eggs, egg yolks and cheese. Flan mixture can be prepared to this point 1 day in advance.

- Preheat oven to 275 degrees. Spray six small oven-proof ramekins with vegetable cooking spray. Divide the flan mixture between the ramekins and place in a hot water bath. Bake for 1-1/2 hours, or until a toothpick inserted into the flan comes out clean.

To Finish and Serve:

- Invert flans and pop them out of the ramekins.

Banana Tart

Serves: 6

Banana Tart:

6-8 each medium bananas, just ripe *(not overripe or green)*

1 each medium lemon, juiced

1 cup butter, at room temperature

1-1/2 cups brown sugar

1 cup granulated sugar

1/4 cup dark rum

1/4 teaspoon cinnamon

1/4 teaspoon salt

3 each vanilla beans, split, seeds scraped

16 ounces puff pastry

All-purpose flour for dusting

Finish:

Double English cream *(optional)*

Rum-raisin ice cream *(optional)*

For the Banana Tart:

- Preheat oven to 400 degrees.

- Peel and slice bananas 1/8-inch thick and 2-inches in length. Sprinkle lemon juice on top to keep from browning.

- Using a mixer with a paddle, beat together the butter, sugars, rum, cinnamon, salt and seeds scraped from vanilla bean. Beat until thoroughly incorporated but not fluffy. Divide the butter mixture evenly between 6 smooth-sided Teflon-coated 3-inch diameter tart pans, filling them approximately half full.

- Place the tart pans in the oven until caramelized. Remove from oven and allow to cool slightly. Place the sliced bananas in a flower shape or a feathered circle in each tart pan. Place back in oven and cook for 2 more minutes.

- Roll out the puff pastry, using flour to prevent sticking, and cut into six, 4-inch rounds. Tuck one pastry circle in around the bananas and down the inside of each of the tart pans.

- Bake for 18 minutes until pastry is golden brown.

To Finish and Serve:

- Invert pans while still warm onto individual serving plates and pop out the tarts. Garnish with double English cream or rum-raisin ice cream, or both.

GUENTER SEEGER

ATLANTA, GA

American Express Best Chef: Southeast, 1996

With 40 years in professional kitchens under his belt, Guenter Seeger appreciates the importance of food aesthetics. His sense of the aesthetic provides a cornerstone for his culinary style.

"There is the technical part of cooking; you need to know the basics," he says. "But there also has to be a sensitivity, where you know how to keep harmony among the ingredients and not step outside of the boundaries. Without the harmony, it will all crash."

Classically trained in Europe, Seeger has the technical part down pat, and his upbringing near Baden Baden, Germany, a spa town with a rich cultural heritage, developed his artistic tendencies.

Seeger grew up in a family that brokered produce, specializing in cultivated strawberries, raspberries, plums, white asparagus and wild berries. The highlight of their week, Sunday brought the whole family (Seeger has one brother and two sisters) together for lunch.

"When you grew up in the country, in another generation when things were slower, a big part of that culture was eating. People worked to eat. Here eating is more entertainment. We'd sit down to braised meat and spaetzle; a Sunday without dumplings was a disaster. There would be potato salad, seasonal vegetables and garnishes. It was a big deal, a celebration."

As much as he relished the weekly feast, that wasn't what set Seeger on the road to international fame as a chef.

"I don't want to romance it. I can't say I was dreaming when I was six that I was going to be a chef. My mother decided I was going to be an apprentice. There was no discussion. Now, I believe she knew more about me than I did."

At the age of 13, Seeger began his career in a hotel in the Black Forest area in a work/school program. At 16, he passed both the written and practical cooking tests and went on to take his first job in Switzerland.

"It was an amazing event for me, like moving to another world," he says. "For the first time I was exposed to big hotels and restaurants and classical French cuisine."

Continental cuisine with an emphasis on classical French. But after a trip to Alsace, where he experienced contemporary French cooking in restaurants such as Auberge dl'Ill and Aux Armes de France, he completely changed his style of cooking.

"This was an important step. In eight years I went from zero to having a restaurant that was among the top 20 in the country. It was pioneer work. The challenge was creating a restaurant with

For ten years he worked in the Swiss towns of Interlaken, St. Moritz and Lucerne. At the same time, he also continued his formal education learning restaurant management, the bar business, purchasing and wines.

Knowing it was time to strike out on his own, Seeger moved back to Germany and opened his restaurant Hoheneck in Phorzeim at the gateway of the Black Forest. In the beginning, he featured

its own identity. Americans are open to new ideas, Germans aren't. To introduce them to another kind of food is difficult."

Difficult as it may have been, Seeger soon commanded universal attention. Including the Michelin guide, which awarded him one star — a distinct honor for any restaurant, but particularly for one outside of France.

After a vice-president of the Regent Hotel Company dined at Hoheneck, he convinced Seeger to go international and take over the kitchen at the Regent in Washington D.C.

"I was young and it sounded like a dream job," recalls Seeger. "I'd done my restaurant and wanted another challenge. Once again, I had the opportunity to be exposed to new things, a new country. It was a top hotel and fabulous to work for, but they had financial problems from the start."

When the hotel closed, Seeger planned to return to Germany, but Horst Schulze, general manager of the Atlanta Ritz-Carlton and a fan of Seeger's cuisine, convinced him to come on board, so he moved south. In his twelve years at the Ritz, Seeger made the Dining Room a top draw, garnering the Mobil 5 Star Award, the AAA Five Diamond Award and the Triple Crown Award.

It wasn't always easy. For ten of those years he literally cooked in a hallway because the hotel did not have adequate kitchen facilities at the time. "You don't think about it, you just do it," says Seeger.

He looks back on his time at the Ritz as transitional. Much of the raw material he could rely on obtaining in Europe was simply not available. Instead, he learned to adapt and redevelop recipes and encourage local producers to grow specialty fruits, vegetables and herbs, bake artisanal bread, make boutique cheeses and raise high end game, meat and poultry. Seeger was, in fact, one of the founders of the Georgia Organic Growers Association.

For the past six years, Seeger has captained his own ship, the appropriately named Seeger's in the Buckhead section of Atlanta.

"When I opened myself up to the possibility of owning a restaurant again, the locale chose me," he explains. "I didn't want to be in an office building or a strip mall."

The converted bungalow on Paces Ferry Road bookends one of the most glamorous stretches of real estate in Atlanta. It is a commanding two-story space, both sleek and intimate, with white walls, rich cherry paneling and a color scheme of claret red, warm gold and gray. The attention to detail is staggering. From the stunning arrangements of locally grown organic flowers to the portholes into the magnificent kitchen with its custom-made six foot by eight foot Morice stove, it epitomizes Seeger's signature blend of opulence and restraint.

On the subject of restraint, he says, "My style comes closest in spirit to the Japanese, not the ingredients or the techniques but the simplicity and spontaneity."

A series of artful photos he designed for a calendar in the early eighties illustrates the sensuality of Seeger's creations. They hang in a hallway on the restaurant's bottom floor. Colorful pristine foods, prepared and raw, are nestled into monochromatic curves of nude human bodies. This amazing evocation matches his culinary presentations that include golden grilled squab with date chutney, glazed carrots and a cumin crisp or Nantucket scallop brochette with smoky bacon mousse and braised romaine.

There aren't many out-of-the-restaurant pursuits for Seeger. He enjoys traveling but rarely does. He alleviates stress with a martial arts program. Seeger loves listening to music, but mostly he works. When he does take a break, Seeger spends time with his wife Laureen, a litigator for a major corporation, and their two daughters, Angela and Grace. He also has two grown daughters from a previous marriage.

Says Seeger, "I've done a lot in my life and I'll continue to work just as hard in the future. Progress and bettering yourself, it is a lifelong evolution."

Tuna Tart with Sesame Crisp and Cucumber Salad

Serves: 6

Sesame Crisps:

1 **sheet** phyllo dough,
   thawed if frozen

1 **tablespoon** honey

3 **tablespoons** melted butter

1 **tablespoon** sesame seeds

Cucumber Salad:

1 **each** European cucumber
   peeled, seeded and finely
   chopped

1 **teaspoon** salt

2 **tablespoons** grapeseed oil

1 **tablespoon** rice vinegar

Sauce:

1 **each** egg yolk *(pasteurized)*

1 **tablespoon** plum wine

3/4 **cup** white soy sauce*

1 **tablespoon** lemon juice

1/2 **cup** pecan oil

Salt and pepper to taste

Tuna Tartare:

6 **ounces** tuna *(sashimi quality)*,
   very finely chopped

2 **tablespoons** minced spring
   onion

3 **tablespoons** chopped pine nuts

For the Sesame Crisps:

- Brush the phyllo pastry with the honey and the melted butter. Sprinkle with sesame seeds. Cut the pastry into 2-1/2-inch rounds with a cookie or biscuit cutter. Place on a baking sheet and bake at 400 degrees until golden brown, approximately 2 to 3 minutes. Let cool until ready to assemble dish.

For the Cucumber Salad:

- Salt the chopped cucumber and let stand for 1 hour. Rinse with warm water and dry thoroughly with paper towels, squeezing if necessary to remove as much liquid as possible. Mix the chopped cucumbers with the grapeseed oil and rice vinegar. Set aside until ready to assemble dish.

For the Sauce:

- Mix the egg yolk, wine, soy sauce and lemon juice together in a small bowl. Slowly whisk in the oil until emulsified. Season to taste with salt and pepper.

For the Tuna Tartare:

- Mix the chopped tuna together with the spring onions, the pine nuts and 6 tablespoons of the sauce. Spoon the tuna mixture into six 2-1/2-inch cookie cutters or other round molds.

To Finish and Serve:

- Unmold the tuna mixture onto six serving plates. Top each round with a sesame crisp. Place a small scoop of the cucumber salad on top of each sesame crisp.

* Available at Asian specialty markets

Guenter Seeger's Beverage Recommendations

Tuna Tart with Sesame Crisp
and Cucumber Salad
Robert Weil Riesling
Kabinett 2001
page 183

Loup de Mer Poached in
Sake, Japanese Plum
Puligny Montrachet
Domaine Leflaive 1997
page 185

Roasted Pheasant with
Fall Vegetables
Gevrey-Chambertin ler Cru
Domaine Claude Dugat 1996
page 187

Golden Delicious Apple Beignet
with Tahitian Sauce
Domaine de Beaumalric,
Muscat de Beaumes de
Venise 2001
page 189

Kiwi with Goat
Yogurt Sorbet
Paolo Saracco,
Moscato d'Asti 2001
page 189

Cheese Course
Turley "Haynes
Vineyard" Zinfandel,
Napa Valley 1992
page 191

Loup de Mer Poached in Sake, with Japanese Plum

Serves: 6

Fish:

6 each Loup de Mer fillets, 5 ounces each *(may substitute bass or grouper)*

6 each fermented plums*

1/2 cup dry sake

Salt to taste

2 tablespoons olive oil

1 tablespoon white soy sauce*

1 tablespoon yuzu juice*

2 tablespoons butter

For the Fish:

- Preheat oven to 350 degrees. Place the fish fillets and the plums in a heavy, non-reactive ovenproof pan. Cover with the sake and season with salt. Poach until opaque and slightly firm, approximately 15 minutes. Carefully remove the fillets and the plums from the pan to a platter and hold in a warm place until needed. Add the olive oil, white soy sauce and yuzu juice to the pan in which the fillets were poached and reduce over low heat for 3 to 4 minutes. Whisk the butter into the liquid a small amount at a time to form an emulsion.

To Finish and Serve:

- Place 1 fillet and one plums on each of six serving plates. Spoon the sauce around the plate.

* Available at Asian specialty markets

Seeger's Tea Service

Enjoy a unique tea ceremony to top off an evening of fine dining.

Green Tea

Dragonwell Lung Ching: Delicate, with a light aroma of chestnut from the tender buds and young leaves of superior grade tea grown in China's Lung Ching province. *(China)*

Jasmine Dragon Phoenix Pearls: Delicate, slightly sweet, with a floral flavor. The jasmine blossoms are hand-rolled, and the silver down of young tips give this tea a pearl-like shine. *(China)*

White Tea

Drum Mountain White Cloud: Light yet complex with a nutty flavor and natural sweetness. *(China)*

Oolong Tea

Ti Kaun Yin "Iron Goddess of Mercy": Beautiful, full-bodied with a distinctive orchid flavor and fruity aroma. *(Taiwan)*

Black Tea

Sikkim – Temi Estate: A very smooth flavor and a light amber color. Region is located between Darjeeling and Nepal, at an elevation of 8,000 feet.

Pureh: A pronounced earthy flavor and a deep red color. It is aged in Chinese caves and dates from the Tang Dynasty. *(China)*

Roasted Pheasant with Fall Vegetables

Serves: 2

Pheasant:

1 each pheasant
2 slices fatback *(thin slices)*
1/4 cup olive oil
Salt and pepper to taste

Vegetables:

2 cups assorted vegetables:
  carrots, turnips, rutabaga, blue
  potatoes, mushrooms and figs
2 tablespoons butter

For the Pheasant:

• Preheat oven to 375 degrees. Place the fatback on the pheasant breast and secure with string. Rub the pheasant with the olive oil and season with salt and pepper. Roast the pheasant for about 35 minutes. Let the pheasant rest in a warm spot for 10 minutes.

For the Vegetables:

• Bring a large pot of salted water to a boil. Blanch the vegetables for 1 minute in the boiling water and drain immediately. When the pheasant is removed from the oven to rest, melt the butter in a sauté pan. Add the vegetables and cook until heated through.

To Finish and Serve:

• Place the pheasant on a platter and arrange the vegetables around the pheasant. Serve immediately.

Share Our Strength

Each year, Guenter Seeger hosts a gourmet 5-star dinner at his restaurant with the proceeds to benefit Share Our Strength. S.O.S. is one of the United States' premiere anti-hunger, anti-poverty charitable organizations.

For the event, Seeger call on some of his 5-star award-winning buddies including Daniel Boulud, Charlie Trotter, Thomas Keller, Jean-George Vongerichten, Masa Takayama, Julian Serrano and Patrick O'Connell.

The star-studded line-up produces a multicourse meal that has diners flying in from all over the country, happy to fork out big bucks knowing they will enjoy a once-in-a-lifetime culinary experience and have the opportunity to do some good for the less fortunate.

For more information call
(404) 846-9779

Golden Delicious Apple Beignet with Tahitian Sauce

Serves: 6

Apple Beignets:

1-1/3 cups all-purpose flour, sifted

12 ounces dark beer
  (ideally Hoegarden)

1/4 cup sugar

Salt to taste

1 each egg yolk

2 each egg whites

2 tablespoons peanut oil

3 each golden delicious apples

2 tablespoons flour,
  for dredging the apples

2 teaspoons cinnamon

2 tablespoons sugar

Tahitian Vanilla Sauce:

1 pint heavy cream

1/3 cup sugar, divided in half

1 pinch salt

1/2 each Tahitian vanilla bean

4 each egg yolks

Sesame Tuiles:

1/2 cup sugar

1/3 cup all-purpose flour

3 tablespoons ground
  sesame seeds

7 tablespoons chicken stock

7 tablespoons melted butter

1-1/2 tablespoons whole
  sesame seeds

For the Apple Beignets:

- In a large bowl, combine the flour and beer. Whisk until the batter is smooth. Add the sugar, salt, and egg yolk to the batter. Whisk until combined. Allow the batter to rest for 30 minutes.

- Whip the egg whites to soft peaks. Fold the egg white meringue into the batter. Refrigerate. Heat the peanut oil to 350 degrees. Peel and core the apples. Cut them into 1/2-inch-thick slices. Coat the apples with flour. Dip them in the batter until covered. Do not fry the apples until ready to serve the dessert. Fry them in the oil until golden brown. Immediately toss them in cinnamon sugar. Assemble dessert per the "To Finish and Serve" instructions below.

For the Tahitian Vanilla Sauce:

- Combine the heavy cream, half of the sugar, salt and vanilla bean in a heavy saucepan. Whisk the remaining sugar and the egg yolks together in a mixing bowl. Bring the cream mixture to a boil. Whisk a small amount *(1/2 cup)* of the hot cream mixture into the egg yolk mixture. Whisk the egg yolk mixture into the cream mixture in the saucepan. Cook over low heat, stirring constantly, until the mixture is slightly thicker than the consistency of heavy cream and coats the back of a spoon, about 7 or 8 minutes. Strain into a clean metal bowl through a fine-mesh strainer. Cool the metal bowl in an ice bath. Refrigerate until needed.

For the Sesame Tuiles:

- Combine the sugar, flour and ground sesame seeds in a large bowl.

- Whisk to evenly distribute ingredients. Slowly add the chicken stock while whisking constantly. Then slowly add the butter while whisking. Whisk until the mixture is uniformly mixed. Mix in the whole sesame seeds. Refrigerate the batter at least 1 hour.

- Preheat oven to 350 degrees and line a sheet pan with parchment paper. Spread the batter in a thin layer in 4-inch circles on the parchment paper. Bake until golden, approximately 12 to 15 minutes. Remove from oven and cool.

To Finish and Serve:

- Spread some of the Tahitian vanilla sauce on each of six dessert plates. Arrange a mound of the just-fried apples on top of the sauce. Use a sesame tuile to garnish each plate.

Lavender Marinated Kiwi with Goat Yogurt Sorbet

Serves: 8

Kiwis:

1 cup simple syrup

2 teaspoons lavender flowers

5 each kiwi, peeled and sliced
1/4-inch thick

Sorbet:

1 quart of plain goat's milk yogurt

1/2 cup sugar *(more to taste, if desired)*

1 cup simple syrup

1 teaspoon vanilla

pinch of salt

For the Kiwis:

Add the lavender flowers to simple syrup and warm over medium-low heat. Remove from heat and pour the syrup *(including the flowers)* over the kiwis. Stir gently and cover. Let sit at room temperature overnight.

For the Sorbet:

Mix the yogurt and sugar together until the sugar is dissolved. Add simple syrup, vanilla and salt. Mix thoroughly. Freeze in an ice cream maker according to manufacturer's directions.

To Finish and Serve:

Divide the kiwis into eight serving bowls. Form a quenelle of sorbet and place on top of kiwis. Drizzle with a bit of the liquid left from the kiwis.

Selection of Cheeses

1. Everona, Sheeps Milk

- Rapiden, Virginia. A hard, aged raw milk cheese that is excellent in place of Romano or, served at room temperature for munching along with a Cabernet. Winner of several American Cheese Society awards.

2. Willow Hill Farm Aged Organic, Sheeps Milk

- Milton, Vermont. Semi-ripened soft sheep cheese that is buttery with an herby finish. Can be further ripened in the fridge to a runny, earthy delicacy.

3. Parè d' Auge, Cows Milk

- Normandy, France. Square cut cheese reminiscent of the cobblestone paves *(bricks)* in an old French town. Earthy cheese with a supple pâtè.

4. Valdeon, Cows Milk, Goats Milk

- Spain. Rich and creamy blue cheese. Wrapped in chestnut leaves.

5. Blue del Re, Cows Milk

- Italy. Salty blue cheese that is crumbly and slightly stronger and more ammoniated than a Forme d'Ambert.

6. Mt. Tan Cowgirl Creamery, Cows Milk

- Point Ray's Station, California. This elegant, triple-cream round is the Cowgirl's signature, aged cheese. It is firm, yet buttery and smooth with a mellow, earthy flavor reminiscent of mushrooms.

7. Gaperon, Cows Milk

- France. A dome-shaped, semi-hard with garlic and cracked peppercorns that infuse the cheese with most of its flavor; has a rind of natural mold and is hung over an open flame during the aging process, giving the cheese its smoky qualities.

8. Greenhill, Aged Cows Milk

- Sweetgrass Dairy, Thomasville, Georgia. Soft-ripened with a white, bloomy rind; rich and smooth.

9. Arome de Lyon, Cows Milk

- France. A round semi-hard cheese from the Lyon region; aged and adorned with marc *(damp skins, seeds and stalks left after pressing grapes for making Marc de Bourgogne)*. Fruity, floral and sweet tastes.

10. Vera Pagliettina, Cows Milk, Sheeps milk

- Italy. Resembles a flattened brie. Tastes similar to camembert with a fresher, younger tang.

11. Camembert, Cows Milk

- France. Soft and pale yellow with a rough white and gold-flecked crust. A rich, buttery flavor, it ripens quickly and must be eaten at its prime.

12. Manchester Round, Cows Milk

- Zingerman's Dairy, Manchester, Michigan. A white-mold ripened cream cheese made similarly to a Camembert. Has a modestly forward flavor, buttery texture and a delicate tickle of pepperiness at the finish.

The Cheese Course

Seeger's cheese course features a selection of anywhere from 10 to 15 varieties. They range from mild to pungent, young to aged and include both regional American and imported cheeses made from cow, goat and sheep milk as well as combinations thereof. They are carefully served at optimum temperature.

According to the season, the cheeses might be accompanied by raisins simmered in port; baked apples and pears; or pear, peach or apple chutneys.

MICHAEL SCHLOW

BOSTON, MA

Michael Schlow is unusual among James Beard Award-Winning chefs. Rather than possessing a single culinary style, he has two, and they are showcased in his Boston restaurants. Schlow describes them as "left brain and right brain."

Radius, featuring contemporary French cuisine, is about symmetry and precision. Via Matta is rustic Italian, all about warmth and nurturing. While they are obviously very different, says Schlow, "These are the two cuisines I've studied my entire career."

Professional baseball's loss was the food world's gain when Michael Schlow traded a promising career as a pitcher for chef's whites. The route from one to the other, however, wasn't direct. Schlow attended college on an athletic scholarship, but after suffering an arm and shoulder injury and realizing that path was closed to him, he found himself at loose ends. Partly because he loves horses, and partly to rehabilitate his arm, Schlow went to work training harness horses. He even briefly considered becoming a veterinarian. Then his mom suggested he think about cooking school, and something clicked.

"We've always been a family of foodies," says Schlow. "Ours was the house where the whole neighborhood congregated for sleepovers and meals. My mom made garam masala from scratch and cooked Szechuan food when everyone else was making chop suey. I was only ten years old when I first tasted sushi. Back then, if you ate fish at all, it was frozen fish sticks or salmon if you were dining out."

He enrolled in New Jersey's Academy of Culinary Arts and never looked back. "You learn the basics in school but you don't graduate ready to be a chef," he says. "What's important is who you work with afterwards. That's where you learn kitchen culture, the heritage, the tradition, the time honored techniques."

For Schlow, it was famed Tuscan chef Pino Luongo who became his mentor. Schow helped Luongo open a couple of restaurants in Manhattan and then went on to take up the post of executive chef for Luongo at Sapore di Mare on Long Island. "The experience really opened my eyes to how much Italian influence there is in French cuisine whether the French want to admit it or not," says Schlow. "Duck a la orange actually originated in Italy. Working at Sapore was also instrumental in teaching me to be a restaurateur as well as a chef."

At Sapore di Mare Schlow met his friend and future business partner, Christopher Myers. Myers, the general manager of a Boston restaurant looking to replace a chef, contacted Schlow. Schlow passed on the opportunity but remembers Myers saying to him, "We have to do this in Boston someday."

"Someday" would prove to be far in the future. Schlow continued to hone his skills, getting more and more deeply involved in contemporary French cuisine during stints at 75 Main in the Hamptons, restaurant Ariel & Michael back in New York and at The Ryland Inn in New Jersey.

In 1995 Myers talked Schlow into moving to Boston and heading up Café Louis. Not long after, the pair cooked up Radius. The location, a turn-of-the-20th century bank building downtown, had previously housed an old time German-American restaurant. Schlow and Myers had something completely different in mind.

The high ceilinged, semi-circular foyer of the bank is Radius' main dining room. The old, ornate detailing juxtaposed with the sleek red, grey and white decor is stunning. In the basement, the bank safe is now used for wine storage.

"We wanted a great restaurant, graceful and hospitable but not pretentious," explains Schlow. "I think we succeeded. It's not a serious restaurant, but we are serious about the food and making people happy. We bend over backward to accommodate."

Radius' cuisine is clean and precise. "I'm maniacal about cutting techniques. I teach my assistants to cut backward, like a surgeon does, so there are no raw edges."

Schlow's Radius menu isn't fussy. Rather it is full-flavored, relying on seasonal produce, local seafood and some lusty proteins such as calves liver, short ribs, venison, foie gras and steak tartare.

In essence, Schlow says, "We lighten French up. Flavors are intense and we attempt to make the presentations beautiful."

Schlow's and Myers' long held plan to introduce authentic Italian to Boston finally came about in 2002 when they opened the big, buzzing Via Matta. With sidewalk tables, busy bar, and colorful art — including giant paintings of tarot cards — it feels like it could be on the Via Veneto in Rome.

"Boston's North End is an Italian enclave. It's packed with Italian-American restaurants. This is something different. We started slow with the menu because we wanted people to get used to it," says Schlow.

It didn't take long for Bostonians to warm up to the rigorously authentic line-up that includes porchetta, bistecca alla

fiorentina, thin-crust pizzas, savory pastas and an all-Italian wine list.

Seasonality is important to Schlow and it ties into his two different cuisines in a big way. "As far as Radius is concerned, in the summer I think Provencal. For Via Matta, in the winter I think soup like ribollita and papardelle with rabbit. In the summer I think food from the Amalfi coast."

He insists that he plays no favorites between his two culinary offspring. "I make no judgment between the restaurants. They are very different but have in common that we use the best ingredients and keep things uncomplicated. Complicated is not a synonym for creative."

An extrovert, Schlow doesn't hide in the kitchen. He wants to know what guests think of the food and isn't shy about asking. "He is phenomenal on the floor," says Radius events manager June Mariani. "He tries to make it to each table, chats with the guests and really pays attention to what they have to say."

When he is not at one of the two restaurants, Schlow enjoys golf, music, movies and gardening and, yes, baseball — he is an avid New York Yankee fan. He also believes in giving back to the community by participating in charitable events including returning to New Jersey each year for a Dinner of Hope benefiting children with AIDS.

Schlow was recently asked whom he would like to come back as if he were reincarnated. He didn't even hesitate, "I want to come back as me. I'm really happy."

Happiness for Schlow is being busy. He and Myers have recently opened an upscale seafood restaurant, Great Bay, which he describes as being in the spirit of Aqua and Le Bernadin but more relaxed. But it is Radius and Via Matta that express him best. "I'm so lucky having the two restaurants. I'd hoped to build both and see them to fruition and I did. They speak to both parts of me. It's my goal to always exceed expectations."

Perona Farms Smoked Salmon Tortes

Serves: 6

Tortes:

72 each potato disks,
1/8-inch thick

Olive oil, thyme, rosemary
and black pepper to taste

54 each 1-inch smoked salmon
disks,1/8-inch thick *(preferably
from Perona Farms)*

54 each English cucumber slices,
cut into 1-inch disks, 1/8-inch
thick

4 teaspoons gribiche sauce
(see recipe below)

1 teaspoon osetra caviar
(or more, if you like)

Gribiche Sauce:

(makes 1 cup)

3/4 cup olive oil

1/4 cup sherry vinegar

1 teaspoon chopped tarragon

1 teaspoon chopped parsley

1 teaspoon chopped dill

1 teaspoon sliced chives

1 teaspoon chopped chervil

Salt and pepper to taste

Finish:

1 each cooked egg yolk *(chopped,
patted dry with a paper towel and
passed through a fine-mesh sieve)*

4 tablespoons chopped avocado
*(with lime juice and salt
added to taste)*

For the Tortes:

- Cut the 1/8-inch-thick potato slices with a just slightly larger ring mold *(1-1/4-inch)* first. Then use a 1-inch ring mold to cut a 1-inch disk. Save the outside ring for the garnish. Sauté the 1-inch potato disks in olive oil seasoned with thyme, rosemary and black pepper until just tender, taking care not to tear or crumble the disks. Drain. Slowly fry the outside rings in hot oil until golden brown, drain and reserve for the garnish.

- On each of six serving plates, alternate layering the potato, salmon, and cucumber disks, until you have used four slices of potato, three slices of salmon and three slices of cucumber for each "torte." Each plate will consist of three tortes. Place the tortes off the center of each plate. Top each torte with gribiche sauce and a bit of caviar.

For the Gribiche Sauce:

- Combine all ingredients together in a small bowl and whisk to blend.

To Finish and Serve:

- Sprinkle a diagonal line of egg yolk powder on each plate near the tortes. Place 1/6 of the chopped avocado mixture opposite the tortes on each plate. Place three crispy potato rings in the avocado mixture on each plate so they stand up.

Michael Schlow's Beverage Recommendations

Perona Farms Smoked
Salmon Tortes

NV Bollinger Special Cuvée

page 197

Olive Oil Poached Duck

1998 P. Granger Julienàs

Grand Reserve

page 199

Halibut with Wild Mushrooms

2000 Etienne Sauzet

Puligny-Montrachet

Les Reférts

page 201

Maine Diver Scallops

1997 J.J. Prüm Riesling

Spatlëse Graacher

Himmelreich

page 203

Goat Cheesecakes with

Huckleberries

2001 Coppo

Brachetto d'Acqui

page 205

Olive Oil Poached Duck

Serves: 2 as an entrée, 4 as an appetizer

Duck:

4 cups olive oil

2 each duck breast, cleaned of
  skin and fat

Salt and pepper to taste

Spinach Purée:

1 cup heavy cream

6 bunches spinach, washed,
  stems removed

Salt and pepper to taste

Spiced Honey:

1 cup honey

1 each star anise

1 each cinnamon stick

2 each cloves

1 each chipotle pepper
  *(dried, smoked jalapeño pepper
  available in specialty section of
  some supermarkets)*

Cashews:

4 tablespoons sugar

1 teaspoon cayenne pepper

1 cup cashews

Star Anise Vinaigrette:

1 cup balsamic vinegar

2 each star anise, toasted

2 tablespoons canola oil

Cucumber Salad:

2 each English cucumbers,
  peeled and diced

3 each scallion greens, julienned

Rice wine vinegar

Extra-virgin olive oil

Salt and pepper to taste

For the Duck:

- Over a low flame, heat up the olive oil in a deep casserole until it reaches approximately 140 degrees, then turn it off. Season the duck breasts with salt and pepper and place them in the oil. After 8 minutes, remove the duck from the oil and let rest.

For the Spinach Purée:

- Simmer the heavy cream in a small, heavy saucepan over low to medium heat until reduced by 2/3. Blanch the spinach leaves in salted, boiling water for 30 seconds and then quickly plunge in ice water. Squeeze out the excess liquid and blend in a blender in small batches with the cream. When the purée is smooth, cool it down over a metal bowl of ice. Season to taste with salt and pepper.

For the Spiced Honey:

- Heat up the honey in a saucepan. Just before it boils, remove from burner. Add the spices and the chipotle and let steep for as long as desired *(at least 1 hour)*. When you are satisfied with the intensity of the flavor, slowly heat the honey up again and pour it through a strainer.

For the Cashews:

- In a large non-reactive sauté pan, melt the sugar over low heat, stirring frequently with a wooden spoon. When the sugar has melted and turned a pale golden color, add the cayenne and the cashews, and then stir until all of the cashews are evenly coated. Spread the cashews onto a non-stick surface, such as a Silpat® mat or a Teflon® cookie sheet, to cool. When cooled, chop and reserve for use in cucumber salad.

For the Star Anise Vinaigrette:

- Simmer the balsamic vinegar in a small, heavy, non-reactive saucepan over medium heat until reduced by 3/4. Lightly toast the star anise in a sauté pan and then let cool. Put the star anise in a coffee grinder or grind with a mortar and pestle until finely and evenly ground. Add the ground spice to the balsamic vinegar reduction and cover it with the canola oil *(do not mix the oil into the vinegar, just pour it in gently)*.

For the Cucumber Salad:

- Toss the cucumbers with the chopped spicy cashews, julienned scallions, rice wine vinegar and extra-virgin olive oil. Season to taste with salt and pepper.

To Finish and Serve:

- To assemble, heat up the spinach purée over low heat and place a circle of it on each plate. Put 2 spoonfuls of the cucumber mixture in the middle of the spinach. Brush the still-warm duck breast with the spiced honey mixture and slice it thinly and evenly the short way across the breast. One duck breast yields one entrée serving, or two appetizer servings. Spoon a little of the star anise vinaigrette around the spinach.

Halibut with Wild Mushrooms

Serves: 4

Carrot Reduction:

1 cup carrot juice

1 teaspoon curry powder

Salt and sugar to taste

Truffle Vinaigrette:

6 tablespoons balsamic vinegar

1 each shallot, minced

1 teaspoon chopped thyme

10 tablespoons truffle oil

Salt, pepper, and chopped chives
   to taste

Turnips:

1 cup diced turnips

2 tablespoons butter

1 tablespoon sugar

Salt and pepper to taste

Carrots:

1 cup diced carrots

Olive oil

Salt and pepper to taste

Green Beans:

1 cup cut green beans

Olive oil

Salt and pepper to taste

Mushrooms:

1 tablespoon olive oil

1 tablespoon butter

2 cups assorted wild mushrooms
   *(chanterelles, black trumpet,
   shiitake and oyster mushrooms
   work well)*

1 each shallot,
   peeled and quartered

Pinch chopped thyme

1 tablespoon lemon juice

Salt and pepper to taste

Halibut:

4 each 6-ounce halibut fillets,
   skinned

Salt and pepper to taste

2 tablespoons olive oil

2 tablespoons butter

1 tablespoon chopped thyme

1 tablespoon lemon juice

For the Carrot Reduction:

- Place carrot juice and curry powder in a saucepan. Simmer over low to medium heat until reduced by 2/3. Season to taste with salt and sugar. Keep warm.

For the Truffle Vinaigrette:

- In a saucepan, reduce balsamic vinegar over medium heat by half. In a bowl, combine all the ingredients, but do not mix well *(leave broken)*.

For the Turnips:

- Cook the turnips in the butter and sugar until golden brown. Keep warm.

For the Carrots:

- Cook the carrots in the olive oil over low heat until tender. Keep warm.

For the Green Beans:

- Cook the green beans in the olive oil over low heat until tender. Keep warm.

For the Mushrooms:

- Heat the oil and butter in a large sauté pan over medium heat. Sear the mushrooms and the shallot for 2 minutes. Add the turnips, carrots and green beans, a pinch of thyme and the lemon juice. Keep warm.

For the Halibut:

- Season the halibut with salt and pepper. In a large sauté pan over medium heat, heat the oil and then place the fillets top-side *(non-skin side)* down until they appear golden around the edges. Flip the fillets, add the butter and thyme and cook, basting, for 1 minute. Add the lemon juice and remove the fish from the pan.

To Finish and Serve:

- Put 1/4 of the vegetable mixture in the center of each of four serving plates, and then place the halibut on top of the mushrooms on each plate. Ring the plates with the truffle vinaigrette and the carrot reduction.

Chef on the Spot

Do you have a guilty food pleasure?
"Almond Joy™ candy bars, New York City pizza and Nathan's™ hot dogs"

Is there a food you don't like and why?
"Oatmeal, you need to ask?"

What kitchen gadget do you most rely on?
"At home it's my toaster oven. In the restaurant it would have to be our high-speed blender."

What is your culinary philosophy?
"Don't crowd the plate with too many flavors. Come up with new and interesting ways to present approachable foods."

Maine Diver Scallops

Serves: 6

Endive:

4 heads Belgian endive,
   bottoms trimmed

Salt and pepper to taste

1 tablespoon oil

1/2 cup white wine

2 cups fresh-squeezed
   orange juice

1/4 each vanilla bean

1/4 cup vegetable stock
   (may substitute water)

Apricot Purée:

12 each dried apricots

3 cups orange juice

1/4 cup white wine

Scallops:

6 each Maine diver scallops
   (approximately 1/2 pound total)

Salt and pepper to taste

1 tablespoon oil

1 tablespoon butter

1 tablespoon chopped thyme

Juice of 1 lemon

Finish:

1 teaspoon sliced and blanched
   almonds

2 tablespoons whole almonds,
   toasted and salted

1 each carrot, cut into 1/8-inch
   dice, blanched and shocked

1 each celery, cut into 1/8-inch
   dice, blanched and shocked

1 tablespoon veal glace

For the Endive:

- Cut the heads of endive in half length-wise, season them with salt and pepper, and place them cut-side down in a warm sauté pan with the oil. Allow them to cook undisturbed until a golden caramel color begins to appear around the edges. Add the white wine and cook over low to medium heat until reduced to almost dry. Add the orange juice *(it should come slightly more than halfway up the endive)* and the vanilla bean *(both the seeds scraped from the pod and the pod itself)* and cook until reduced by 1/2. Remove endive from liquid, reserving liquid. Allow both the endive and the liquid to cool to room temperature. Cut each endive head in half lengthwise once more, and return them to the cooled reduction. To serve warm, heat up the endive in 3/4 cup cooking liquid and 1/4 cup vegetable stock.

For the Apricot Purée:

- In a separate pan, cover the apricots with orange juice and wine, and cook over low heat until the apricots are plumped. Remove four of the apricots, halve them and reserve. Place the remaining apricots in a blender with as little of the poaching liquid *(approximately 1/2 cup)*, as necessary to allow them to purée easily. When the purée seems smooth, pass it through a fine-mesh strainer into a bowl and cool it immediately over an ice bath *(set the bowl with the purée in it into a larger bowl filled with ice)*.

For the Scallops:

- Season scallops with salt and pepper to taste. In a heavy sauté pan over medium heat, heat the oil and then place the scallops in the pan, making sure they sit upright like small drums. Allow them to caramelize, keeping an eye on the edges to see if they're getting too dark *(anything past golden is undesirable)*. When the desired color is achieved, flip the scallops and add the butter and chopped thyme. Briefly baste the scallops. Add the lemon juice and remove pan from heat.

To Finish and Serve:

- Rewarm the endive and add the sliced almonds to it. Place one of the scallops on top of each of the endive pieces. Garnish with whole almonds, carrots, celery, halved apricots, apricot purée and the veal-reduction.

Raw endive will make your hands, and in turn, anything you touch, taste bitter. Be sure to clean your cutting board, knife and hands well after handling.

Goat Cheesecakes with Huckleberry Ice Cream

Serves: 6

Cheesecakes:

5 ounces cream cheese

4 ounces goat cheese

1/2 cup granulated sugar

2 teaspoons lemon juice

Zest of 1 lemon

2 each large eggs

1 cup crème fraîche
  (may substitute sour cream)

1/8 teaspoon salt

Buckwheat Tuiles:

7 ounces melted butter

2 cups light-brown sugar

1/2 cup granulated sugar

10-1/2 ounces coconut milk

7/8 cup all-purpose flour

7/8 cup buckwheat flour

2 pinches salt

Huckleberry Ice Cream:

1 pint huckleberries

3-1/2 cups milk

1 cup granulated sugar

12 each egg yolks

6 tablespoons Trimoline or
  corn syrup

2 tablespoons fresh lemon juice

1 pinch salt

Huckleberry Jam:

8 ounces fresh or frozen
  huckleberries

1 cup granulated sugar

1 teaspoon powdered pectin or
  SureJell®

For the Cheesecakes:

- Preheat oven to 350 degrees. Prepare six 2-1/2-inch ring molds with aluminum foil on the bottom and halfway up the sides of the molds. Place the molds on a sheet pan.

- Combine cream cheese, goat cheese, sugar, lemon juice and zest in the bowl of a tabletop mixer. Using the paddle attachment, cream these ingredients until smooth, scraping the bowl often. Add the eggs one at a time, scraping the bowl often. Fold in the crème fraîche and salt, and strain through a fine-mesh strainer. Pour into the rings, filling them 7/8 full.

- Place the sheet pan into the oven, fill the pan with water to come half-way up the sides of the molds. Bake for approximately 10 minutes, rotate the pan, and bake for approximately 8 minutes or until just set. Cool to room temperature and then refrigerate until cold. *(Remove the foil when cool and replace with squares of parchment paper since the lemon will react to the aluminum foil.)*

For the Buckwheat Tuiles:

- Combine the melted butter, sugars and coconut milk and whisk until incorporated. Combine flours and salt. Add flour mixture to wet ingredients and mix until just combined. Chill. Preheat oven to 325 degrees. Using a 3-inch round template *(a piece of cardboard or plastic mat with a 3-inch circle cut out)*, on a non-stick baking pan, spread the batter thinly over the template and scrape off the excess batter to make the tuiles. Bake for 7 minutes or until very golden brown. Cool and store in an airtight container. Crisp the cookies prior to serving by putting them on a baking sheet in a 200 degree oven for 5 minutes.

For the Huckleberry Ice Cream:

- Purée the huckleberries in blender and set aside. In a saucepan, heat the milk, half of the sugar and salt to the boiling point and set aside. Whisk egg yolks and remaining sugar together in a bowl. Slowly whisk the hot milk into the yolk mixture, then return the mixture to the saucepan. Cook the milk and egg mixture over medium heat, stirring constantly, until mixture is steaming and coats the back of a wooden spoon. Strain into a bowl set over ice and whisk the mixture to release the steam and bring down the temperature quickly to prevent curdling. When chilled, add 1 cup of the huckleberry purée and lemon juice. Freeze according to the manufacturer's instructions for your ice cream machine.

For the Huckleberry Jam:

- Combine the huckleberries and sugar in a non-reactive saucepan. Place over medium heat. When warm, add the pectin. Bring to a boil and cook to 210 degrees. Cool the mixture to room temperature. Place 3/4 of the mixture in a blender and purée. Add this mixture back into the rest and chill.

To Finish and Serve:

- Garnish each of six serving plates with the remaining huckleberry purée left over from the ice cream. Unmold the cheesecakes and place one in the center of each plate. Center a tuile on top of each and place a dollop of huckleberry jam in the center. Place a scoop of huckleberry ice cream on the jam.

RICK BAYLESS
CHICAGO, IL

Humanitarian of the Year, 1998

All-Clad Metalcrafters Outstanding Chef, 1995

American Express Best Chef: Midwest, 1991

How does a kid from Oklahoma end up as Mexico's unofficial culinary ambassador to the United States? According to Rick Bayless, that unlikely career recipe goes back four generations.

The future chef's great grandparents and grandparents owned grocery stores in the Midwest and he describes his grandmother as, "an amazingly good country cook." Every summer, during peach season, she'd gather the grandchildren and spend four days with them picking and processing the fruit into pickled peaches, peach butter and peaches canned in simple syrup. Peach cobbler all year 'round was the reward for their efforts.

Bayless' parents owned a barbecue restaurant, and as a boy Rick cooked both at home and in the restaurant. "It was a passion for me," he explains, "but for my family it was more of a business."

When his dad went to the commercial produce market, Bayless tagged along. "Back then, it was really a farmer's market where they brought in their stuff and we'd deal directly with them. That really marked me strongly. Today one of the things our restaurants are known for is locally grown produce and cooking with the seasons."

His first trip to Mexico at age 14 was a revelation. "Growing up in a barbecue restaurant in a town where barbecue was considered our local food; I already had a sense of the role food plays in a community, but in Mexico I discovered that the regional foods are far more complex and distinct than in the United States."

For nearly six years, the couple immersed themselves in Mexican culture and cuisine by exploring, researching and taking copious notes. "We loved the openness of the society and generosity of spirit you find throughout the country and the way people open their doors to you when you express interest in something, especially food."

It all culminated in 1987 when the Baylesses penned their first cookbook *Authentic Mexican: Regional Cooking From the Heart of Mexico*. Observes Bayless, "At that point I fully intended to write serious cookbooks and teach cooking, but I knew it would be hard to make a living that way."

Thus colorful and casual Frontera Grill, hailed by many food writers and critics as the best Mexican restaurant in the U.S., was born. Topolobampo, a more upscale version of the wildly successful original, opened next door in 1989.

"It was the right time and the right place," says Bayless, "Chicago has a huge Hispanic population, over a million people, so this is a good place to do what we do. Most people here have some connection to the local Mexican population so our clientele knows the real thing."

In college Bayless majored in Spanish language, literature and Latin American culture while working in the catering side of the family restaurant. He earned a doctorate in anthropological linguistics from the University of Michigan. Although intending to become a Spanish teacher, the siren call from South-of-the-Border led to what he calls "the best possible job I could have gotten." A California-based Mexican restaurant chain hired Bayless as a consultant taking him and his new wife Deann to every part of Mexico.

The restaurants are as close to the real thing as it gets, though Bayless is careful to say, "We base all our food on traditional recipes; handmade tortillas, sopes with fillings such as plantains in sour cream, fresh and cooked salsas, sauces, moles, grilled seafood, meats and poultry, stews, tamales wrapped in banana leaves, but we are not perfectly reproducing the food since we use mostly local ingredients."

He has a great deal of respect for his adopted cuisine. "Mexican food is very simple in presentation and very complex in preparation. I spent many years mastering that complexity. After all, it took hundreds of years to perfect that balance of flavor."

The Bayless family, including daughter Lanie, shares a spacious home in a renovated turn-of-the-twentieth-century tavern in the Bucktown area of Chicago. From the original tin Heileman's Old Style Beer® sign still hanging in front to the glorious vegetable and herb garden, wood decks and outdoor kitchen in back, it creates a highly personal environment.

The garden and kitchen are familiar to fans of Rick's PBS television series *Mexico — One Plate at a Time*. The rest of the comfortable and family-oriented house showcases stunning Mexican folk art, ceramics and oil paintings. In the basement prep kitchen Bayless readies dishes for the TV show and in the greenhouse grows micro greens for the restaurant.

Says wife Deann, "With any older building, there's always a project. We tackle a major one each year."

It's surprising that the couple even finds time to do that. Between running the restaurants, producing the Frontera product line, writing, teaching, surviving the hectic schedule involved in taping the TV series, coordinating the annual staff visit to Mexico and the other trips the Baylesses make each year, including an annual Christmas trek to Oaxaca, it's a busy life. But, somehow, they manage.

The house boasts a phenomenal sound system, and favorite CDs such as Tito Puente's *Mambo Birdland*, Isaac Delgado's *Forbidden Cuban in the '90s* and *Putumayo Presents Mexico* are always playing. Rick contends that one thing most people don't know about him is that he is a dancing fool and the Baylesses throw parties at the drop of a...well, sombrero. Yoga is another favorite way of keeping the stress down.

When Bayless cooks at home, he says he never does the same dishes that are featured at the restaurants. "We prepare a wide variety of dishes, things we pick up on our travels." Thai and Japanese foods are favorites.

Looking ahead, Bayless claims there will be no more restaurants in his future. "The two we have are totally infused with our personalities." Still, he intends to keep authoring articles and books, doing the television series and continuing to educate the world about the nuances and traditions of real Mexican cuisine — to which Bayless fans can only shout, "Ole!"

Ceviche Clasico

Serves: 8

Ceviche:

1 pound fresh snapper, bass, or halibut, skinless, cut into 1/2-inch cubes or slightly smaller

3/4 cup fresh lime juice

1 each white onion, medium, chopped into 1/4-inch pieces

1 pound tomatoes, chopped into 1/4-inch pieces

2 to 3 each Serrano chiles or 1 to 2 jalapeños, stemmed, seeded and finely chopped

1/3 cup chopped cilantro *(leave a few leaves whole for garnish)*

1 to 2 tablespoons extra-virgin olive oil

Salt to taste

3 tablespoons fresh orange juice

Finish:

1 each large avocado or 2 small, peeled, pitted and diced

Tostadas, tortilla chips or Saltine crackers for serving

For the Ceviche:

- In a 1-1/2-quart glass or stainless steel bowl, combine the fish, lime juice and onion. You'll need enough juice to cover the fish and allow it to float somewhat freely; too little juice means unevenly "cooked" fish. Cover and refrigerate for 6 to 8 hours, until a cube of fish no longer looks raw when broken open. Pour into a colander and drain off the lime juice.

- In a large bowl, mix together the tomatoes, chiles, cilantro and olive oil. Stir in the fish, then taste and season with salt, usually about a teaspoon, and orange juice *(the sweetness of the orange juice helps balance some of the typical tanginess of the ceviche)*. Cover and refrigerate if not serving immediately.

To Finish and Serve:

- Just before serving, stir in the diced avocado, being careful not to break up the pieces. For serving, you have several options: set out the ceviche in a large bowl and let people spoon it onto individual plates to eat with chips or Saltines; serve small bowls of ceviche *(I like to lay a bed of frisée lettuce in each bowl before spooning in the ceviche)* and serve tostadas, chips or Saltines alongside; or pile the ceviche onto chips or tostadas and pass around for guests to consume on these edible little plates. Whichever option you choose, garnish the ceviche with leaves of cilantro before setting it center stage.

Rick Bayless' Beverage Recommendations

Ceviche Clasico
Oregon Pinot Gris from the Willamette Valley
page 211

Jicama Salad with Red Chile and Lime
Spanish Albarino or a Torrontes from Argentina
page 213

Tortilla Soup with Shredded Chard
Marlborough New Zealand Sauvignon Blanc
page 213

Whole Fish Braised with Tomatoes, Capers, Olives and Herbs
Barbera d'Asti or Chianti Classico
page 215

Charcoal-Grilled Pork Loin with Red Chile Sauce
Côtes-du-Rhône, or a lighter style Syrah
page 217

Buttered Crêpes with Caramel and Pecans
20- or 30-year-old Tawny Port
page 219

Jicama Salad with Red Chile and Lime

Serves: 8

Jicama Salad:

1 pound jicama

3 each oranges, seedless

2 each small cucumbers, seeds removed, sliced diagonally 1/4-inch thick

6 each radishes, thinly sliced

1/3 cup fresh lime juice

1/2 teaspoons salt

Finish:

2 teaspoons dried powdered guajillo chile (*may substitute any other powdered hot chile*)

2/3 cup pickled red onions (*optional*)

1/3 cup roughly chopped cilantro, plus a sprig for garnish

For the Jicama Salad:

- Peel away the brown skin and fibrous exterior layer of the jicama. Cut the jicama in half and slice into 1/4-inch-thick slices. Cut the slices in half diagonally. Cut stem and blossom end off oranges. Working close to the flesh, cut away the rind and all white pith. Cut oranges in half, then slice crosswise into 1/4-inch-thick slices.

To Finish and Serve:

- Mix the vegetables, fruit and lime juice in a large bowl. Marinate 20 minutes, and season with salt. Pile the vegetables and fruit onto a serving platter and drizzle with accumulated juices. Sprinkle with powdered chile, top with the optional pickled onions, and sprinkle with cilantro. Garnish with the cilantro sprig.

Tortilla Soup with Shredded Chard

Serves: 4 to 6

Tortilla Soup:

4 to 6 each tortillas, preferably stale store-bought ones

1/3 cup vegetable oil

4 to 5 each dried pasilla chiles, stemmed and seeded

2 cloves garlic, unpeeled

1 each tomato, large

1 tablespoon olive oil

1 each white onion, sliced 1/8-inch thick

6 cups broth, preferably chicken stock

Salt to taste

Finish:

2 cup shredded Mexican Chihuahua cheese (*or any other melting cheese, such as brick or Monterey jack*)

1 each lime, large, cut into 6 wedges

4 cups thinly sliced red chard, loosely packed

For the Tortilla Soup:

- Slice tortillas into 1/8-inch-wide strips. Heat 1/3 cup of vegetable oil in a medium-sized skillet over medium heat. Add about 1/3 of the tortilla strips and fry, turning frequently, until they are crisp on all sides. Remove and drain on paper towels. Fry remaining strips.

- Cut chiles into 1-inch squares using kitchen shears. Reduce heat under the oil to medium-low. Let cool a minute, then fry the squares briefly to toast them; remove and drain on paper towels. Place 1/3 of the chiles in a small bowl, cover with hot water and rehydrate for 30 minutes, stirring regularly. Drain and discard the water. Set aside the remaining fried chiles.

- While the chiles are soaking, roast the unpeeled garlic on an ungreased griddle or heavy skillet over medium heat, turning occasionally, until blackened in spots and soft. Cool; then slip off the skins.

- Broil the tomato on a baking sheet 4 inches below a very hot broiler until blackened and blistered, about 6 minutes; flip and broil the other side. Cool, then peel, collecting any juices.

- In a 4-quart pot, heat the olive oil over medium-low heat. Add the onion and fry until brown, about 10 minutes. Purée the rehydrated chiles along with the garlic, tomato and 1 cup of broth; purée until smooth. Raise the temperature under the pot to medium-high. Press the tomato-chile mixture through a medium-mesh strainer into the fried onion. Stir for several minutes as the mixture thickens. Mix in the remaining 5 cups of broth, then simmer uncovered over medium-low heat, stirring occasionally, for 30 minutes. Season with salt.

To Finish and Serve:

- Make mounds of the fried tortilla strips, fried chiles, cheese and lime on a large platter. Before serving, reheat the soup, add the sliced chard and simmer until the chard is tender, 5 or 6 minutes. Ladle into warm soup bowls and pass the garnishes.

Whole Fish Braised with Tomatoes, Capers, Olives and Herbs

Serves: 4 to 6

Fish:

1 each snapper or grouper,
  4 pounds, scaled and cleaned

Juice of 2 limes

Salt to taste

Sauce:

1/4 cup extra-virgin olive oil

1 each medium white onion,
  thinly sliced

4 cloves garlic, finely chopped

3 pounds ripe tomatoes, peeled,
  cored and chopped into 1/2-inch
  pieces

4 each bay leaves

1-1/2 teaspoons oregano, dried,
  preferably Mexican

3 tablespoons finely chopped
  flat-leaf parsley leaves, plus a
  few sprigs for garnish

1 cup green olives, pitted,
  preferably Manzanillo olives

1/4 cup capers, drained and
  rinsed

3 each jalapeño chiles, pickled,
  stemmed, seeded and thinly
  sliced, or 6 whole pickled
  guerro/largo chiles

Salt to taste

For the Fish:

• Cut 2 parallel diagonal slashes across each side of the fish, starting the first one near the top of the head and angling down toward the tail; cut down through the flesh to the backbone. Put the fish into a large baking dish. Drizzle both sides with the lime juice and sprinkle liberally with salt, about 1/2 tablespoon per side. Cover and refrigerate for about an hour *(but no more than 4 hours)*.

For the Sauce:

• In a 4- to 5-quart pot, heat the oil over medium heat. Add the onion and cook, stirring regularly, until just beginning to brown, about 5 minutes. Add the garlic and cook 1 minute more, stirring several times. Raise the heat to medium-high and add the tomatoes, bay leaves, oregano, chopped parsley, half of the olives, half of the capers and half of the chiles. Simmer briskly, stirring frequently, for about 5 minutes to evaporate some of the liquid. Reduce the heat to medium-low and stir in one cup of water. Simmer for 15 minutes. Taste and season with salt, usually about 1 teaspoon.

For Baking the Fish:

• Preheat the oven to 350 degrees. Lightly oil a roasting pan large enough to hold the fish comfortably. Remove the fish from the lime mixture and lay in the pan. If the tail sticks out of the pan, crimp a piece of oiled aluminum foil around it to prevent burning. Cover the fish with steaming tomato sauce. Bake in the center of the oven until the flesh flakes when firmly, gently pressed at the point where the body meets the head, just above the gills — a total of 50 to 55 minutes.

• Using two sturdy metal spatulas, carefully transfer the fish to a large serving platter. Tip up the baking pan to collect the sauce and spoon it over the fish. Sprinkle with the remaining olives, capers and chiles and decorate with sprigs of parsley.

To Finish and Serve:

• Carry the platter to the table. Set out a sharp knife *(a boning or filleting knife works best here)* and the two spatulas. Scrape the tomato sauce away from the body of the fish so you can see where you are cutting. Use the knife to cut an outline of the meatiest part. Starting where the head meets the flesh *(and following the head shape)*, cut from the top of the fish down to the gill area, cutting all the way down to the bone. At the gill area, turn the knife's direction 90 degrees and cut straight down the length of the fish to the tail. Turn the fish so that you're facing its top. Now, holding the knife horizontally, slice into the meat just above the backbone, starting where the head meets the flesh and continuing all the way to the tail. Keep cutting farther and farther until you reach the cut you made down the length of the fish. The top fillet is now free.

• Cut the fillet into 3 pieces, then use a spatula to transfer the pieces to dinner plates. Generously spoon sauce over each piece. Lift off the now-exposed skeletal structure starting at the tail and holding down the bottom fillet with the spatula. The second fillet is now ready to cut into thirds and serve with the sauce.

Charcoal-Grilled Pork Loin with Red Chile Sauce

Serves: 6

Red Chile Sauce:

8 each dried ancho chiles, stemmed, seeded and deveined

3 tablespoons lard or vegetable oil

1/2 each onion, diced

3 cloves garlic, peeled

1-2/3 cups broth, *(preferably pork)*, plus a little more for thinning the sauce

1/2 teaspoon cumin seeds

1 each bay leaf

1/2 teaspoon dried oregano

1/4 teaspoon dried thyme

2 tablespoons cider vinegar

1 cup freshly squeezed orange juice

1 tablespoon sugar

1/2 teaspoon salt

Pork:

2 to 3 pounds pork loin, lean boneless with a thin cap of fat on one side *(pork tenderloin also works well)*

4 tablespoons cider vinegar

Finish:

Salt and sugar to taste

1/2 cup green olives, meaty, preferably Manzanillos

Several pickled jalapeño chiles

1 slice onion, broken into rings

Several orange slices, grilled

For the Red Chile Sauce:

- Tear the ancho chiles into flat pieces. Heat 2 tablespoons of the lard or oil in a medium-sized skillet over medium heat. Add several of the chiles and quickly fry, a couple of pieces at a time, toasting them for a few seconds on each side. Drain well and cover with boiling water. Weight with a plate to keep the chiles submerged and let soak for several hours or overnight to rid them of any harshness.

- In the same skillet, fry the onion and garlic over medium heat, stirring occasionally, until well browned, about 8 minutes. Scoop out the onion and garlic, draining as much fat as possible back into the pan, and place in a blender.

- Drain the chiles, squeezing them gently to remove all of the soaking liquid. Add to the onion mixture in the blender, along with 2/3 cup of the broth. Grind the cumin and bay leaf in a mortar or spice grinder, and add them to the blender along with the oregano, thyme and vinegar. Blend until smooth, then strain through a medium-mesh sieve.

- Heat the remaining tablespoon of lard or oil in a large saucepan over medium-high heat. When quite hot, add the chile purée and stir constantly for 5 to 7 minutes, until it is a thick deep burgundy mass.

- Stir in the remaining cup of the broth and the orange juice. Partially cover, reduce the heat to medium-low and simmer for about 45 minutes. Season with sugar and salt, then cool.

For the Pork:

- Mix together 1/4 cup of the cooled chile sauce and the vinegar. Cover and refrigerate the rest of the chile sauce. If the pork loin consists of 2 pieces tied into a double thickness for roasting, untie them and place in a non-corrosive container. Pour on the sauce-vinegar mixture and coat well. Cover and refrigerate at least 12 hours, turning the meat in the marinade several times.

- About 2 hours before serving, remove the meat from the marinade and set it out to come to room temperature. Build a charcoal fire and let it burn until only medium heat. Position the grill about 6 inches above the coals and brush it with a little oil. When the fire is right, remove the pork from the marinade and lay it on the grill, fat-side down. Turn it periodically until it feels firm and reaches an internal temperature of about 150 degrees. This cooking process should take about 50 minutes to an hour.

To Finish and Serve:

- Warm the chile sauce in a small saucepan, thinning it with a little broth if necessary to achieve a light consistency *(like moderately thin barbecue sauce)*. Season to taste with salt and sugar. Thinly slice the meat, then overlap the slices on a warm platter. Spoon the sauce over the top and garnish with the olives, chiles, onion rings and orange slices. Serve immediately.

Buttered Crêpes with Caramel and Pecans

Serves: 4

Crêpes:

1 each 1/2-inch piece cinnamon stick *(or about 1/2 teaspoon ground)*

3 each cloves

1 cup milk

2 each large eggs

1/4 teaspoon salt

1 teaspoon sugar

1/2 teaspoon vanilla extract

2/3 cup all-purpose flour

1 tablespoon unsalted butter, melted

Oil for frying

Goat Milk Caramel with Spirits *(Cajeta)*:

1 quart goat's milk

1 cup granulated sugar

1 tablespoon corn syrup

1/2 inch piece cinnamon stick

1/4 teaspoon baking soda

1 tablespoon grain alcohol or sweet sherry, rum or brandy

Filling:

8 tablespoons unsalted butter

1 cup roughly chopped pecans

1-1/2 cups Goat Milk Caramel *(see recipe above)*

Finish:

Assorted berries

Mint sprigs

For the Crêpes:

- Pulverize the cinnamon and cloves in a mortar or spice grinder, then place in a blender or food processor with all the remaining crêpe ingredients except the butter. Process until smooth, stopping the machine once to scrape down the sides. With the machine running, pour in melted butter. Set aside to rest for 2 hours. Before using, thin with a little water, if necessary, to the consistency of heavy cream.

- Set a 7-inch skillet or crêpe pan over medium to medium-high heat and brush lightly with oil. When hot, pour in about 1/4 cup of the batter and quickly swirl it around to coat the bottom. Immediately pour the excess back into the blender.

- Cook until the edges begin to dry, about 45 to 60 seconds. Loosen the edges with a knife and trim off the irregular part. Using your fingers or a narrow spatula, flip the crêpe *(it should be golden brown)*. Cook about 1 minute longer, until golden brown underneath, then remove to a plate. Continue until all of the batter is used, greasing the pan from time to time and stacking the finished crêpes on top of one another with sheets of plastic wrap to separate. Cover with plastic wrap.

Goat Milk Caramel with Spirits *(Cajeta)*:

- In a large heavy-bottomed saucepan or kettle, combine the milk, sugar, corn syrup and cinnamon and bring to a simmer, stirring. Dissolve the baking soda into the mixture; reduce over medium heat. When the bubbles start changing from small, quick bursting ones to larger, glassier ones — 25 to 40 minutes — reduce the heat to medium-low. Stir frequently, washing the spoon each time, until the mixture thickens into a caramel-brown syrup that's a little thinner than corn syrup.

- Strain the syrup through a fine-mesh sieve into a small bowl or wide-mouth jar. Let cool a few minutes, then stir in the alcohol. Cool completely before covering. Store in refrigerator.

For the Filling:

- Melt the butter in a medium-sized skillet over medium-low heat. Add the pecans and stir frequently for about 10 minutes, until nuts are toasted and the butter is browned. Remove the nuts with a slotted spoon, and set the skillet of browned butter aside.

- Lay out a crêpe with the most-attractive side down and brush with the browned butter. Spoon a scant tablespoon of the caramel on one side. Fold in half and press gently to spread out the filling. Brush the top with butter. Fold in half again to form a wedge and brush with butter again. Lay in a buttered decorative baking dish. Repeat the buttering and filling with the remaining crêpes, arranging them, slightly overlapping, in 2 rows in the baking dish. Cover with foil and scrape the remaining caramel into a small saucepan.

To Finish and Serve:

- About 20 minutes before serving, preheat the oven to 325 degrees. Bake the crêpes in the oven for 20 minutes to warm them through. Heat the remaining cajeta in the small saucepan over medium-low heat. Drizzle it over the warm crêpes, sprinkle with the nuts and assorted berries and top with a sprig of mint. Serve at once.

JOACHIM SPLICHAL

LOS ANGELES, CA

American Express Best Chef: California, 1991

Los Angeles restaurant Patina is a dining magnet for entertainment world celebrities, in the culinary arena, chef/owner Joachim Splichal is a star in his own right.

Casual observers might marvel at the business empire Splichal has built since opening Patina in 1989. However, a closer look reveals that whether he knew it or not he has been a celebrity chef in training since he was a boy.

Born in Spaichingen, Germany, Splichal grew up in the business. His father and grandfather were innkeepers and chefs. The family's inn had 17 rooms and the restaurant seated 400 people, serving typical German home cooking, and, Splichal says, "I always helped out, running errands, setting up for parties, arranging the wine cellar and working in the on-premise butcher shop."

After graduating from high school he enrolled in a Swiss hotel school. "I had no sense of wanting to cook. I wanted to get into management." However, his first job as a desk clerk in

Holland was an eye-opener. "I didn't speak enough Dutch, so they gave me the worst duties and I hated it. But I had a girlfriend and wanted to stay in Holland."

In order to do so, he took a job in a restaurant. "I knew chopping but I sure wasn't a chef," he remembers. "I picked up the basic stuff and did a lot of reading in order to educate myself as quickly as possible."

When the relationship ended, Splichal looked for employment at a number of Swiss hotels. He was hired at the St. Moritz at the very bottom of a hierarchy of 55 chefs. "I replaced people when they were off. It was so structured that at lunch the staff were seated according to their positions. I didn't care for that; I was long-haired and a bit rebellious," he says. Still, there were perks. "I worked in the morning and evening and skied in the afternoon. Although they paid peanuts, it was great."

From there he went to the Grand Hotel Royale in Stockholm where he learned both Swedish and some French cooking. Off-season he headed for Tunis where there was another girlfriend. Then it was back to Switzerland working in the kitchen at Mont Cervin in Zermatt, at the foot of the Matterhorn, and skiing at every opportunity.

Splichal realized he had reached a turning point. "I had worked in a lot of kitchens, big hotels and small regional restaurants," he recalls. "But I knew I had to go to France to learn refinement."

He went through the application process again and was offered a position at La Bonne Auberge in Antibes. There, Splichal attained the technical finesse he sought and, more importantly, met legendary Chef Jacques Maximin whom he calls his greatest culinary influence. "He was the star in France; the Alain Ducasse of his day." Maximin offered him the position of saucier at his restaurant Chantecler at Nice's Hotel Negresco. Splichal was only 23 years old.

"The kitchen staff was a bunch of French guys, all older than me and they'd been there forever," says Splichal. "Six months after I arrived Jacques promoted me over all of them to sous chef. It was difficult, a tremendous challenge. I had to fight them every step of the way."

He almost gave in to the pressure, considering a career in photography, but finally, "I put my foot down and ended up traveling all over the world with Jacques picking up experience and languages." Eventually, though, Splichal came to understand he was at a career standstill. With Maximin he'd always be the number two guy.

"In 1981 I decided to go to the U.S. and got a job as opening chef at the private Regency Club in Los Angeles. At this point my culinary style started to develop. All I learned in the many countries where I had been was mixing up in a big bowl. Provencal was the main influence — straightforward, good food. I started using my own recipes using fresh produce, olive oil and juices which reflected my training with Jacques."

The Regency Club was a bastion of rich Republicans, movie stars, politicians, CEO's and CFO's of major corporations — precisely the people who would be likely to invest in an entrepreneurial chef's restaurant venture.

At this point, Splichal had met French-born Christine Mandion. Her formidable education, including an MBA in international management, made for a marital match made in heaven. The pair opened the hugely successful 7th Street Bistro in downtown LA. "I had what I was going to do in my mind for a long time. We did a five-course lobster meal, a five-course vegetable meal. Nobody did that. All the chefs in LA were using pasta. I used potato; potato lasagna, potato canneloni."

A developer tapped Splichal to go into a center in Beverly Hills. The experience was mixed, he says. "The restaurant's decor was 20 years ahead of its time. We had great critical acclaim but the guy didn't have a plan, he was overextended. The center didn't work so the restaurant didn't work. The biggest lessons you learn come out of failure."

The Splichals regrouped. He consulted with various hotels, developing menu concepts and doing private parties, maintaining his contacts. They found a location that was perfect for

what they wanted to do, made the deal and raised investor money. "We called it Patina because we knew it was just going to get better with age," he says.

Christine was in the front of the house, Splichal in the kitchen. The couple's dream restaurant was packed from the day they opened. "What I did was combine French techniques with everything that makes up California cuisine: Mexican, Japanese, Italian, Korean...."

In the midst of 1989's recession, Splichal formed the Patina Group and began opening his more casual and moderately priced Pinot Restaurants. "I was afraid to have just a high-end restaurant and felt we needed to do something more neighborhood and rustic to give our clients a choice."

At the same time, catering took off and the Splichals moved into the museum-cafe business covering all ends of the economic spectrum. Splichal says, "I never had a precise strategy, it was all about my seeing a good market. We were the first to see opportunity downtown and now we have eight restaurants there."

The Patina juggernaut shows no sign of slowing down. "We've got many things in the works, says Splichal. "Our company is growing tremendously but you always have to be in control and maintain consistency."

Considering his workload, Splichal manages to get in plenty of quality time with Christine and their seven-year-old twins (Nick & Stef's Steak House is named after the pair). "I hang out with my family. There's no pressure, no timelines. We make pizza, grill a steak or cook a stew."

They share a spacious Mediterranean-style home in San Marino hung with a spectacular collection of contemporary art. There is a huge multi-purpose party room/kitchen studio/guest house by the pool. In addition to a wood-fired grill and pizza oven, the structure houses Splichal's collection of antique food molds and art deco martini shakers. An adjacent wine cellar holds 2,000-plus bottles. He plays tennis, practices yoga and still skies every chance he gets. Jokingly, Splichal says when he retires he wants to cook twice a week for 12 people at $200 a head, cash up front.

More seriously, he confides that he intends to explore wine-making. Given Splichal's track record, there's little doubt there will eventually be a well-regarded Patina wine label.

Pizza With Pears, Prosciutto, Gorgonzola and Arugula

Serves: 4

Pizza Crust:

5 cups all-purpose flour, sifted

1 teaspoon salt

1-3/4 cups warm water

1 package dry active yeast

3 tablespoons olive oil

Pizza:

1/4-pound thinly sliced
  prosciutto

1 each fresh pear, thinly sliced

6 ounces grated Gorgonzola

Finish:

1 bunch fresh arugula, cleaned
  and separated

For the Pizza Crust:

- Combine 4-1/2 cups of the flour and the salt together in a large glass mixing bowl and set aside. In a separate bowl, stir together warm water and yeast until yeast is dissolved. Form a small well in the middle of the flour and salt. Pour the water and yeast mixture into the well and combine with a fork. When dough begins to form, turn out onto floured surface. Gently knead additional flour into the dough, a little at a time, until dough is no longer sticky and forms into a ball. Place ball of dough into bowl, cover with a damp cloth and place in warm, dry area to rest and rise.

- When dough has doubled in size, punch dough down in the bowl, then place deflated dough onto floured surface and gently knead dough approximately 25 times. Gently form into a ball and return once again to the bowl, cover with damp cloth and place in warm, dry area to rest and rise again

- When doubled in size, lightly grease a shallow cookie sheet with olive oil. Place dough onto a floured surface and gently knead dough into the shape of the cookie sheet. Gently transfer dough to greased cookie sheet and let rest for approximately 15-20 minutes for a thicker crust. If you prefer thinner crust, rest dough on cookie sheet for 7-10 minutes.

For the Pizza:

- Preheat oven to 425 degrees. Bake dough for approximately 10 minutes, or until edges of crust begin to turn light brown. Remove crust from oven and top with prosciutto, pear and Gorgonzola. Return topped pizza to oven and finish baking for approximately 5-7 more minutes until edges of crust turn golden brown.

To Finish and Serve:

- Remove pizza from oven and top with arugula. Let cool and slice.

Wild Mushroom Scrambled Eggs

1/2 cup clarified butter

3 ounces shiitake mushrooms,
  cut in pieces

3 ounces chanterelle mushrooms,
  cut in pieces

3 ounces oyster mushrooms,
  cut in pieces

3 shallots, peeled and diced

Salt, pepper and nutmeg to taste
  (optional)

12 large eggs, beaten

1 cup heavy cream or half & half

Heat up a non-stick pan over medium-high heat. Add 1/4 cup of the clarified butter. Add the mushrooms and sauté them. Once the mushrooms get some color add the shallots. Season them with salt and pepper. In a separate pan, whisk together the eggs and cream and season to taste with salt, pepper and nutmeg. Now you might need to add a little bit more of the clarified butter, because you will add the eggs. Add the beaten eggs to the mushrooms and stir them with a wooden spoon until they look firm and shiny.

Cold Pea Soup with Shrimp Cake

Serves: 4

Cold Pea Soup:

2 each medium shallots, chopped

1 teaspoon olive oil

1 each boiling potato, about 4 ounces, peeled and cut into 1/2-inch pieces

1 teaspoon salt

3-1/2 cups water

3-1/2 cups baby peas

Salt and pepper to taste

Shrimp Cake:

1/2 pound rock shrimp *(may substitute frozen peeled and deveined shrimp)*

1/2 each red onion, finely chopped

2 tablespoons chopped chives

Salt and pepper to taste

1 tablespoon olive oil

Finish:

1/4 cup crème fraîche or sour cream

Fresh chervil to garnish

For the Cold Pea Soup:

- In a 3-quart heavy saucepan over moderate heat, cook the shallots in the olive oil, stirring, until softened, about 2 minutes. Add the potato, salt, and water and simmer, covered, until the potato is tender, about 15 minutes. Add the peas and simmer, uncovered, 2 minutes. Chill the soup immediately in an ice bath. Purée in batches in a blender, then force through a very fine sieve into a saucepan. Season with salt and pepper. Chill until ready to serve.

For the Shrimp Cakes:

- Chop the shrimp very fine. Mix with the red onion, chives, salt and pepper. Form 1-inch round cakes. Heat the olive oil in a non-stick skillet until hot. Sear cakes, drain on paper towels, and keep warm until ready to serve.

To Finish and Serve:

- Ladle the cold pea soup into each of four soup bowls. Drizzle each bowl of soup with crème fraîche or sour cream. Place several warm shrimp cakes in each bowl of soup. Garnish with sprigs of chervil.

Bibb Lettuce and Endive with Roasted Pecans, Maytag Blue Cheese and Italian Parsley with Champagne Vinaigrette

Serves: 4

Champagne Vinaigrette:

2 tablespoons Champagne *(optional)*

1 tablespoon Dijon mustard

1/3 cup Champagne vinegar

1 each shallot, finely diced

1 cup extra-virgin olive oil

Salt and pepper to taste

Salad:

1 cup pecan halves

1 tablespoon olive oil

Kosher salt to taste

1 head Bibb lettuce, nice leaves only, cleaned and washed

2 heads Belgian endive, large outer leaves only, cleaned and washed

1/2 bunch Italian parsley, leaves only

Ground black pepper to taste

Finish:

6 ounces Maytag blue cheese, crumbled *(may substitute any blue cheese)*

For the Champagne Vinaigrette:

- Combine the Champagne, mustard, Champagne vinegar and shallot in a blender and mix until smooth and starting to emulsify. Slowly drizzle extra-virgin olive oil into blender while running until smooth and emulsified. If vinaigrette seems too thick, add a little cold water and blend to a thinner consistency. Season to taste with salt and pepper.

For the Salad:

- Toss pecan halves in olive oil. Spread out on a baking sheet and bake at 350 degrees for about 5 to 7 minutes, or until the nuts are pale golden brown and aromatic. Season the roasted pecans lightly with salt. Let cool. Chop them roughly. In a salad bowl, mix the Bibb lettuce, endive and the parsley. Very lightly season with salt and pepper.

To Finish and Serve:

- Arrange the mixture nicely on each of four salad plates. Crumble the blue cheese and sprinkle it and the pecans over the top of each salad. Drizzle the champagne vinaigrette over the salads.

Casserole of Chicken with Market Vegetables and Morning Herbs

Serves: 4

Chicken:

1 each roasting chicken, 4 pounds

Kosher salt to taste
(may substitute fleur de sel)

Ground black pepper to taste

1/4 cup chopped fresh thyme

1/4 cup olive oil

Vegetables:

2 each yellow beets or red beets

2 each large carrots, peeled and
cut into 1-1/2-inch chunks

2 each large turnips, peeled and
cut into wedges

1 each celery root, peeled and cut
into 1-inch chunks

6 each shallots, peeled and
cut in half

6 each Yukon Gold potatoes, cut
in half *(about 2-1/2 to 3 pounds)*

1/4 cup olive oil

Salt and pepper to taste

Finish:

2 cups chicken stock

2/3 cup extra-virgin olive oil

1/2 cup chopped parsley

2 tablespoons chopped sage

For the Chicken:

- Preheat the oven to 350 degrees. Season the chicken with salt, pepper and the thyme. In a large roasting pan on the stovetop, heat the oil over medium heat. Place the chicken into the hot pan, breast down. Sear the chicken for approximately 5 to 7 minutes on each side until golden brown. Transfer the roasting pan with the chicken from the stovetop to the oven. Roast in the oven, breast side-up for approximately 15 minutes. Turn the chicken over and roast for another 15 minutes. Continue to turn the chicken over every 15 minutes until chicken has roasted for approximately 1 hour total. If the oven gets too hot during roasting, reduce temperature to 325 degrees.

For the Vegetables:

- While the chicken is roasting, cook the beets in boiling salt water until tender. Cool slightly, peel and cut into wedges. Blanch all of the remaining vegetables in boiling water for 5 to 7 minutes; shock the blanched vegetables in ice water. In a large casserole dish, mix 1/4 cup of olive oil with blanched vegetables. Season the vegetables with salt and pepper. Toss to coat with oil. Place vegetables in oven and roast for 15 to 20 minutes; remove vegetables from the oven.

To Finish and Serve:

- Remove chicken from the roasting pan and keep chicken warm. Add stock to the roasting pan and bring the stock to a boil on the stovetop over medium heat. Skim the fat from the stock. Add the beet wedges to the boiling stock and cook until the beets are hot. Mix the roasted vegetables with 2/3 cup of extra-virgin olive oil and the chopped herbs. Place the chicken on a serving platter. Surround with the vegetables and the beets.

Rib-Eye Steak with Roasted Shallots and Vinegar Sauce with Wild Mushrooms and Home Fries

Serves: 4

Home Fries:

4 ounces butter

2 each large potatoes, peeled and cut into pieces about 3 inches long and 1/2 inch wide

Wild Mushrooms:

5 each large shallots, peeled and cut into quarters

2 ounces butter

1 pound wild mushrooms, sliced thin

Steaks and Sauce:

3 tablespoons olive oil

4 each rib-eye steaks, 12 ounces each, seasoned with salt and pepper

6 ounces butter

5 each large shallots, peeled and cut into quarters

1 cup red wine vinegar
(may substitute sherry vinegar)

1 cup heavy cream

2 tablespoons chopped chives

For the Home Fries:

- Melt the butter in a large heavy sauté pan over medium heat. Cook the potato pieces in the butter until golden brown, approximately 10 to 15 minutes. The potatoes need to be turned often during cooking to ensure even cooking. Drain on towels. Keep warm until ready to assemble dish.

For the Wild Mushrooms:

- Cook the shallots in the butter until tender and translucent. Add the wild mushrooms and sauté until mushrooms are soft.

For the Steaks and the Sauce:

- Heat up a heavy sauté pan over high heat. Add the olive oil. Put the steaks into the hot pan and start searing over high heat. After 1 minute, turn down the heat to medium high. Add 2 ounces of the butter and stir in well. This will give the steaks a nice crust and flavor. Add the shallots and cook them with the steaks. Once the steaks reach medium-rare, take them out and keep warm. Continue cooking the shallots until translucent and caramelized. To make the sauce, add the vinegar to the pan and bring to a boil. Cook until reduced by half, and then add the cream and cook until reduced by half again. Finish the sauce by adding the remaining 4 ounces of butter. Stir until the butter is completely dissolved.

To Finish and Serve:

- Serve the steaks individually with home fries, sautéed wild mushrooms, and sauce.

Warm Wild Berries with Vanilla Ice Cream and Vanilla Bean Whipped Cream

Serves: 4 to 6

Vanilla Bean Whipped Cream:

1 cup cold heavy cream

1/2 **each** vanilla bean
(may substitute 2 teaspoons vanilla extract)

1 tablespoon powdered sugar

Warm Wild Berries:

1/2 cup honey

2 **tablespoons** white wine, preferably Chardonnay

1 cup fresh blueberries

1 cup elderberries
(May substitute with double the amount of blueberries)

1 cup strawberries

1 cup fresh blackberries

Finish:

High-quality vanilla ice cream, such as Hägen-Daz®
(2 scoops per person)

4 **each** mint sprigs

For the Vanilla Bean Whipped Cream:

• Put the cream into a mixing bowl. Slice the vanilla bean open and scrape the vanilla seeds out of the bean with a small kitchen knife and mix with the cream. Beat the cream until you have a soft peaks. After 30 seconds of beating, add the powdered sugar. Set in refrigerator to chill until ready to serve.

For the Warm Wild Berries:

• Heat the honey in a saucepan. Boil for 1 minute. Add the white wine and mix well. Boil for another minute. Add the blueberries and elderberries. Mix well to coat all, and boil for another minute. Add the strawberries, mix well to coat all berries, and boil for another minute. Add the blackberries, mix well to coat all berries, and boil for another minute. Remove from heat.

To Finish and Serve:

• Place two scoops of vanilla ice cream into each of four to six serving bowls. Pour the warm wild berries over the top of the ice cream scoops. Place a scoop of vanilla bean whipped cream on top of each bowl. Garnish with mint sprigs.

MICHAEL MINA
SAN FRANCISCO, CA

American Express Best Chef: California, 2002

Michael Mina is a man of many kitchens. His sprawling Marin County home has a showplace residential kitchen with granite counters and all the amenities.

In the back of the house, near the patio and pool area, is a commercial kitchen he uses when he and wife Diane, who whips up a potent Bloody Mary, entertain guests. There is another full-sized kitchen at his corporate office for recipe testing and photography. And, of course, his four restaurants, Aqua at the Bellagio and NOBHILL in Las Vegas, Arcadia in San Jose and his flagship Restaurant Michael Mina in San Francisco's historic Westin St. Francis Hotel all have state-of-the-art-kitchens. This is a chef who truly lives to cook.

Laughing, Diane says, "Last Thanksgiving was the first time in ages he wasn't working and he cooked three complete dinners, two for practice and then the real deal. I told him, 'Honey, enough!'"

That little example illustrates the drive and energy that have taken the 35-year-old chef to the top tier of the culinary world.

Though he was born in Egypt, Mina's family moved to Ellensburg, Washington when he was a toddler. The small farming town of 7,000 people is also home to Central Washington State University with a student population of 6,000 where Mina's father worked as controller.

He grew up eating a mixture of Middle-eastern and homegrown American food. "My dad was from Alexandria and liked seafood. My mom was from Cairo where they mostly eat meat. I really didn't like seafood as a kid because Mom cooked it to death. When I grew up and learned how it should be prepared, I fell in love."

In this agricultural wonderland Mina literally learned about food from the ground up. The father of one of Mina's best friends owned a dairy farm. Another buddy's family had a meat packing company, and by the age of 12 or 13 Mina was pitching in with the butchering, making sausage and jerky. Other friends' parents raised potatoes, apples and corn, and he worked part time as a farm hand.

"I was exposed to all these things. At the time it was just the usual, but I realize now how much I learned. When I enrolled at the CIA, we were in meat cutting class and it all came back to me. I could break down a leg of veal without even thinking," he recalls.

Fate gave him a further shove down the career path when a well-traveled, retired English teacher opened a little French restaurant in Ellensburg and, at the age of 15, Mina went to work for him making salads and doing odd jobs. The following year, the owner's health began to fail, and Mina took over more and more of the kitchen duties.

Says Mina, "Finally, he basically gave me the restaurant. I hired three of my best friends to help me and for my last two years of high school did a work-study program. It was great. I was the only kid in town making that kind of money. I had a hot car and a lot of fun."

More than just that, Mina discovered he loved what he was doing. "I was into it. I didn't know where it would take me, but I felt mentally challenged by the speed, pace and pressure. I thrived on it."

With his university background, Mina's father valued higher education and expected his son to as well. "One

night my friends and I were hanging out at the lake. They were all heading for college and excited about it. I just couldn't get into the conversation. The prospect of more school just didn't appeal to me." Mina says.

When he returned home that night, he snapped on the television. As luck would have it, Mina tuned into an episode of *Lifestyles of the Rich and Famous* featuring Jeremiah Tower, the chef/owner of San Francisco's hot Stars restaurant. For the conflicted teenager, it was truly a eureka moment.

"I'd always wanted to live in San Francisco; I had a poster of the city in my bedroom, and here was this chef having a great career there. A week later I told my dad that's what I wanted to do. He told me I was out of my mind."

The Mina family finally reached an agreement; Michael would spend a year at the University of Washington in Seattle and after that, well, father and son would renegotiate.

Arriving in Seattle, the reluctant collegiate promptly secured a job atop the city's landmark Space Needle. "I was so much more into that than school — and Dad could tell."

His stint in the revolving eatery turned the trick, says Mina.

Realizing his true calling, Mina began considering culinary schools and, unbeknownst to him, his father was evaluating them as well, flying to New York to check out the Culinary Institute of America. The senior Mina was impressed with what he saw and suggested Michael apply there.

Mina's experiences at the Institute were golden. On weekends he traveled to Manhattan to work at Charlie Palmer's esteemed Aureole restaurant. For his externship, he worked in the pastry shop of Beverly Hill's famed Hotel Bel Air under Chef George Morrone. After graduation he returned to Los Angeles and continued to work with Morrone.

In 1991, Morrone, Mina and businessman Charles Condy opened Aqua in San Francisco. Mina became executive chef in '93. In the ensuing years he has racked up every conceivable honor for himself and the restaurant, opened seven more restaurants, and all the while continued to hone his signature style of seafood.

"There is so much you can do with fish. Starting by using European techniques, I'm open to everything, but always keep a balance of acidity, sweetness, spice and fat in my recipes. And

the seafood is always the best and freshest."

Deciding to go in a different direction, Mina left Aqua San Francisco and immediately threw himself into developing his eponymous new showcase restaurant Michael Mina. "I've spent ten years developing in new ways and now I'll focus on those," explains Mina. "The restaurant has a high energy level and the food, service and décor are on a high level as well. There is a definite Mediterranean influence in the food, the greatest hits are still featured and there are tasting menus. We've worked through every detail. A woman in Italy handcrafted all our china."

In addition, he founded The Mina Group, which forms management partnerships with hotels and resorts. All this is possible because, "I learned from Charlie Palmer and George Morrone to grow the people around me, build them up and keep the team together. I've had the same core of employees for ten years."

Despite his commitment to raising the bar, family remains a huge part of Mina's life. He and Diane have two sons, Sammy and Anthony, who ensure their comfortable home is abuzz with activity. Says Diane, "It's only two years old but it already has some scars from living."

And in the middle of it all, in the kitchen in front of the stove, Michael Mina is doing what he does best.

Caviar Parfait

Serves: 4

Potato Cakes:

2 each small russet or other baking potatoes

1/4 cup assorted chopped herbs: chervil, chives, parsley and tarragon

1 each egg

1 tablespoon salt

1 tablespoon potato starch*

Peanut oil, for frying

Egg Salad:

7 each hard-boiled eggs

2 teaspoons chopped parsley

2 teaspoons minced red onion

Salt and pepper to taste

Whipped Crème Fraîche:

1-1/2 cups crème fraîche**

2 teaspoons chopped lemon zest

2 teaspoons chopped chives

Salt and pepper to taste

Dill Oil:

2 tablespoons salt

1/2 bunch dill, stems removed

1/2 cup canola oil

Finish:

Cooking oil spray *(such as Pam)*

7 ounces smoked salmon *(cold smoked)*, minced as needed

4 ounces osetra caviar *(may substitute other type of caviar if osetra is not available)*

For the Potato Cakes:

- Bake the potatoes in a 375 degree oven until tender but not soft, approximately 20 minutes. Let cool. Peel and grate the potatoes using a hand grater. Mix in the herbs, eggs, salt and potato starch. Mix well. Shape the mixture into 4 cakes in 3-inch diameter molds about 1/2-inch high. Cookie cutters or PVC pipe both work well for this purpose. If the cakes are not wet enough to stick together, add some additional beaten egg, although one egg should be sufficient. Chill in refrigerator for at least 1 hour. Do not fry the cakes until just before serving. At that time, heat oil in a deep fryer to 360 degrees. Deep fry the cakes until golden brown. Assemble the parfaits as instructed in the "To Finish and Serve" section below.

For the Egg Salad:

- Push the hard-boiled eggs through a mesh strainer. Do not use a mesh that is too fine. Add the parsley and red onion, then mix well and season to taste. Reserve 1/4 cup for garnish. Refrigerate egg salad until needed.

For the Whipped Crème Fraîche:

- Place all ingredients into a metal bowl and whip with an electric mixer until stiff. Refrigerate.

For the Dill Oil:

- Bring a small pot of water to a boil, then add the salt. Add the dill to the boiling water, stirring to immerse. Boil the dill for 45 seconds, strain and shock in an ice bath. This will help the dill retain a bright green color. Squeeze all of the water out of the dill and chop roughly. Place the dill in the blender along with the canola oil. Blend the dill and oil on high speed for 1-1/2 to 2 minutes, or until the oil turns a bright green color and the mixture is well blended.

To Finish and Serve:

- Use four 3-inch diameter ring molds that are 2-inches tall. Spray the molds lightly with the cooking spray. Starting with the egg mixture, measure 2 tablespoons *(loosely scooped)* into each mold. Using a small glass or a flat whisk handle, gently press the egg mixture down so that it flattens the eggs. Repeat the same process of flattening the ingredients as you add them. Add the salmon and then add the crème fraîche. Refrigerate for at least 1 hour. Preparation up to this point can be done the day before as long as the molds are covered tightly with plastic.

- When you are ready to serve, fry the potato cakes in 360 degree oil until golden brown. Hold in a warm oven if needed. Spread 1 ounce of caviar on top of each parfait, working gently. Sprinkle about 1 tablespoon of the reserved egg mixture on each plate. Place a potato cake in the center of the plate. Gently press the bottom of each parfait to "release" the seal and carefully shake the parfait out through the bottom of the mold onto the potato cake. Make sure to work close to the plate. Repeat for all servings. Garnish with the dill oil.

* Potato starch is available in the kosher section of most grocery stores.

** Crème fraîche is available in the specialty dairy section of most grocery stores.

Chilled Maine Lobster Salad with Spicy Avocado Purée and White Basil Vinaigrette

Serves: 4

Tomato Water:

20 each Roma tomatoes, coarsely chopped

Spicy Avocado Purée:

1 each avocado

1/4 cup tomato water *(from above)*

1/4 teaspoon rough chopped jalapeño, seeded

1 tablespoon lime juice

Salt and pepper to taste

Tomato Gelée:

5 each gelatin sheets
(may substitute 1-1/2 tablespoons powdered gelatin)

2 cups tomato water *(recipe above)*

White Basil Vinaigrette:

1 cup canola oil

1/3 cup champagne vinegar

1 bunch basil

Salt and pepper to taste

Lobster:

2 each 1-1/2 pound lobsters

Finish:

Micro celery or mixed baby greens

Salt and pepper to taste

Cherry tomatoes cut in half

Lime sections

Fresh basil, cut chiffonade

Bell peppers cut into 1/8-inch dice

For the Tomato Water:

- Using a food processor, purée the tomatoes. Line a strainer with two layers of wet cheesecloth and place the strainer over a bowl. Place the purée in the strainer and let it sit overnight in the refrigerator.

For the Spicy Avocado Purée:

- Peel and remove the pit from the avocado. Place the avocado and rest of ingredients in a blender and blend until smooth. Season to taste with salt and pepper.

For the Tomato Gelée:

- Combine the gelatin and 1/4 cup of cold water and let sit for 2 minutes or until soft. In a medium pot, bring the tomato water to a boil. Scoop the dissolved gelatin from the water that it softened in and whisk it into the tomato water. Remove from the heat and pour the mixture into a flat pan to a depth of 1/4-inch. Let chill in refrigerator until fully set. This can be done one day in advance. Once the gelée is fully set, cut it into 1/4-inch cubes. Keep refrigerated until ready to assemble dish.

For the White Basil Vinaigrette:

- Combine all ingredients in a small non-reactive saucepot and heat gently over low heat. Steep over low heat for about 5 to 7 minutes, until the mixture takes on the basil flavor. Strain the mixture through a fine-mesh strainer. Season to taste with salt and pepper and chill.

For the Lobster:

- Grasp the head of one lobster with one hand and the tail with the other hand. Twisting firmly in different directions remove the head from the tail. Twist both arms from the lobster. Repeat with second lobster. Bring 2 gallons of water to a boil in a large stockpot. Cook the tails first by placing them in the boiling water and cooking for 5 minutes. Remove the tails from the water and immediately place in a large bowl of ice. Repeat the same process with the claws, cooking them for 6 minutes. Chill well. Carefully hold the tail down on a cutting board. Using a sharp knife, cut straight down the back of the tail and gently remove the meat from the shell. Remove any veins that remain. Repeat with second lobster tail. To clean the claws, hold a claw flat on a cutting board. Using the back of a large knife, gently tap the shell in the middle section until it cracks. Carefully remove the meat so that it doesn't tear. Repeat with remaining claws.

To Finish and Serve:

- Place a 4-inch circle of the avocado purée in the center of each of four chilled dinner plates. In a mixing bowl, pour in the vinaigrette and toss the micro celery or baby greens in it. Season to taste with salt and pepper then remove the greens and set aside. Place the lobster meat in the vinaigrette and mix it enough to coat, then season to taste. Place one half of one lobster tail meat on the plate on top of the avocado purée. Place the greens on top of the lobster tail, then place the lobster claw meat from one claw on top of that. Garnish the plates with remaining garnishes and the diced tomato gelée. Sprinkle the plates with vinaigrette and serve immediately.

Poached Crown of Shrimp with Oregon Morel Mushroom Ragout, Green Asparagus Coulis and Madeira Mushroom Cream

Serves: 4

Shrimp:

24 each shrimp
(approximately 15-16 per pound)
1 bunch chives

Sauce:

1 tablespoon olive oil
5 each shallots, sliced
1/2 pound morel mushrooms
1/2 cup Madeira
1 cup chicken stock or broth
1 cup heavy cream
Salt and pepper to taste

Purée:

12 each green asparagus spears,
with tough ends cut off
1 cup chicken stock or broth
Salt and pepper to taste

Ragout:

12 each white asparagus spears,
with tough ends cut off
1/2 pound morel mushrooms
2 tablespoons butter
1 bunch thyme, chopped

Finish:

1 tablespoon butter
1/2 cup white wine
Salt and pepper to taste

For the Shrimp:

- Peel and devein the shrimp, reserving the shells for the sauce. Blanch the chives in salted boiling water for 1 minute, then cool immediately. Lay 3 to 4 chives across a cutting board horizontally *(keep the chives close together as they will be used as string to tie the shrimp)*. Working with 6 shrimp at a time, place the tails 1/2-inch above the chives *(the shrimp should be vertical to the chive string)*. Gently bring the two ends of the chives together and very carefully tie a knot. Stand the shrimp up *(tails pointing up)* and adjust the shrimp into a crown formation. Repeat with remaining shrimp.

For the Sauce:

- In a large saucepan, sear the reserved shrimp shells in olive oil. Add sliced shallots and morel mushrooms. Sauté for 12 to 15 minutes over medium heat or until the moisture created by the mushrooms is gone. Add the Madeira and cook until liquid is reduced by 80 percent. Add the chicken stock and cook until the total amount of liquid is reduced by 1/2. Finally, add the cream and simmer for 10 minutes. Season to taste with salt and pepper then strain the sauce through a fine-mesh strainer. Reserve.

For the Purée:

- In salted boiling water, blanch green asparagus until tender. Cool immediately in ice water. Once asparagus is cooled, cut into 1-inch pieces. Place the chicken stock in a blender. Add the asparagus and blend until mixture is smooth, yet relatively thick. Season to taste with salt and pepper.

For the Ragout:

- In salted boiling water, blanch the white asparagus until tender, then cool immediately in ice water. Rinse the mushrooms and cut into bite-size pieces. Sauté the mushrooms in butter for about 5 to 7 minutes. Cut the cooled asparagus in 1-inch pieces. Toss the mushrooms and asparagus together in a mixing bowl, along with freshly chopped thyme.

To Finish and Serve:

- Preheat oven to 450 degrees. In a large sauté pan with an oven-proof handle, combine butter and white wine. Season the deveined shrimp crowns with salt and pepper and place in pan. Cover, place in preheated oven, and bake for approximately 10 minutes. While the shrimp is baking, heat the ragout and the purée in separate pans over medium-low heat. On each of four dinner plates, form a circle with the purée, smoothing it with the back of a spoon. Place the ragout on top of the purée. Remove the baked shrimp from the pan, reserving the remaining liquid from the pan and pouring it in a separate saucepan on the stove. Place one crown of shrimp directly on top of the purée on each plate. Add the morel sauce to the saucepan with the reserved shrimp liquid and bring to a boil. The sauce will thicken as you continue to boil; cook sauce until desired consistency is reached. Spoon sauce over each shrimp crown and serve immediately.

Potato-Crusted Snapper with Lobster-Stuffed Potatoes, Lemon Beurre Blanc and Osetra Caviar

Serves: 4

Potato-Crusted Snapper:

6 each russet baking potatoes, peeled

2 pounds butter

1/4 cup potato starch *(available in kosher section of the grocery store)*

4 1-1/4 pound Thai snapper *(or regular snapper)* fillets

Lemon Beurre Blanc:

4 each shallots, sliced

1 pound cold butter

1 cup white wine

1/2 cup lemon juice

2 tablespoons lemon zest

1 teaspoon black peppercorns

1 each thyme sprig

1/4 cup heavy cream

Salt to taste

Additional Items:

Lobster-Stuffed Potatoes:
Recipe on page 248

Mirepoix:
Recipe on page 248

Finish:

2 tablespoons minced chives

1 tablespoon osetera caviar

4 each baby leeks, blanched and scored 1/2-inch from the top

5 ounces mascarpone cheese, whipped until stiff

For the Potato-Crusted Snapper:

- Using a 1-inch ring mold or cookie/biscuit cutter, cut "logs" out of the raw potatoes. Cook the potato "logs" in a pot of salted water on low heat *(do not boil)* until they become translucent all the way through when sliced. This will take about 5 to 8 minutes. Strain and cool completely. Once cooled, slice the logs into 1/8-inch-thick rounds. In a saucepan, melt the butter on low heat to make clarified butter. Let the butter bubble gently for a few minutes. Skim the fat solids off the top. Pour the remaining clear liquid off, leaving the milky liquid in the bottom of the pan. The clear liquid is clarified butter. In a large bowl, mix 2 cups of the melted clarified butter and the potato starch. Set aside the remaining clarified butter for the fish. Gently add in the sliced potatoes, stirring to coat. Do this in a timely manner before the butter has time to solidify.

- Lay each snapper fillet out on a lined baking sheet, placing the two sides of the skin-side of the fish up, leaving no gap between the two fillets. Starting at the tail, start shingling the potato disks along the fish to resemble fish scales. When complete, place the fish in the refrigerator for at least 1 hour.

For the Lemon Beurre Blanc:

- Sweat the shallots in 2 tablespoons butter over low heat until translucent, about 2 minutes. Add the wine, lemon juice, lemon zest, peppercorns and thyme. Simmer until the pan is almost dry. Stir in the cream and simmer for 1 minute. Remove pan from heat and slowly whisk in the remaining cold butter in small increments. Strain through a fine-mesh strainer and keep warm.

To Cook the Fish:

- Fill a large sauté pan over medium-high heat with 1/4-inch of clarified butter and heat until a test piece of potato sizzles. Carefully remove one fish fillet at a time from the baking sheet, season both sides with salt and pepper and gently place fish, potato-side down, in the pan. Try not to move the fish too much until the potato crust starts to turn a golden brown, adding more clarified butter as needed. The fish should be 80-90 percent cooked through once the crust turns golden brown. Carefully flip the fish to finish cooking. Remove from the pan and place on a warm plate.

To Finish and Serve:

- In a medium saucepan on low heat, carefully heat the buerre blanc with the mirepoix and chives until warm. Do not boil. Reheat the stuffed potatoes in a 350 degree oven until heated through, about 3 to 5 minutes. Just before plating the fish fillets, stir 1/2 tablespoon of caviar into the buerre blanc. Spoon about 2 tablespoons of sauce into the center of the plate and spread into a large circle. The circle should be large enough to see the sauce when the fish is placed on top. Place three halves of stuffed potatoes around the fish. Heat the baby leeks in salted water or a little stock and butter, and fan one out on top of each fish. Place a dollop of mascarpone cheese on top of the leek and garnish with a scoop of caviar.

Root Beer Float with Sassafras Ice Cream

Serves: 8

Root Beer Sorbet:

2 cups simple syrup
  *(2 parts sugar plus 1-1/2 parts
  water, bring to a boil and let cool)*

2 cups root beer syrup*

3 cups water

1 cup sugar

Lemon juice to taste

Sassafras Ice Cream:

4 cups heavy cream

2 cups milk

2 each vanilla beans

15 each egg yolks

1 cup sugar

1 tablespoon sassafras, filé or
  powdered root

Finish:

2 liters root beer

For the Root Beer Sorbet:

- Mix all ingredients together. Freeze in an ice cream machine according to manufacturer's instructions.

For the Sassafras Ice Cream:

- In a large pot, combine the cream, milk and vanilla beans over medium heat and bring to a boil. Place the egg yolks in a large mixing bowl and whisk in sugar until it is smooth. Pour a little cream mixture into yolks and whisk, then pour the egg mixture back into cream mixture, whisking constantly. Continue to whisk until yolks are completely combined. Strain and cool. Add the sassafras powder to the mixture and freeze in an ice cream machine according to manufacturer's instructions.

To Finish and Serve:

- In each of eight tall glasses, alternate scoops of root beer sorbet and sassafras ice cream. Pour root beer soda over them. Serve immediately!

*Available at home brewing supply stores

Chocolate Chip Cookies

Makes 2 to 3 dozen

Cookies:

1 pound butter, softened

1-1/2 cups sugar

1-3/4 cups brown sugar

4 each eggs

1-1/2 tablespoons vanilla extract

4 cups flour

1-1/2 teaspoons baking soda

1-1/2 teaspoons salt

1 pound walnuts, chopped

2 pounds chocolate chips

For the Cookies:

- Preheated oven to 325 degrees. Using a hand mixer or stand mixer, cream together the butter, sugar and brown sugar until smooth. Add the eggs one at a time and mix on low speed until incorporated. While still mixing, add the vanilla extract. Mix the flour, baking soda, and salt together in a bowl. Slowly add the dry ingredients to the creamed butter and sugar in 3 to 4 separate additions. Turn mixer off. With a spoon or spatula, stir in chopped walnuts and chocolate chips.

- Using a small ice cream scoop or a 2 tablespoon-size scoop, scoop out portions of the dough and place well-spread onto a baking sheet. Bake for 12 to 15 minutes or until golden brown around the edges and slightly cooked in the middle.

To Finish and Serve:

- Take out of the oven and cool on the sheet pan for 2 minutes. Remove from the sheet pan and finish cooling cookies on a cooling rack.

Michael Mina's Beverage Recommendations

Caviar Parfait
Light Champagne
page 239

Chilled Maine Lobster Salad
with Spicy Avocado Purée and
White Basil Vinaigrette
Austrian Gruner Veltliner
page 241

Poached Crown of Shrimp with
Oregon Morel Mushroom Ragout,
Green Asparagus Coulis and
Madeira Mushroom Cream
White Burgundy
page 243

Potato-Crusted Snapper with
Lobster-Stuffed Potatoes,
Lemon Beurre Blanc and
Osetra Caviar
German Riesling
page 245

Lobster-Stuffed Potatoes

For the Potato-Crusted Snapper with Lobster-Stuffed Potatoes, Lemon Beurre Blanc and

Osetra Caviar recipe. Page 245

Lobster-Stuffed Potatoes:

2 pounds russet potatoes
 (can use scraps from cutting logs)

1 cup heavy cream

2 tablespoons butter

1/2 tablespoon chopped tarragon

Salt and pepper to taste

1 cup chopped lobster meat

10 each small red potatoes,
 approximately 2-inches in
 diameter

Oil to coat

1 pound rock salt

1/4 bunch thyme

For the Lobster-Stuffed Potatoes:

• Boil the potatoes until cooked through. Put potatoes through a ricer or food mill. Once the potatoes are riced, add the cream, butter and tarragon and season with salt and pepper to taste. Chill well, then add the chopped lobster meat. Place mixture into a pastry bag. Set aside.

• Preheat oven to 350 degrees. Toss the red potatoes with oil to coat. Spread the rock salt out onto a baking sheet and spread the thyme evenly on top. Next, place the potatoes on the baking sheet and bake for 10 minutes, or until just cooked through. Allow to cool until you can easily handle them. Using a sharp paring knife, cut the red potatoes in half. Cut a small slice from the bottom so that each half will stand up straight.

• Using a melon baller, scoop out the insides of the red potatoes to form small cups. Pipe or spoon in the lobster-mashed potatoes to fill each potato cup. Keep warm until ready to plate.

Mirepoix

For the Potato-Crusted Snapper with Lobster-Stuffed Potatoes, Lemon Beurre Blanc and

Osetra Caviar recipe. Page 245

Mirepoix:

2 tablespoons equal parts carrots, leeks and celery, cut into 1/8-inch dice

For the Mirepoix:

• Blanch the carrots, leeks and celery for 45 seconds in boiling salt water then plunge in ice water to halt the cooking process.

SUSAN SPICER

NEW ORLEANS, LA

American Express Best Chef: Southeast, 1993

Compared to many chefs who seem to have been born with spatulas in hand, New Orleans-based chef Susan Spicer took the long route to the kitchen.

Though briefly considering culinary school after graduating from high school, she didn't go to work in a professional capacity until almost ten years later. When she did, however, her rise to national culinary prominence was meteoric.

A navy brat, Spicer's family settled in New Orleans when she was five. Her Danish mother was, and is, an enthusiastic cook whose repertoire includes everything from pastry and cookies to bami goreng and other Indonesian dishes she learned while the clan was stationed in Holland.

The Spicers entertained frequently and because Susan was the youngest girl among the seven Spicer siblings, she was recruited to do a lot of the prep work for dinner parties.

Her dad put the kibosh on plans to enroll at the Culinary Institute of America. "He said, 'you must be insane; it's way too hard a life,'" Spicer recalls.

Instead, she entered the University of New Orleans where she lasted a year. "I had wanderlust," confesses Spicer. "Once I left school I traveled around the country, lived for a while in California and went to Europe."

The global gadabout worked in a succession of jobs that included secretary, cocktail waitress, record store clerk and, finally, graphic designer. As for the food angle, Spicer says, "Sure, I always liked to eat, but not in a conscious way as if I were storing up the experience to use later."

All that changed in 1973. That was the year her dad had a stroke and Spicer settled back in New

Orleans. "My then-boyfriend and I met another couple. She was a great cook and we'd hang around and just cook for fun," she says. Pamela Westbrook-Calhoun, the "great cook," decided she wanted to pursue food professionally and, after apprenticing with a local chef and studying at La Varenne cooking school in Paris, started a catering business and taught cooking classes.

Using her graphics skills, Spicer typeset Westbrook-Calhoun's ads and in exchange took classes from her. Says Spicer, "The classes were very technique-oriented rather than product or

The good news is we'll be closed, so you have the Fourth off. The bad news is you don't need to come back to work after that."

Although being fired stung, it might have been the best thing that could have happened to Spicer.

Daniel Bonnot, chef at New Orleans' renowned Louis XVI restaurant in the Marie Antoinette Hotel then hired Westbrook-Calhoun. She, in turn, reintroduced him to Spicer, who had known Bonnot when she worked at the hotel years

recipe-oriented." In short it was the perfect launch pad for a chef-to-be.

In 1979, Westbrook-Calhoun was hired at a downtown New Orleans restaurant and persuaded Spicer to join her in the kitchen. Looking back, Spicer says, "Up to that point, working in a restaurant had never occurred to me. I liked the graphic arts but wasn't terribly creative at it and I wanted to do something where I *could* be creative. Cooking was just that, hard work but fun and interesting."

Three months later, just before the Fourth of July, the boss told the pair, "I have good news and bad news.

before as a cocktail waitress. "We used to flirt a little," she admits, smiling. "I started asking Daniel questions and looking at his culinary books. He paid attention to my interest and became a mentor to me."

Fast-forward three years. The owner of Marie Antoinette bought another hotel and, deciding to open a bistro-type restaurant there, tapped Spicer for the job. She says, "I'd only been cooking three years but I was a good employee, had the initiative to do things like clean the walk-in. I guess I have the workaholic gene."

The spring before the bistro, Savoir Faire, was to open, Spicer went to Paris for a ten-day promotional event at the Hotel Sofitel. "I was so excited by the food I saw that I worked up the nerve to ask if I could come back and work. They told me summer was slow and to wait until September."

But Savoir Faire was slated to open in September, so when Spicer got back to New Orleans she decided to go for broke. "I returned to Paris in May, just showed up at the Sofitel. It was the ballsiest thing I'd ever done."

It also proved a pivotal experience for Spicer, helping prepare her for the venture ahead. Back at Savoir Faire she had to hire people and tell them what to do — a daunting task for the fledgling chef, she notes, since most of them had resumés much longer than hers. Bonnot and Spicer co-wrote the menu for Savoir Faire and she executed the dishes. That's when she came up with her signature cream of garlic soup recipe. "In those days you couldn't buy peeled garlic, so the dishwashers had to do it. They'd look at me with this baleful expression, like 'I can't believe you're making me do this,'"Spicer recalls.

Savoir Faire was an authentic French-style bistro featuring classic dishes and initially was very successful, but things started to change. It was the heyday of Paul Prudhomme and blackened this 'n' that, and hotel ownership pressed Spicer to go in the same direction. She felt differently, "I had certain standards and my instincts were good. I knew what I wanted to produce and the Cajun thing wasn't for me."

On the loose again, Spicer took advantage of the time to return to California and France. Back in New Orleans she worked briefly at the Meridien and then opened the Bistro at Maison de Ville in the French Quarter. Here, she continued polishing her culinary style, which has its roots in her French training but borrows lightly from Asia, the Mediterranean and Creole tradition. She rarely mixes influences in a single dish, preferring to keep things pure. "I'm not very good at articulating what my food is about," she says. "I appreciate foods from around the world and cook what I like to eat."

A lot of other people like to eat it, too. The year before she left the Bistro to open her own restaurant, Bayona (named for the original Spanish moniker of Dauphine Street where the restaurant is located), *Food & Wine* magazine named Spicer one of the best new chefs.

Bayona, which opened in 1990, is a picturesque Creole cottage with a secluded brick courtyard in back. The one-of-a-kind environment, combined with Spicer's compelling menu and a *Wine Spectator* award-winning cellar has made the restaurant an international destination.

Not one to rest on her laurels, in 2000, Spicer went back to her bistro roots and with three partners opened Herbsaint in New Orleans' business district. The following year, she debuted Cobalt, which specializes in regional American food. With both restaurants up and running, she spends most of her time at Bayona.

Spicer downplays her personal life, which includes a boyfriend and two cats. She shrugs, "I'm a creature of habit. I get up in the morning and I come to work."

Nevertheless, this habitual creature has some interesting things lined up to break the monotony. Her future slate includes a succession of culinary events in which she'll participate, a lot of travel and writing a cookbook in which she'll spill her culinary secrets.

Crayfish Pie

Serves: 8

Cornmeal Pie Dough:

3 cups all-purpose flour

3/4 cup cornmeal

1 tablespoon sugar

1-1/4 teaspoons salt

9 ounces butter,
  cut into small pieces

1/2 cup sour cream

1/4 cup ice-cold water
  (or more as needed to work dough)

Crayfish Filling:

1/2 each onion, finely diced

1/2 stalk celery, finely diced

1/2 bulb fennel, finely diced

7 tablespoons whole butter

1 teaspoon minced garlic

2 tablespoons flour

1/4 cup shrimp stock
  (may substitute clam juice)

1-1/4 cups heavy cream

Zest of 2 lemons

Juice of 1 lemon

1 pound crayfish tails

2 each scallions, finely sliced

1 tablespoon chopped parsley

Salt, pepper, Tabasco and
  Worcestershire Sauce to taste

Finish:

Crispy fried bacon bits as desired
  (optional)

Finely diced jalapeño peppers as
  desired *(optional)*

Sliced scallions as desired
  (optional)

For the Cornmeal Pie Dough:

- Mix dry ingredients together in the bowl of a food processor. Pulse to combine. Add the butter pieces one at a time to the dry mix, pulsing quickly to mix. Transfer the mixture to a large bowl. By hand, work in the sour cream and ice water, small amounts at a time. The dough should be soft and pliable, but not sticky. Adjust with flour to desired consistency. Divide the dough into eight equal parts. Chill for at least 1 hour.

- Preheat oven to 350 degrees. After dough is chilled, roll each piece of dough out very thinly. Blind bake* the pie crusts in eight 4-ounce tart pans or gratin dishes. Bake for 10 to 12 minutes. Remove the beans and foil from the tart pans; bake 1 to 2 minutes longer to finish. Dough should no longer be translucent. Do not get too much color on them now because they will be baked again.

For the Crayfish Filling:

- Sauté the onion, celery and fennel in 3 tablespoons of the butter. Add garlic; cook 5 minutes. Sprinkle with flour just to coat lightly. Stir to combine. Add the stock, cream, lemon zest and juice. Cook approximately 10 minutes to reduce the cream a bit. In a separate pan, sauté the crayfish tails in the remaining 4 tablespoons of butter. Add the scallions and parsley. Add the crayfish to the cream mixture. Adjust the seasonings with salt, pepper and Tabasco. Add 1 tablespoon of Worcestershire Sauce if desired. Fill each pre-baked cornmeal pie shell with 1/2 cup of filling. Bake the pies for 10 to 15 minutes, until hot and bubbly.

To Finish and Serve:

- Garnish with crispy bacon bits, diced jalapeño and/or sliced scallions, if desired.

* To blind bake, line the dough in each pan with foil and put dry beans or coffee beans on top of the foil, so that there is weight to hold up the sides of the tart during the baking process.

Chef on the Spot

What is your favorite comfort food?

"Ice cream."

Do you have a guilty food pleasure?

"LOTS of ice cream."

Is there a food you don't
like and why?

"Kidneys, they taste like pee."

What is always in your
home refrigerator?

"Mustard, lime pickles, barbecue
sauce, condiments of every kind
and spring water. The water in
New Orleans is awful."

Do you cook at home? What kind
of dishes do you prepare?

"Simple things — steak and
salad, or pasta."

Where and when was your
most memorable meal?

"It was outdoors in
Turkey. There was roast
lamb, eggplant, delicious
tomatoes and olives.
Also, my first dinner at
Lutèce with braised
Belgian endive, Dover
sole meunière, perfect
haricots verts with
shallots and gratin
dauphinois — the
quintessential
French meal."

Bayona Fried Oyster and Spinach Salad with Rosemary-Dijon Dressing

Serves: 4

Rosemary-Dijon Dressing:

2 **tablespoons** finely chopped shallots

1/4 **cup** red wine vinegar

1 **tablespoon** Dijon mustard

1 **tablespoon** lemon juice

1 **cup** olive oil

1 **tablespoon** lightly chopped fresh rosemary
(or 1 teaspoon dry)

Salt, pepper and Tabasco sauce to taste

Oyster and Spinach Salad:

1 **pint** oysters, shucked *(about 24)*

2 **cups** bread crumbs

4 **tablespoons** mixed dried herbs
(parsley, sage, rosemary and thyme)

1 **cup** egg whites, beaten until light and foamy

Olive oil for cooking

Finish:

6 **cups** spinach, washed

6 **each** button mushrooms, medium-size

1/2 **bunch** scallions, sliced

For the Rosemary-Dijon Dressing:

- Place the shallots, red wine vinegar, Dijon mustard and lemon juice in a small bowl. Whisk together, then slowly whisk in oil until dressing is creamy in consistency. Stir in rosemary and season with salt, pepper and Tabasco. Add more oil if flavor is too sharp.

For the Oyster and Spinach Salad:

- Drain the oysters and dry thoroughly on paper towels. In a bowl, combine the bread crumbs and mixed dried herbs. Dip the oysters first in the egg whites and then in the herbed bread crumbs to ensure an even coating. Lay the oysters on a tray in one layer and set aside or refrigerate *(uncovered)* until ready to cook.

- Heat the oil in a large, heavy sauté pan over medium-high heat. Sauté the oysters until golden brown *(should take 1 to 2 minutes on each side)*

To Finish and Serve:

Divide the spinach between each of four salad plates. Slice the mushrooms and arrange the slices around the spinach. Divide the oysters evenly among the four plates. Drizzle with the dressing and sprinkle with scallions. Serve immediately.

Crispy-Skin Snapper with Asparagus Cream and Crabmeat Rice

Serves: 4

Asparagus Cream:

1/2 pound asparagus

1 tablespoon butter

1/4 cup chopped shallots

1 cup heavy cream

1 cup fresh chopped
  spinach leaves

Salt and pepper to taste

Crabmeat Rice:

2 tablespoons butter

1/4 cup finely chopped onion

1/4 cup finely chopped celery

1 cup raw rice *(Spicer uses Ellis
  Stansel Louisiana-grown rice)*

1 teaspoon salt

1 cup diced button or
  shiitake mushrooms

1/4 cup 1/4-inch diced butternut
  squash or carrots, blanched in
  boiling water until crisp tender

1/2 cup lump crabmeat

1 tablespoon finely minced
  tarragon

1/4 cup finely chopped scallion or
  chives

Crispy-Skin Snapper:

4 each red snapper fillets,
  6 ounces each, skin on and
  scales off

Salt and pepper to taste

2 tablespoons olive oil

For the Asparagus Cream:

- Trim asparagus tips about 3 inches long. Blanch in boiling water and then immediately shock the tips in ice water and set aside. Cut the remaining asparagus stalks into 1/4-inch rounds until you reach the tough, woody part of the stem. You should have about 1 to 1-1/2 cups. In a 1-quart pot, melt the butter, then add the shallots and asparagus stems and sweat over medium heat for about 3 minutes. Add cream and bring to a boil. Reduce heat and simmer for about 10 to 15 minutes, until asparagus pieces are tender and liquid is reduced by about half. Add the spinach and cook about 2 more minutes.

- Remove from heat and let cool. Drain, reserving both the solids and the liquid. Place the asparagus and one-half of the liquid in a blender and blend. Then add the remaining half of the reserved liquid to the asparagus mixture while the blender is running. Strain the mixture through a fine strainer, pushing down with a ladle to extract all the cream. You should have about 1/2 cup of sauce. Season to taste with salt and pepper.

For the Crabmeat Rice:

- Melt 1 tablespoon of butter in a small pot and sweat the onion and celery over medium-low heat for about 3 to 5 minutes. Add the rice and stir. Cook rice, stirring for about 3 more minutes, then add 1-1/2 cups of water and salt and bring to a boil. Reduce heat and cover the pot. Simmer gently for 16 minutes, until rice is cooked. Remove from heat and let the rice sit, covered, for about 5 minutes. Remove rice from pot and let cool.

- Melt the remaining tablespoon of butter in a sauté pan over medium-high heat and sauté the mushrooms until golden brown. Then add the diced squash or carrot and cook for 2 minutes. Add the crabmeat and then the cooked rice, and stir gently over medium heat until warmed through. Stir in tarragon and scallions or chives, and taste for seasoning. Keep warm while the fish is cooking.

For the Crispy-Skin Snapper:

- Season the fish on the meat side with salt and pepper. In a non-stick sauté pan, heat the oil until very hot, then add the fish fillets, skin-side down, to the hot pan. You may wish to press the fish with a plate to keep the skin in contact with the pan. Cook over medium-high heat until the skin is golden brown and crispy and the fish is cooked about 1/2 to 3/4 through. Check at least once to make sure the skin is not burning and adjust heat if needed. Finish cooking on the meat side *(do not overcook)*. Turn off the heat when fish is just barely cooked through.

To Finish and Serve:

- Place a drizzle of warm asparagus cream on each of four serving plates. Spoon or mold a portion of crabmeat rice onto each plate. Warm the asparagus tips and arrange on the plates as well. Then add the crispy-skin snapper fillets, skin-side up, and serve immediately.

Grilled Skirt Steak with Thai Salad and Chile-Lime Sauce

Serves: 4

Grilled Skirt Steak:

2 tablespoons sweet soy sauce*
(*Indonesian style*)

2 tablespoons grated or minced
lemon grass

2 tablespoons minced garlic

1 tablespoon chile paste *(sambal
oelek)*, or fresh, finely minced
Thai chiles

2 tablespoons vegetable oil

1 teaspoon sesame oil

1 pound skirt steak, good-quality
(*like Niman Ranch*)

Thai Salad:

1 teaspoon soy sauce

1 teaspoon fish sauce*

1 tablespoon minced shallot

1 teaspoon minced ginger

Juice of one lime

2 tablespoons vegetable oil

1 teaspoon sesame oil

1 each cucumber, seeded and cut
into julienne

1 each carrot, peeled and cut
into julienne

1/2 cup scallions, split lengthwise and cut into julienne

1/2 cup fresh basil, mint and
cilantro, torn into small pieces

1 cup rice noodles

Oil for frying

Chile-Lime Sauce:

1 cup bottled sweet chile sauce*

Juice of one lime

1 teaspoon fish sauce*

1 teaspoon sweet soy sauce*

A little sugar, if necessary to
balance flavors

Finish:

1 each avocado, sliced

For Grilled Skirt Steak:

- Whisk together all ingredients except the steak. Add the steak and turn to coat with marinade. Set aside for at least 15 minutes.

- Preheat grill or broiler. Remove meat from marinade. Grill or broil the meat to desired temperature *(rare or medium-rare is best for tenderness)*, approximately 3 minutes on each side. Let the meat rest for about 5 minutes.

For Thai Salad:

- Whisk together first 7 ingredients in a small bowl. In a second bowl, mix together the remaining ingredients, except the rice noodles. Set aside until ready to assemble and serve. Fry the rice noodles in 375 degree oil until crispy, about 15 seconds. Set all aside until ready to assemble and serve.

For Chile-Lime Sauce:

- Whisk together all ingredients in a small bowl.

To Finish and Serve:

- Slice the meat on an angle, and arrange on individual serving plates or a large platter, alternating with slices of ripe avocado. Toss the Thai salad with the rice noodles. Place the salad and noodles in a high, tight pile on top of beef. Serve immediately with chile-lime sauce on the side.

* Available at Asian specialty markets

Chef's Tip

When sautéing, home cooks rarely get the pan hot enough and have trouble sufficiently browning the meat or fish they are cooking. You have to be patient and wait until the oil in the pan is almost smoking before you add the meat or fish. Also, be sure to pat the meat or fish dry before adding to the pan.

If you prefer using butter rather than oil to sauté, make sure the butter is clarified.

Pecan-Crusted Rabbit with Tasso Cream Sauce and Smothered Greens

Serves: 4

Tasso Cream Sauce:

4 tablespoons vegetable oil

1 each yellow onion, medium dice

1 each carrot, medium dice

1 each celery stalk, medium dice

1-1/2 cups white wine

1/2 cup Crystal hot sauce

1 tablespoon Worcestershire sauce

1 tablespoon thyme

2 quarts game stock
(may substitute chicken stock)

1 quart heavy cream

1/4 cup Creole mustard

Juice of 2 lemons

Salt and pepper to taste

1/2 cup finely diced tasso ham*
(may substitute any spicy ham)

1/2 each yellow onion, small dice

Smothered Greens:

3 tablespoons smoked bacon fat

1 each medium onion, chopped

2 tablespoons minced garlic

2 cups chicken stock

3 to 4 pounds greens, such as
mustard, turnip or collard,
stemmed, washed and chopped
*(a mixture of all three is best, or you
can add red chard, beet tops, kale or
other hearty greens)*

1/4 cup cider vinegar

Salt, pepper and
hot sauce to taste

Pecan-Crusted Rabbit:

2 each rabbits, whole and fully
deboned *(your butcher will do this)*

1 cup pecans, pulsed in a food
processor until finely chopped

1 cup flour

2 tablespoons thyme

1 tablespoon paprika

Salt and pepper to taste

4 each egg whites,
whipped until foamy

1/4 cup clarified butter or
vegetable oil for sautéing

For the Tasso Cream Sauce:

- Heat 2 tablespoons of the vegetable oil in a heavy sauté pan over medium-high heat. Add the onion, carrot and celery and cook until caramelized, making sure to cook until deep brown in color. Deglaze the pan with the wine, Crystal hot sauce and Worcestershire. Add the fresh thyme. Continue cooking until reduced by two-thirds. Add the game stock. Continue to cook the mixture until its total volume is reduced by three-fourths. Strain.

- In a separate pot, simmer the cream until reduced by one-half. Add the reduced cream to the game stock mixture. Continue cooking until reduced to nappe *(mixture evenly coats the back of a spoon)*. Finish the sauce by whisking in the Creole mustard, lemon juice, salt and pepper to taste. Sauté the diced tasso ham and onion in the remaining vegetable oil until translucent. Add to cream sauce. Adjust seasonings to taste.

For the Smothered Greens:

- Melt bacon fat in a wide, heavy-bottomed pan. Sauté onions for about 5 minutes, without allowing them to brown. Add garlic and cook 2 more minutes. Add the chicken stock, stir in the greens and cook over medium-high heat until wilted, about 5 minutes. Cover pan and cook for approximately 10 minutes, then remove cover and turn heat up to evaporate some of the liquid in the pot. Taste for bitterness. If still bitter, reduce heat and cook a little longer. When greens taste good, sprinkle in vinegar and season to taste with salt, pepper and hot sauce. Keep warm until ready to serve.

For the Pecan-Crusted Rabbit:

- Once the rabbits are deboned, the bones may be used to make a game stock. Trim the tenderloins and remove the silver skin and set aside. The legs should be pounded out to an even thickness for cooking.

- Combine the chopped pecans, flour, thyme and paprika. Season the pounded legs with salt and pepper. Dredge in the frothy egg whites and then dredge them in the pecan-flour mix. Season the rabbit tenderloins with salt and pepper. Dust them with a bit of flour. Heat clarified butter or oil in sauté pan over medium-high heat. Cooking in 2 batches, sauté both the legs and the tenderloins until golden brown, about 3 minutes on each side.

To Finish and Serve:

- Arrange the pecan-crusted rabbit pieces on a serving platter, surrounded with the smothered greens. Serve with tasso cream sauce.

* Available in the deli section of some specialty food stores

Danish Rice Pudding with Strawberry Sauce

Serves: 12

Danish Rice Pudding:

1 quart milk

3/4 cup rice *(raw white or basmati)*

1/2 cup sugar

1/2 teaspoon almond extract

1/2 cup sliced and toasted
almonds

6 tablespoons sherry

2 cups heavy cream

Strawberry Sauce:

4 ounces dried strawberries

1/2 cup Pinot Noir

1 tablespoon sugar or currant jelly

For the Danish Rice Pudding:

• Scald milk in a heavy saucepan. Add the rice and bring
to a simmer over medium heat and cook for 10 to 15
minutes. Reduce heat to low, cover pan and cook until
all of the milk is absorbed. Stir in sugar, almond
extract, almonds and sherry and chill. Once rice is
chilled, whip the cream until stiff peaks form and fold
it into the rice mixture.

For the Strawberry Sauce:

• Place the strawberries in a small pot with the wine, 1/2
cup water and the sugar or jelly. Bring to a boil. Reduce
the heat and simmer until the strawberries are tender
and the juice is syrupy, approximately 10 minutes.

To Finish and Serve:

• Serve the strawberry sauce warm or cold with the chilled
rice pudding. Or, you may use fresh berries tossed with a
little sugar, if necessary, in place of the strawberry sauce.

CHRISTINE KEFF
SEATTLE, WA

American Express Best Chef: Northwest/Hawaii, 1999

Introducing new flavors to Seattle diners has become a way of life for Christine Keff. When she opened her first restaurant, Flying Fish, in 1995, local seafood restaurants were modeled on East Coast fish houses featuring simple, traditional preparations.

Keff brought a distinct and exciting Asian sensibility — curries, coconut milk, chiles, sesame and soy — to the usual sea suspects. Enthusiasts have packed the place ever since.

Her newest venture, Fandango, just across the street from Flying Fish in the picturesque Belltown neighborhood, offers a completely different and equally fresh fare. The menu stars the cuisine of Latin America, particularly Mexico, Brazil, Argentina, Bolivia, Peru and Cuba, and she is now educating her customers in the intricacies of mole and pipian sauces. Both restaurants reflect her extensive travels and the culinary style she has developed over the years. "I'm not subtle," explains Keff. "I like big flavors. I also feel if you really understand where a cuisine comes from, you will be able to interpret it with grace and intelligence."

In philosophy and distance, it's a long way from Bakersfield, California, where Keff was born.

"I've read about chefs who grew up cooking at grandma's knee, but that wasn't me," Keff says.

Her New Orleans-bred father taught her mother the Cajun-Creole gamut from red beans and rice to pecan pie. Apart from that, Mom made tuna casserole, used iceberg lettuce and relied on canned vegetables. "It was the usual 'Fifties stuff'". Mom would have liked to teach me some kitchen skills, but I wasn't interested. I was out playing ball."

Keff describes herself as an uptight, A-student in high school who instinctively felt that she needed to let go and loosen up. She did so by enrolling at Immaculate Heart College, a hotbed of '60s-style ferment. The college was run buy 240 renegade nuns (including the iconic Corita Kent) who had left the church but stayed together as a community. "I went in wearing a pleated skirt and loafers and left barefoot, in overalls," Keff chuckles.

Keff graduated with a degree in mathematics, which might have doomed her right back into the conservative world. In fact, her dad suggested she interview with oil companies for the position of salary manager. In the meantime, however, she accepted a job in a restaurant making salads two days a week. She says, "I loved the camaraderie, the intensity and I never looked back."

After working three years in Los Angeles, she decamped to New York. "My then-lover was a commercial artist who got a job there and I followed."

It was a good move. Through a combination of perseverance, luck and good timing, Keff talked herself into an apprenticeship right at the top of the heap — the legendary Four Seasons restaurant.

Keff's mentor there was Chef Seppi Rengli and she has nothing but praise for

his tutorship. "Seppi has such receptiveness and openness along with an almost maternal connection with food. He also truly believes women make better cooks than men; they just need to be toughened up for the commercial kitchen."

Toughening up also meant taking initiative. "You get assigned a certain station in the kitchen and if you don't go on and learn new stuff on your own time that's where you'll stay. So I did. It was a great place to work but when he felt you were ready, Seppi would move you on, line up another job for you and gently kick you out of the nest."

After leaving the Four Seasons she worked with a company that opened one of the first Southwestern restaurants in New York. Keff stayed up all night making sweet tamales and Mexican hot chocolate to take to the interview. A smart move — she bagged the job and also began her love affair with bold, spicy food that culminated with the opening of Fandango.

Eventually, she burned out, not from the spices, but the unrelenting pressure. She decided to take a year, travel and see where it would eventually lead. For five months she roamed the U.S. and then, for four months, toured on the cheap through Asia and Indonesia. "We shopped the markets, cooked in people's homes and ate street food. It was the best thing I ever did."

Ultimately she faced a critical decision. Torn between settling in Charleston or Seattle, Keff finally opted for the later because her brother, a physical therapist, and his wife lived there. For seven years she toiled in restaurants around the city, including a stint as executive chef at McCormick & Schmick where she learned the business end of running a restaurant. "Management there made us very aware of budget and numbers. It was an impressive education." Keff decided it was time to strike out on her own.

One of the secrets to Keff's success is that she isn't really on her own — she's deliberately surrounded herself with an intensely stable and loyal staff that has literally become a family. Explains Flying Fish waiter Eugene Chang, "She's so passionate about what she does. It shows not only in the food but in

her working relationships which are incredibly positive." Keff strongly advocates personal empowerment, which not only gives her staff autonomy, but also affords her time away from the restaurants.

And that's all to the good. Keff freely admits she's a homebody, and the home she shares with partner Mary Jean Kotleba on Puget Sound in West Seattle is architecturally and visually spectacular. The open

plan, light-filled contemporary two-story residence with a wood deck jutting directly over the waves presents a view of islands and snow-capped mountains that looks like a travel poster.

At this boating heaven, Keff alternates kayaking with playing squash and hiking. A long-term goal is to hike some of the countries long trails like the Pacific Crest, if she says, laughing, her knees hold out — an occupational hazard among long-standing chefs. Her newest interest, black-and-white photography meshes nicely with her love of travel. Mexico is a favorite destination; as often to work and do research as for relaxation. Eventually, when she and Kotleba retire, they plan to spend half the year traveling. Keff also plans on getting more involved with charitable work. "We help raise money for the March of Dimes, Northwest AIDS Foundation and Share Our Strength, but I'd like to be more directly involved with the recipients."

Meanwhile, Keff says, she is moving more and more into teaching by conducting workshops, seminars and cooking classes that help spread the word on her signature mix of local product with Asian and Latin American influences. It continues the education process she started when she opened her first, very personal, restaurant.

Whole Fried Rockfish

Serves: 4

Marinade:

1 **stalk** lemon grass,
   tender white portion

4 **tablespoons** fish sauce

4 **tablespoons** lime juice

3 **each** bird chiles, finely sliced

1 **clove** garlic, finely sliced

Sauce:

1/2 **each** whole pineapple, peeled,
   cored and chopped

2 **each** anchovy fillets

2 **cloves** garlic, chopped

2 **tablespoons** lime juice

2 **tablespoons** fish sauce

2 **tablespoons** sambal
   (garlic-chile sauce)

1/4 **bunch** mint, chopped

Fish:

Vegetable oil for frying
   (enough to fill pan, covering fish)

1 **whole** 4-pound Pacific rockfish,
   or other soft-fleshed white fish,
   gutted and scaled *(may use two
   fillets, for convenience)*

Salt and pepper to taste

1/2 **box** cornstarch

Finish:

8 **sheets** rice paper

1 **bunch** Thai or Italian basil

1 **bunch** mint

1 **bunch** cilantro

1 **each** lime, cut in wedges

For the Marinade:

- Finely slice the lemon grass, cutting across the grain. Put the lemon grass, fish sauce, lime juice, bird chiles and garlic into a blender and process until very smooth, approximately 5 minutes. Set aside.

For the Sauce:

- Place the chopped pineapple in a food processor with all of the other sauce ingredients. Process to a coarse purée. Set aside.

For the Fish:

- Find a pan large enough to allow the fish to lay fairly flat and add vegetable oil to a depth that will cover the fish. Heat the oil to 350 degrees. Rinse the fish and cut 1/2-inch-deep slits in the sides about 2-inches apart. You should have about 3 or 4 cuts on each side. Rub some of the marinade into each cut and salt and pepper the fish generously inside and out. Dredge the fish in the cornstarch, coating entire surface inside and out. When the oil is at 350 degrees, slide the fish in carefully and fry until the flesh is cooked at the bone, about 7 to 10 minutes. Turn head away when placing fish in hot oil — it will sputter and pop. When done, remove from the oil and drain on towels.

To Finish and Serve:

- While the fish is cooking, dip the rice papers in a bowl of hot tap water one at a time until soft enough to fold in quarters. Place flat between cool, moist towels. Arrange the rice papers on a platter with the herbs and lime wedges. Place the hot fish on the platter. Pass the sauce separately. Guests will pull chunks of crispy fish off the bone and wrap them in a softened rice paper with herbs, a squeeze of lime and some of the sauce.

Christine Keff's Beverage Recommendations

Whole Fried Rockfish

Sara Lee Arrowood

Pinot Blanc 1997

page 271

Grilled Radicchio Salad with

Chevre and Balsamic Syrup

Kay Simon Washington State

Chinook Chardonnay 1999

page 273

Smoked Oyster and

Chipotle Chowder

Kay Simon Washington State

Chinook Chardonnay 1999

page 273

Thai Curry Sea Scallops

with Black Rice Cake and

Green Papaya Salad

Elk Cove Willamette Valley

Pinot Noir 2000

page 275

Beef Short Ribs with

Red Chile Sauce

Fandango Mojito

page 277

Toasted Coconut Cream

Torte with Cherry Ice

Cream

Pedro Ximenez

Don PX Manzanilla

Muscatel

page 279

Grilled Radicchio Salad with Chèvre and Balsamic Syrup

Serves: 8

Salad:

2 **heads** radicchio, rinsed and
dried thoroughly

1 **each** red or sweet onion, peeled
(*peel off any damaged outer rings*)

1/3 **cup** olive oil

1/4 **cup** basil leaves

2 **cloves** garlic, chopped

2 **tablespoons** lemon juice

Salt and pepper to taste

4 **tablespoons** crumbled Chèvre

Syrup:

1/2 **cup** balsamic vinegar

For the Salad:

- Quarter the radicchio through the stem. Cut the onion into 8 wedges, leaving the core of the onion intact. Place the olive oil, basil, garlic and lemon juice in a blender and purée for approximately 2 minutes. Season to taste with salt and pepper. Toss the radicchio and onion in the oil dressing and set aside.

- Preheat grill to 350 degrees. Remove the radicchio and onion from the marinade and grill slowly until the outside is fairly charred and the inside is softened. Place the radicchio and onion in a bowl with the crumbled Chèvre and pour the leftover marinade over the mixture. Toss to coat.

For the Syrup:

- Put the balsamic vinegar in a small saucepan and reduce over low to medium heat until you have about 2 tablespoons of syrup that is fairly thick, approximately 3 minutes. Cool.

To Finish and Serve:

- Divide the salad among eight serving plates and drizzle the balsamic syrup over the top of each serving.

Smoked Oyster and Chipotle Chowder

Serves: 8

Chowder:

60 **each** oysters, shucked, with
their liquid

1 **cup** wood chips, soaked in
water overnight

2 **tablespoons** butter

2 **tablespoons** sliced shallots

2 **tablespoons** sliced leek, white
part only

1/4 **cup** dry white wine

2 **cups** fish stock

2 **cups** half and half

2 **teaspoons** finely chopped
chipotle chiles in adobo*

Finish:

2 **tablespoons** chopped cilantro

Salt and pepper to taste

For the Chowder:

- Separate the oysters from their liquid, reserving the liquid (*you should have about 3/4 cup*). Drain the wood chips and set up a smoker using a steamer pan. Place the wood chips in the bottom pan, the oysters in the perforated pan and the lid on top. Put the smoker on a burner and turn the heat on high. When the chips start to smoke heavily (*ensure room has good ventilation*), reduce the heat to medium and smoke the oysters until they are firm.

- Melt the butter in a saucepan and sweat the shallots and leeks until transparent. Add the white wine and reduce by 1/2. Add the oyster liquid, fish stock and half & half and simmer for 10 minutes. Transfer 2 cups of the liquid to a blender and add 15 of the smoked oysters. Blend until smooth and return the mixture to the saucepan. Stir in the chipotles. Simmer for 10 more minutes; strain.

To Finish and Serve:

- Add the remaining smoked oysters and the cilantro. Season to taste, heat through.

* Available in Latin markets or specialty sections of grocery stores

Thai Curry Sea Scallops with Black Rice Cake and Green Papaya Salad

Serves: 4

Curry Paste:

1/4 **pound** fresh galanga*, peeled *(may substitute additional ginger if not available)*

1/4 **pound** fresh ginger, peeled

3 **teaspoons** ground turmeric

1/4 **pound** shallots, sliced

1 **head** garlic, peeled and chopped *(about 8 cloves)*

1/2 **bunch** cilantro *(or 1 small bunch)*

Juice of 2 limes

5 **each** Thai bird chiles*, stems removed

1/2 **cup** peanut or canola oil

Scallops:

2 **tablespoons** peanut or canola oil

20 **each** large sea scallops

Salt to taste

1-1/2 **tablespoons** fish sauce*

6 **tablespoons** curry paste

2/3 **cup** chicken stock

1/2 **cup** coconut milk

2 **tablespoons** cornstarch

2 **tablespoons** water

Black Rice Cakes:

1/2 **cup** yellow Thai curry paste

1/2 **teaspoon** salt

1/2 **teaspoon** pepper

5-1/2 **cups** water

2 **cups** glutinous Thai black rice

Green Papaya Salad:

1/2 **each** green papaya, julienned

1 **each** zucchini, julienned

1 **each** yellow squash, seeds removed, julienned

1/2 **each** carrot, peeled and julienned

2 **each** Thai bird chiles, sliced thinly

Juice of 2 limes

1 **clove** garlic, chopped

2 **tablespoons** fish sauce*

For the Curry Paste:

- Thinly slice all vegetables, cutting across the grain. Mix together. Place all curry paste ingredients except the oil in a food processor and grind. Add just enough oil to make a paste. Continue to grind until paste is smooth, about 5 minutes.

For the Scallops:

- Place half of the oil in a large non-stick skillet. Heat to smoking. Season the scallops with salt and fish sauce. Add scallops to the pan, one by one. Sear the scallops on one side, turn, and sear on the other side. This process should take approximately 4 to 5 minutes; the scallops will be medium-rare.

- Add curry paste and remaining oil to a pan and heat over medium heat for 5 minutes. Add chicken stock and bring to a boil. Then add the coconut milk and continue to simmer. Mix together cornstarch and water to make a slurry. Stir in bit by bit until the sauce is thick enough to coat a spoon. Strain and set aside in a warm spot on the stove or in a warm water bath.

For the Black Rice Cakes:

- Put the yellow curry paste, salt, pepper and the water in a blender and mix for a few seconds. Place in a bowl and let stand for about 30 minutes, stirring every 15 minutes. Let rest for another 20 minutes, covered. Put the mixture in a heavy-bottomed pot and bring to a simmer. Add the rice, cover and cook until tender and thick. Spread on a sheet tray and let cool. When cooled, cut into 3-inch circles with a ring mold.

For the Green Papaya Salad:

- Combine all ingredients in a bowl.

To Finish and Serve:

- Place five scallops on each of four serving plates. Garnish with a black rice cake and a small serving of the green papaya salad.

* Available at Asian specialty stores

The Fandango Mojito

Serves: 1

5-6 **mint leaves**, fresh and medium to large in size

2 **ounces** white rum

1 **ounce** simple syrup

1-1/2 **ounces** lime juice, fresh squeezed

Full a pint glass with ice cubes, tear mint leaves and place in glass. Add rum, simple syrup and lime juice. Shake or stir vigorously and transfer to serving glass.

Beef Short Ribs with Red Chile Sauce

Serves: 4

Ribs:

1 to 1-1/2 pounds beef short ribs

1/2 each white onion, coarsely chopped

1 each whole head of garlic, cut in half

4 quarts water, salted

Sauce:

16 each large guajillo chiles

3 each large ancho chiles

3 each large tomatoes

15 cloves of garlic, large (*do not peel*)

1/2 each white onion, cut into 1/2-inch slices

3 tablespoons lard, shortening or corn oil

2 teaspoons ground cumin

1 teaspoon dry oregano

1/2 teaspoon black peppercorns

3 each whole cloves

1/2 cup white vinegar

2 teaspoons salt, or to taste

For the Ribs:

- Place the short ribs, onion and garlic in a large pot and cover with the salted water. Bring the water to a gentle boil over medium heat. Reduce heat and continue cooking for approximately 50 minutes, until the meat is fully cooked and somewhat soft. Separate the meat from the broth, reserving and straining the broth. This can be done one day ahead if desired.

For the Sauce:

- While the meat is cooking, clean the chiles by removing the seeds and veins. Roast the chiles lightly in a dry sauté pan over medium heat. Soak the toasted chiles in 4 cups of hot broth taken from the pot in which the ribs were cooked. Allow the chiles to soak for 25 minutes. Place the chiles with the broth in which they were soaking in a blender and blend until you achieve a very smooth sauce. Strain the sauce. After straining, return the solids to the blender and add another cup of broth. Liquefy again, and strain again, this time discarding the solids. Set aside.

- Roast the tomatoes under the broiler until the skins blacken and the tomatoes become soft. Char the garlic cloves, with skins on, and the onion slices in a dry sauté pan until the cloves and the slices are black on both sides. Peel the roasted garlic cloves. Roughly chop the roasted onion, tomatoes and garlic. Liquefy in a blender until very smooth. Set aside.

- Heat the lard (*or shortening or oil*) over high heat, letting it smoke lightly. Add the chile sauce. Cook for approximately 5 minutes, stirring occasionally. Add the tomato purée and cook for an additional 10 minutes.

- In a spice grinder (*or coffee grinder*), grind together the cumin, oregano, pepper and cloves. Add the mixture to the chile sauce.

- Add the ribs, vinegar, and 3 cups of the meat broth to the chile sauce in a large pot. Cook for 50 minutes over low heat, leaving the pot uncovered to enable the mixture to reduce and become thicker. Add salt to taste.

To Finish and Serve:

- Serve the ribs with plenty of the sauce and accompany with tamale de olla.

Tamale de Olla

Serves: 6

6 ounces lard or shortening

2 teaspoons baking powder

1-1/2 pounds dry, course masa for tamales (*rehydrate masa with 1-3/4 cups hot water*)

1 cup cool chicken broth

Salt to taste

1-1/2 cups filling of choice (*i.e. leftover stewed meats with a little sauce, etc.*)

In a mixer, beat lard with baking powder until light and creamy. Slowly incorporate the cooled masa to the lard, then add 3/4 cup broth. Continue beating for another minute, until a 1/2 teaspoon dollop floats in a cup of cold water.

Beat in enough additional broth to give the mixture the consistency of soft cake batter. Season with salt to taste.

Preheat oven to 400 degrees. Pour half of the batter into a greased 10-inch pie plate. Spread the filling over the top evenly. Cover the filling with the remaining batter.

Bake in the upper 1/3 of the oven for 25 minutes. Then reduce the oven temperature to 300 degrees. Cover lightly with foil and continue baking until the center springs back when pressed lightly and the top is golden brown, approximately 20 minutes.

Let stand a few minutes before cutting into wedges.

Toasted Coconut Cream Torte with Cherry Ice Cream

Serves: 8

Torte:

5 tablespoons butter, diced

1-1/4 cups powdered sugar, sifted

3 each small eggs, at room temperature

1-1/2 teaspoons baking powder

1/2 teaspoon salt

1-3/4 cups sifted flour

1 cup coconut milk

Coconut Cream Filling:

1 cup coconut milk

2 cups heavy cream

3 each egg yolks

6 tablespoons sugar

3 tablespoons cornstarch

6 tablespoons ground unsweetened coconut

1 cup sweetened flaked or shredded coconut

For the Torte:

- Line the bottom of an 8-inch round cake pan with parchment paper. Preheat over to 300 degrees.

- Cream the butter and powdered sugar together in a mixing bowl until light and creamy, scraping the sides of the bowl frequently. Add the eggs, one at a time, beating several minutes after each addition and scraping the sides of the bowl frequently.

- Combine the dry ingredients in a bowl. Gently fold into the butter and egg mixture. Add coconut milk, 1/3 cup at a time, and fold in until completely blended.

- Pour the batter into the cake pan. Bake for approximately 30 minutes. Let cool.

For the Coconut Cream Filling:

- In a pan over medium heat, scald the coconut milk with 1 cup of the cream. In a separate bowl, whip the egg yolks together with the sugar and the cornstarch. Whisk a small amount of the hot cream mixture into the whipped egg yolk mixture to settle it. Then whisk in remaining cream mixture and stir until well blended. Pour the entire mixture back into the saucepan and place over medium heat and simmer for 3 minutes, stirring constantly. Remove pan from heat. Add the ground unsweetened coconut. Let cool slightly. Cover with plastic wrap and chill.

- In a large bowl, whip the remaining cream until peaks form. Remove the chilled coconut cream mixture from the refrigerator and whip until smooth. Gently fold the coconut cream mixture into the whipped cream.

- Toast the sweetened coconut on a sheet pan in a 300 degree oven until light brown, stirring occasionally. Let cool.

To Finish and Serve:

- Cut the cooled torte into 3 layers. Spread 1/3 of the filling in between each layer, and use the last 1/3 to frost the entire torte. Gently pat the toasted coconut onto the sides and top of the torte. Serve with cherry ice cream.

Cherry Ice Cream

Makes: 3 quarts

Ice Cream Base:

2 cups heavy cream

1 cup whole milk

1/2 cup sugar

4 each egg yolks

Cherry Base:

5 cups Bing cherries

1 cup sugar

1 cup water

For the Ice Cream Base:

In a large saucepan, mix together and then scald the cream, milk and 1/4 cup of the sugar. In a mixing bowl, whip the egg yolks and the remaining 1/4 cup of sugar until smooth and almost white. Temper the yolk mixture by whisking in a small amount of the hot cream mixture. Whisk in the rest of the cream mixture. Pour through a fine-mesh sieve into a stainless-steel mixing bowl. Place the bowl in an ice bath and refrigerate overnight.

For the Cherry Base:

Bring all ingredients to a boil and cook for 2 minutes and refrigerate overnight. Pour into a blender and blend very briefly, just enough to break up large pieces; do not purée.

To Finish and Serve:

Combine the ice cream base and cherry base. Freeze in an ice cream maker according to manufacturer's instructions.

JULIAN SERRANO

LAS VEGAS, NV

American Express Best Chef: Southwest, 2002

American Express Best Chef: California, 1998

It seems fitting that two great Spanish artists share the stage at the Bellagio Hotel's premiere restaurant. The explosively colorful art of namesake Pablo Picasso perfectly matches the culinary pyrotechnics of Chef Julian Serrano.

Ironically, Serrano, who has been enormously influential in making Las Vegas a world dining destination, came very close to taking a pass on the position that brought him his second James Beard Award. For almost 16 years, Serrano had worked in the kitchen of Masa's, arguably San Francisco's best and best-known restaurant. Then, Vegas impresario Steve Wynn came calling with a near-bottomless budget and promises that Serrano could have free rein with the showcase restaurant Wynn was cooking up.

"I was very impressed with Wynn," says Serrano. "I believed he wanted to create something extraordinary. Still it was a hard call between Vegas and San Francisco, which had been my life for 23 years."

Serrano agreed to consult on the Picasso project but Wynn wanted a hands-on chef. (Although there are many "celebrity chef" restaurants in Las Vegas, only Picasso and Renoir, with Alex Stratta at the helm, have on-site name chefs.) Finally, Serrano's wife Susan made the decision. "She voted for Vegas because it is a more international destination than San Francisco and at that time, there was no other top restaurant in town. Picasso would be it," says Serrano.

The restaurant turned out to be magical, a one-of-a-kind that is both exuberant and elegant. Pablo Picasso's son designed a bright swirling carpet and its colors are reflected in the priceless paintings hung on wood-paneled walls. Overhead is a coved brick-and-beam ceiling. Cozy nooks, screens and over-sized plants provide privacy and swagged French doors look out on Bellagio's famed dancing fountains. Masses of fresh flowers lavished around the room evoke images of a European marketplace.

There was huge public anticipation prior to Picasso's opening, says Serrano. "A lot of people wanted me to change direction. But I made the decision to do the food I know I can do. I didn't want to fail with someone else's ideas. After all, you don't go to Mick Jagger and say, 'Tomorrow, you are going to sing opera.'"

His instincts proved sound. On opening night, people lined up all the way down the strip and Picasso instantly became one of the hottest dining tickets in the world.

Serrano has come a long way from his Madrid birthplace. "Nobody in my family worked in restaurants or hotels, but my father, a civilian, was in charge of the animals for a big navy hospital. He took care of them, killed and butchered them and would marinate the meat for the kitchen. My mother was a housewife who cooked three meals a day 365 days of the year. It was simple food. Some things she did were good, some not so."

As a youth, Serrano had dreams of traveling and soon figured out a way to do it. "I bumped into a friend who was slightly older and mentioned I hadn't seen him around for awhile. He told me he was in hotel school in southern Spain. When I found out the town was Marbella, it was incredible. I had gone there for vacation with my sister and just loved the place."

Serrano was also influenced by another chance encounter. Helping a friend deliver food to a restaurant, he observed the chef chopping, slicing and combining ingredients, and he was intrigued. It also didn't hurt that the Spanish government paid for room, board and tuition at the hotel school. He applied for chef training. Serrano clearly had flair and graduated first in his class.

His first job was in a French restaurant in Marbella. Barely 18 he worked every night and had no time to enjoy the resort atmosphere. He knew no one and had no car, no bike and no television. He calls it "a painful experience."

His next job was better. He worked for the top hotel in the area, but it was Serrano's stint in the Spanish army that became a turning point." It was a great opportunity," he recalls. "I was cooking for the young, unmarried officers and each day I was given money to go to the market and buy ingredients for lunch and dinner. I learned how to handle money, get the best deals, pick out the best vegetables and fish and what was in season."

Still yearning to travel, he went to the Canary Islands and helped open what was one of the biggest hotels in Europe at the time. With job leads in Sweden and South Africa, Serrano decided instead to go to work for the Carnival Cruise Ship line based in Miami."

He recalls, "I *thought* I could speak English but quickly learned otherwise. I was getting off a bus, going through the crowd saying, 'Excuse me, please,' and getting these funny looks. I told a friend about it later and discovered I was actually saying 'Kiss me, please.'"

Continental French food was the order of the day — lobster thermador, escargot, veal Oscar. "Everyone was doing the same thing," remembers Serrano. "Even if you had ideas, you couldn't use them." Nevertheless, he was excited to be on the boat with the opportunity of seeing different places, but after two years he was ready to leave. "Miami was too much like Marbella with the sun and beaches."

Wanting to stay in the states, he improbably landed a job in the only Spanish restaurant in Nashville, Tennessee. Serrano found it tough going." It was difficult, the customers were not open to anything but steak and potatoes. I put calamari on the menu and didn't sell a single order."

Some positive things came out of this experience. Serrano garnered good reviews to add to his resumé and received his green card. He was also given some great advice by a friend who had moved to San Francisco. "He told me, 'don't go south, go north.' I got in the car and headed straight for Northern California."

Settled in San Francisco, Serrano took the helm of Beethoven, a German restaurant. "One of my wife's friends told me I was too talented to spend my life making sauerbraten. At first I was a little mad and told her to mind her own business, but it made me think."

Soon after, he says, the founder of Masa's Restaurant, Masataka Kobayashi, was giving a cooking demonstration at Macy's and he took the opportunity to introduce himself. Says Serrano, "A week after I talked to him, a sous chef position opened up at Masa's. I had looked a long time to work in a restaurant of that caliber. I immersed myself in the job, experimenting in the kitchen at home, dining out, studying."

Seven months later, Kobayashi was found murdered in his home. "We were all in shock," says Serrano. He and Susan headed off for a six-month work and play tour of Europe. "Then my wife got pregnant, so after three months we scrubbed the whole thing and came back to the States. I had a job lined up in New York."

Masa's management, meanwhile, called Serrano's in-laws attempting to reach him and convince him to come back to a restaurant that was in trouble. He accepted, giving himself two years to turn things around. The restaurant's business started to build and it slowly regained its former reputation. The staff was stable and before he knew it 15 years had passed.

"When I felt comfortable, I changed the food, took away butter and cream and made the menu modern and lighter. As a Spanish chef in a French restaurant it made sense to go more Mediterranean. The customers change your direction, too. They order more vegetables and you see what it is they are looking for."

That's the culinary style Serrano took with him to Picasso, clean and focused with pure, balanced flavors. Menu highlights might include poached oysters in a sweet beurre blanc with the salty snap of osetra caviar sprinkled on top or moist lobster whose natural sweetness is underscored by corn flan, corn kernels and corn jus. Other selections include musky, truffle-dusted medallions of aged lamb loin and flaky black bass bathed in court bouillon enhanced with snipped fresh herbs.

There is little down time for the chef. The restaurant is open every day except Wednesday and the norm for Serrano is a 12-hour workday. He travels extensively participating in charity events. When he gets a chance, he plays tennis because it's fast. He claims he does not have time for golf. Serrano's daughter Estefania is also a talented tennis player. Serrano will tell you he always wins when they play, Estefania smiles, knowing better.

When he does have a day off, he says, "I just want to relax with my wife and daughter."

Asked about goals for the future, he says forthrightly, "I'm happy with what I have achieved with Picasso. You get a great gastronomic experience here. We have the whole package. My goal is to continue to keep the restaurant the best that it can be."

Sautéed Darnes of Salmon with Saffron Sauce

Serves: 4

Saffron Sauce:

1/2 tablespoon saffron threads

1/4 cup white wine

1 each large shallot, chopped

4 each peppercorns, whole

1 each bay leaf

1 cup heavy cream

8 ounces butter, cut into
small pieces

Salt to taste

Salmon:

1-1/2 pounds salmon,
skinless fillet

4 tablespoons clarified butter or
vegetable oil

Finish:

1 each small zucchini

1 each zucchini flower

1 each medium tomato, peeled,
seeded and diced

For the Saffron Sauce:

- Put the saffron in a sauté pan and pound with a wooden spoon. Add a little of the white wine or water and cook for 1 minute over low heat. Set aside. In another sauté pan, add the shallot, the rest of the white wine, the peppercorns, and the bay leaf and reduce until the wine is almost gone. Add the cream and cook until reduced by half. Then add the butter slowly, whisking constantly. Add the saffron mixture to the butter mixture and blend. Keep warm

For the Salmon:

- Cut the salmon into twelve 1/2-inch-thick slices. Curve each slice and put a toothpick in the two ends to make a salmon shape and hold in place while cooking. Sauté the salmon in the clarified butter over medium-high heat. Turn once during cooking.

To Finish and Serve:

- Slice the zucchini paper-thin into approximately 15 slices. Cook in boiling water for about 10 seconds. Drain the slices on a towel. Arrange the zucchini slices into the shape of a flower on a serving platter. Place the zucchini flower in the center. Remove the toothpicks from the salmon darnes and place four groups of three salmon darnes each around the zucchini flower. Top each group of salmon darnes with the chopped tomato. Place a spoonful of saffron sauce between each group of salmon darnes.

Warm Lobster Salad with Panache of Tropical Fruit and Citrus Vinaigrette

Serves: 2

Lobster:

2 each lobsters, 1 pound each

Citrus Vinaigrette:

1/8 cup blood orange juice

1/8 cup pineapple juice

1/8 cup lemon juice

1/8 cup lime juice

1 cup extra-virgin olive oil

1 tablespoon port

1/2 cup sherry vinegar

1/8 cup truffle jus, *(may omit if unavailable, or may substitute juice from canned truffles*)*

1 tablespoon honey

Salt and pepper to taste

Panache of Tropical Fruit:

1 each pineapple, finely diced

1 each papaya, finely diced

1 each mango, finely diced

1 each kiwi, finely diced

Salad:

1 bunch mâche lettuce

1 bunch red oak lettuce

1 head Belgian endive

1 each celery root, peeled and cut into julienne

1 each small curly endive

2 leaves treviso
(may substitute radicchio)

Finish:

12 each chervil leaves

12 each pink peppercorns

1 teaspoon lobster oil*
(omit if unavailable)

For the Lobster:

- Tie the lobsters to a wooden stick to keep the tail straight after cooking. Poach the lobsters in a large pot of boiling water for 2 minutes. Remove the lobsters from the water and allow to cool. Remove the tails and cut the tail meat into 1-inch medallions, holding them together while cutting to retain the tail shape. Reserve the lobster meat for serving.

For the Vinaigrette:

- Individually, reduce the blood orange and pineapple juices in a small saucepan over medium heat until each is reduced by half. Reduce the lemon and lime juices together until reduced by half. Combine all of the reduced juices in a mixing bowl and whisk in the olive oil, port, sherry vinegar, truffle juice and honey. Add salt and pepper to taste.

For the Panache of Fruit Tropical:

- Mix all ingredients together in a bowl.

For the Salad:

- Create a bed of salad greens for the lobster-shaped presentation on each of two serving plates. For the head, place the mâche leaves in a semicircle at the top of the plate, and on top of that another semicircle of red oak lettuce, topped with curly endive. In the center of the plate, place the julienned celery root that has been drizzled with vinaigrette. This will be the bed for the lobster medallions. Fan out the Belgian endive at the bottom of the plate, creating a tail, and place one piece of treviso in the center of the endive.

To Finish and Serve:

- Put the lobster meat in a sauté pan with some of the vinaigrette dressing. Heat until warm. Place the lobster medallions on the beds of lettuce to make the shape of lobsters. Place the claws on either side of the "head" section of the salads. Spoon warm vinaigrette over the salads and garnish each with chervil leaves and pink peppercorns. Place one tablespoon of the panache of tropical fruit on top of each of the lobsters.

* Available in gourmet shops

Picassos at Picasso

Pablo Picasso was arguably the most influential artist of the twentieth century. Born in 1881, his ouput was protean and he never limited himself to a specific style. From his early realistic "Blue Period" to the less representative works of his later life, he continued developing, experimenting and learning throughout his life. In his sixties, he mastered the art of ceramics and some of his vases are on display at Picasso at The Bellagio.

Bust of a Man, September 10, 1969
Oil on canvas

Figures II, July 4, 1969
Oil on canvas

Head of a Man, August 3, 1967
Gouache on paper

La Californie, February 18, 1956
Hand-painted glazed ceramic

Le Déjeuner sur l'her be, 1964
Pinkish-red earthenware, painted with slips, glazed

Pierrot, 1917, Brush and black ink on paper

Seated Man, June 28, 1971
Oil on canvas

Still Life with Basket of Fruit and Pitcher of Flowers and Cattails, August 2, 1942
Oil on canvas

Still Life with Flowers and Fruit Dish, September 14, 1943, Oil on canvas

Still Life with Fruit Dish and Yellow Vase, 1963-65
Unique ceramic

Woman with Beret, January 14, 1938, Oil on canvas

Roasted Langoustines with Pistou and Lemon Balsamic Vinaigrette

Serves: 2

Pistou:

1 each small eggplant *(Japanese)*, diced into 1/4-inch cubes

1 teaspoon salt

1 teaspoon pepper

4 tablespoons olive oil

1 clove garlic, chopped

1 each small onion, diced

1 each small red pepper, diced

1 each yellow zucchini, cut into 1/4-inch cubes

1 each green zucchini, cut into 1/4-inch cubes

Langoustines:

6 each langoustines *(prawns)*, may substitute extra-large shrimp *(10-14/pound)*

1/3 cup olive oil

2 tablespoons finely chopped tomato, peeled, seeded

1/2 cup balsamic vinegar

6 each parsley sprigs, minced

2 tablespoons lemon juice

Finish:

4 each green pepper slices, diced

For the Pistou:

- Clean and dice the eggplant 30 minutes in advance and sprinkle with salt and pepper to remove the bitter juice. Put 2 tablespoons of olive oil into a sauté pan and add the garlic, onion and pepper. Cook slowly until tender. In a separate pan, sauté the zucchini and eggplant individually for one minute each in 1 tablespoon of olive oil over medium-high heat. Combine zucchini, eggplant and onions, garlic and pepper. Season to taste with salt and pepper. Keep warm until ready to assemble dish.

For the Langoustines:

- Clean the langoustines, but do not remove the tails. To maintain the curved shape of the langoustine, sauté in the olive oil over medium heat on the curved edge of the pan. Cook until pink and slightly firm. Add the tomato, balsamic vinegar, parsley and lemon juice to the pan and lightly coat the langoustine with the vinaigrette sauce.

To Finish and Serve:

- Set a round mold in the center of the top half of each of two serving plates and fill each with the pistou. Place the langoustines below the pistou in the center of the bottom half of each plate. Lightly drizzle the plates with a few drops of the vinaigrette from the pan. Garnish with diced green pepper.

Loin of Lamb with Crust of Truffles au jus and Potatoes Parmesan

Serves: 2

Lamb Stock:

1 **each** trimmings, meat and
bone, from one rack of lamb

1 **tablespoon** olive oil

1/2 **cup** diced onion

1/4 **cup** diced celery

1/4 **cup** diced carrot

1/2 **tablespoon** tomato paste

Lamb Sauce:

1/2 **cup** diced shallot

1 **cup** red wine *(ideally Merlot)*

1/2 **tablespoon** tomato paste

Salt and pepper to taste

1 **tablespoon** chopped truffle

Potatoes:

2 **each** red potatoes

1 **cup** chicken stock

2 **tablespoons** grated Parmesan
cheese

1 **tablespoon** butter, melted

Lamb:

1 **each** rack of lamb

1 **each** truffle, chopped*

1/4 **bunch** parsley, cleaned and
chopped

1 **each** egg yolk, slightly beaten

Salt and pepper to taste

Truffle oil
(may substitute clarified butter)

Finish:

3 **each** baby carrots, blanched
until barely tender, keep warm

For the Lamb Stock:

- Preheat oven to 350 degrees. Place bones in a small, oven-proof saucepan. Drizzle the bones with 1 tablespoon olive oil. Roast in oven until the bones are browned, approximately 30 minutes. Remove the pan from the oven and add the onion, celery, carrot and tomato paste. Cover the bone mixture with water and simmer for 40 minutes, adding more water to keep the bones covered, if necessary. Strain and skim off fat.

For the Lamb Sauce:

- In a separate sauté pan, simmer shallots and the red wine over medium heat until wine is reduced by half. When reduced, add the prepared lamb stock. Cook over medium heat until reduced by half again. Add salt and pepper to taste. Add 1 tablespoon of the chopped truffle.

For the Potatoes:

- Preheat oven to 350 degrees. Peel the potatoes and carve into cylinders. Slice into 1/8-inch-thick slices. Place the potato slices in a small casserole dish. Add the chicken stock, sprinkle with the Parmesan cheese and butter. Bake the potato mixture for about 25 minutes, or until stock is absorbed and potatoes are tender. Keep warm.

For the Lamb:

- Preheat oven to 300 degrees. Bone out the rack of lamb, reserving the bones and pieces of meat to make the stock. You may have your butcher do this for you. Set aside 1 tablespoon of the chopped truffle for the lamb sauce *(see below)*. Mix the remaining truffle with chopped parsley. Brush the loin of lamb lightly with the egg yolk. Roll the lamb in the chopped truffle and parsley mixture. Season with salt and pepper to taste. Cook the lamb in a sauté pan with a little truffle oil on medium heat. Do not allow the truffle crust to become crispy. Remove from the sauté pan, place in an oven-proof pan and place the lamb in the oven and cook until medium-rare.

To Finish and Serve:

- On one side of the plate, place the potato slices and carrots. Slice the lamb loin in half, and with cut-side up, place on the other side of the plate. Add the lamb sauce between the plate rim and the lamb.

* Available at gourmet markets or online

Napoleon of Vermeer and Milk Chocolate Mousse

Serves: 4 to 6

Mousse:

4 ounces high-quality
milk chocolate, chopped

2 ounces high-quality
dark chocolate, chopped

2 ounces cocoa butter

2 cups heavy cream

1/4 cup Vermeer Dutch
chocolate liqueur

2 tablespoons Godiva® chocolate
liqueur

2/3 cup sugar

5 each egg yolks, slightly beaten

Chocolate Sauce:

8 ounces high-quality
dark chocolate, finely chopped

1 cup heavy cream

6 tablespoons light corn syrup

Whipped Cream:

1 cup heavy cream

Granulated sugar to taste

1 each vanilla bean,
split and scraped

Chocolate Squares:

16 ounces semisweet chocolate

Finish:

Gold leaf *(optional)*

For the Mousse:

- Combine the chocolates and cocoa butter in a medium bowl set over a pot of simmering, but not boiling, water. Stir occasionally to combine. In a separate mixing bowl, combine cream and liqueurs and whip until the mixture forms stiff peaks. Transfer to a container and refrigerate until needed.

- Place the sugar in a small saucepan and combine with enough water to bring consistency to that of wet sand. Place over medium heat and cook to about 235 degrees, the soft ball stage. While the chocolate is melting and sugar is cooking, place the egg yolks into a mixing bowl and with a whip attachment, whip the yolks until they become pale in color and double in volume. Once the sugar has reached the soft ball stage, pour the hot sugar mixture into the egg yolk mixture while whipping, being careful to pour down the side of the bowl to avoid having the sugar flung to the sides of the bowl by the whip. Allow the yolks to whip for several more minutes with the sugar mixture to gain volume.

- Remove the melted chocolate from the heat and, in two parts, fold the egg yolk mixture into the chocolate with a rubber spatula. Next, gently fold in the whipped, chilled cream in two parts. Be careful not to fold too vigorously or the cream will lose volume and the mousse will be flat and runny. Chill the mousse for 2-3 hours before use.

For the Chocolate Sauce:

- Place the chocolate in a mixing bowl. In a small saucepan, combine the cream and the corn syrup. Bring the mixture to a boil and pour over the chocolate. Let the mixture stand for several minutes and then emulsify completely with a wire whip. Refrigerate until needed. Chocolate may be reheated in a water bath or microwave before serving.

For the Whipped Cream:

- Combine the cream, sugar and seeds from the vanilla bean in a mixing bowl. Whip until stiff peaks form.

For the Chocolate Squares:

- Melt the chocolate over a double boiler or in the microwave, stirring until completely smooth. Spread the melted chocolate approximately 1/8-inch thick on a silicone baking sheet or parchment paper. Let cool completely. For each plate, you will need six 2-1/2-inch-square pieces and one 1-inch-square piece of chocolate. Cut the necessary shapes from the cooled chocolate.

To Finish and Serve:

- Pipe even amounts of mousse between each of the six 2-1/2-inch-square pieces of chocolate for each serving, reserving one square for the top layer. Refrigerate the towers until needed. Garnish each serving plate with lines of the chocolate sauce. Place a tower squarely in the center of each plate. Place a quenelle *(A quenelle is an oval formed by using 2 spoons that have been moistened in water)* of whipped cream on the diagonal on the top of each tower. Place a 1-inch square of chocolate on a diagonal in the large end of quenelle and, if desired, finish with a small piece of edible gold leaf.

ROBERT MCGRATH
SCOTTSDALE, AZ

American Express Best Chef: Southwest, 2001

Roaring Fork River cuts through Aspen, Colorado. It's Robert McGrath's favorite fly-fishing spot and also the name of his Scottsdale, Arizona restaurant. McGrath is a walking, talking testimonial to the rugged Western way of life and that's reflected in every aspect of his culinary style. "The one thing we're not," he says, "is stuffy."

Regionalism is a leitmotif for McGrath. Born in Louisville, Kentucky, he was raised on down-home Southern cooking — country ham, sweet potatoes and green beans — and it made an indelible impression. "The further I get away from 'erector set' cooking, the more I'm going back to the kind of food I grew up with."

In his late teens, McGrath landed a summer job in a resort restaurant and liked it so much he pursued a career in cooking rather than going back to school. This was in the days before being a chef was considered a glamorous occupation. McGrath laughingly recalls that at the time the government classified chefs as "domestic laborers." It wasn't until 1984, in the midst of America's food revolution, that the designation was changed to "professional."

"Fine food meant French. No one gave American food respect. The world didn't know what we were doing until we started winning at the Culinary Olympics," McGrath says.

His career trajectory did take him to Europe where he apprenticed under star French chef Christian Frappier and did a six month stage with chef Fredy Girardet. (McGrath says he has nothing against a formal education but feels he personally learned more from doing than sitting in a classroom.)

Returning to the U.S. in 1975, he opened a restaurant in Ocala, Florida called Green Apple. Situated in the middle of Florida's agricultural belt with the Atlantic on one side, the Gulf of Mexico on the other and fresh water lakes all around, McGrath wrote the menu each day based on available product. Dinner was by reservation only with an average check of $70 per person (astronomical for that time), but nevertheless the restaurant was very successful. It was so successful, McGrath says, that in the years he owned it, he only had about ten days off.

By his middle twenties, he was burned out. While his next gig, working as a sous chef for the Disneyland Hotel in Anaheim, doesn't sound like a relaxing alternative, McGrath says it was nonetheless a great experience. Undoubtedly, since he was in charge of the dinner shift for all eleven restaurants in the Magic Kingdom hostelry as well as two banquet kitchens, each capable of turning out 5,000 meals at a time.

While working in Austin and Houston for The Four Seasons (he was the first non-European executive chef the chain had ever hired) his propensity for regional food began to coalesce into a singular style. McGrath — along with other high profile Texas chefs, Dean Fearing, Stephen Pyles, Jeff Blank, Bruce Auden and Robert Del Grande — began subsidizing local farmers and livestock and game ranchers. "The whole idea was to use indigenous ingredients and cooking techniques. We didn't set out to create a specific cuisine. Each of us had our own slant on it."

McGrath's slant was distinctly Western. "It completely reflects my lifestyle," he says. "I love being outdoors and a lot of the things that I cook over a campfire, I've brought into my repertoire. Sure, there'll be a nice sauce and a nice presentation but it's straightforward stuff."

A visit to the Phoenix area in 1991 proved pivotal in his career. McGrath recalls, "I liked the people I met, the things I saw and sensed opportunities. I needed a change and that was it."

McGrath continued to attract national attention as executive chef at Windows on the Green at The Phoenician Resort. "My culinary style really matured while I was there. I didn't have to be elaborate or esoteric. I did fundamental food reflective of Arizona."

When the time came to open Roaring Fork, he put his experiences all together. In his cookbook, *American*

Western Cooking, McGrath talks about the cultural influences Native Americans, Hispanics and the pioneers and cowboys who settled the West brought to the table. His menu reflects those influences, which encompass product and food interpretations from the Mississippi River to California, from Montana

to Texas. Smoke roasting, smoking and grilling are favorite kitchen techniques. Chiles, garlic, beans, fresh seafood, beef, game and robust sauces are key ingredients.

McGrath designed his spacious, L-shaped restaurant. From the foyer with its wood-fire rotisserie spitted with lamb, chicken and suckling pigs emitting sweetly smoky aromas, through the lounge area (a hugely popular local gathering place) to the laid-back, eye-appealing cream and tobacco-colored dining room dominated by an open kitchen, the place exudes Western elegance. The charmingly appropriate accents include antler chandeliers, barbed wire, embossed copper, well-worn leather and a wealth of McGrath's personal mementos.

The James Beard Award came at a critical point in McGrath's life. He had been battling severe viral encephalitis for months. At one time doctors gave him only a slim chance of survival and the staggeringly difficult road back demanded months and months of therapy. The day he was released from the hospital, barely aware of what was going on, he got the call from New York that he had received the award.

Following his recovery he remembers, "I took an inventory of my life and realized other people's perceptions of me didn't matter. What really counts in the end are my family and my restaurant. I believe you can be successful at life and in business and I'm a big advocate of having fun while you're doing both. Here at the restaurant I host a party every night."

The home front includes wife Amy, daughters Montana Lee and Melissa and son Jason. The family enjoys the outdoor life; horseback riding, fly-fishing, camping and rafting. The first week of January signals the annual fishing trip to Colorado, and every other year Robert and Amy charter a boat in the British Virgin Islands, plot a course and set sail for two weeks.

McGrath also belongs to the Charlie Russell Riders, a philanthropic group that supports the Charles Russell Museum in Montana. The group, which includes ex-astronaut Wally Shirra, gets together every September for a trail ride. In the perfect world, he says, he'd have a ranch on the water so he could sail and ride.

The rest of the time McGrath says the family hangs out at home. For dinner he'll fire up his Texas barbecue and smoke roast chicken or steaks, ribs or brisket along with vegetables, especially corn on the cob when it is in season.

For McGrath, it is all about seizing the moment. "After having a life or death experience, I take nothing for granted. There are very few days I don't fully appreciate being alive."

Cast-Iron Cooked Foie Gras with Grilled Pineapple and Red Lentil "Chow-Chow"

Serves: 4

Chow-Chow:

1/2 cup diced grilled pineapple

1/2 cup cooked red lentils

1/2 cup seasoned rice vinegar

2 tablespoons finely chopped red onion

2 tablespoons finely chopped chives

2 tablespoons seeded, finely chopped jalapeño

Kosher salt and fresh cracked black pepper to taste

Balsamic Syrup:

2 cups balsamic vinegar

Foie Gras:

4 each 2-ounce foie gras medallions

Kosher salt and fresh cracked black pepper to taste

Finish:

2 cups wild arugula *(or small organic arugula leaves)*

For the Chow-Chow:

- Mix all of the chow-chow ingredients together in a bowl. Set aside in a cool place.

For the Balsamic Syrup:

- In a small saucepan over medium heat, prepare balsamic syrup by simmering the 2 cups of balsamic vinegar until reduced to 1/4 cup in volume.

For the Foie Gras:

- Season the foie gras with the salt and pepper and sear in a very hot cast-iron skillet. Flip and briefly sear the other side.

To Finish and Serve:

- Toss the arugula and chow-chow together and place in the center of four plates. Place the foie gras on top of the greens and drizzle the balsamic syrup over the top in a crisscross pattern.

"Category 6" Lemonade

Serves: 1

The Roaring Fork River is known for its white-water rafting. White-water rapids are rated according to their difficulty, with 6 being the most difficult.

1 ounce Absolut Citron® Vodka

1 ounce Absolut Kurrant® Vodka

1 ounce Stoli Oranjh® Vodka

1 ounce Bacardi Limon® Rum

1/2 ounce Chambord® raspberry liqueur

3/4 ounce puréed huckleberries *(may substitute blueberries or boysenberries)*

4 ounces lemonade

Ice cubes

1 each lemon slice, orange slice and cherry *(for garnish)*

Mix the ingredients except for the fruit in a shaker with ice, pour into a glass and garnish with fruit.

Adapted from *American Western Cooking from the Roaring Fork* by Robert McGrath.

"Channel Island" Tuna Salad

Serves: 4

Vinaigrette:

1/2 cup extra-virgin olive oil

1/4 cup red wine vinegar

2 tablespoons lemon juice

2 teaspoons finely chopped garlic

1 teaspoon fresh cracked
black pepper

1 cup peeled, seeded and
chopped tomato

2 tablespoons chopped chives

Kosher salt to taste

Salad:

24 each pencil asparagus spears

8 each red bliss potatoes,
cut into quarters length-wise

1 pound medium to large shimp,
peeled and deveined

4 each 3-ounce tuna fillets

Salt and pepper to taste

2 tablespoons extra-virgin
olive oil

8 cups spinach leaves, cleaned

Finish:

2 cups peeled and julienned
roasted red bell pepper*

4 each hard-cooked eggs,
coarsely grated

12 each Kalamata olives

Kosher salt and fresh cracked
black pepper to taste

For the Vinaigrette:

- Prepare the vinaigrette by whisking all ingredients except for the tomatoes and the chives together in a small bowl. Finish with the tomatoes and chives, and then season to taste with salt. Set aside.

For the Salad:

- Separately blanch the asparagus and the potatoes in salted water and chill.

- Season the shrimp and the tuna. Sauté the shrimp and tuna in the olive oil in a medium skillet until the tuna is cooked to medium.

- Divide the spinach leaves into four portions *(2 cups each)*. Toss each portion of the spinach with 1/4 cup of the vinaigrette dressing.

To Finish and Serve:

- Place 1 portion of salad in each of four wide-rimmed bowls. Arrange 1/4 of the vegetables and shrimp in vertical rows over each portion in the following order: potato, red bell pepper, shrimp, asparagus and hard-cooked egg.

- Place 1 tuna piece on the very top of each salad. Randomly place the olives around the salad. Serve 1/4 cup of additional vinaigrette in a small container on the side of each salad.

* Available in jars in the specialty food section of most supermarkets.

Barbecued Onion Soup with Jalapeño Jack Cheese

Serves: 4

Soup:

1 cup smoked yellow onion,
cut into 1/4-inch-thick julienne
(one medium)

1 cup smoked red onion,
cut into 1/4-inch-thick julienne
(one medium)

1 cup chopped smoked leeks
(3 each)

1/4 cup chopped shallots
(one medium)

1/4 cup chopped roasted garlic*
(one medium head)

2 tablespoons vegetable oil

5 cups chicken stock

1-1/2 teaspoons dark
chile powder

1 tablespoon brown sugar

2 tablespoons barbecue sauce

Kosher salt and cracked black
pepper to taste

1 cup chopped green onions
(one bunch)

Fried Onion Julienne:

2 tablespoons all-purpose flour

1 cup vegetable oil for frying

1 cup fine julienne of onion
(one medium)

Finish:

4 each round sourdough
croutons

4 each 1/4-inch-thick slices
jalapeño jack cheese

2 tablespoons chopped chives

For the Soup:

- Sauté the onions, leeks, shallots and garlic in a heavy pan with vegetable oil until a rich golden brown, adding up to 1 cup of chicken stock, 1/4 cup at a time, to prevent burning; then add the chili powder, brown sugar and barbecue sauce.

- Add the remaining chicken stock and cook over medium heat until reduced by 1/3.

- Season to taste and finish with green onions.

For the Fried Onion Julienne:

- In a medium saucepan, heat oil to 350 degrees. Toss onions in flour, shaking off excess. Fry onions in hot oil for 2 to 3 minutes until golden brown.

To Finish and Serve:

- Ladle the soup into four small cast-iron kettles *(or any kind of single-serving soup crock)* and place one crouton on the surface of the soup in each kettle. Place one slice of cheese on top of each crouton and brown under a broiler until melted. Sprinkle with the fried onion julienne and chopped chives.

* Cut the top off of one medium-sized head of garlic and rub with olive oil. Wrap in foil and bake for 15-20 minutes at 350 degrees. Cool. Press roasted flesh out of skins.

Corn Stew with Crabmeat, Mussels and Barbecued Shrimp

Serves: 8

Stew:

1/4 cup vegetable oil or lard

1/2 cup diced red bell pepper

1/2 cup diced green bell pepper

1/2 cup diced poblano chile

1 cup diced white onion

2 tablespoons minced garlic

1 cup diced Yukon gold potatoes

4 cups sweet corn kernels

3 cups water

4 cups lobster stock or clam juice

1/4 cup granulated sugar

1/4 cup dark chile powder

Salt and pepper to taste

1 pound medium to large
  shrimp, deveined

2 tablespoons tomato paste

24 each green-lipped mussels
  *(may substitute black mussels if
  green are unavailable)*

Finish:

Kosher salt and fresh cracked
  black pepper to taste

1 pound lump crabmeat

1/4 cup chopped chives

1 bunch frissée

For the Stew:

- Heat the vegetable oil or lard in a large saucepan or stock pot. Sauté the peppers, onion and garlic until just tender. Add the potatoes, corn kernels, water and lobster stock *(or clam juice)* and simmer for 20 minutes.

- Mix the sugar, chile powder, and salt and pepper to taste together. Rub the shrimp with the mixture, shaking off excess.

- Grill the shrimp over medium-hot flame until pink. Set aside.

- Whisk the tomato paste into the stock mixture in the saucepan and add the mussels. Simmer for another 10 minutes.

To Finish and Serve:

- Season to taste. Add the crabmeat and chopped chives. Finish with the grilled shrimp and garnish with the frissée.

Roasted Rack of Lamb with Rosemary-Cider Sauce and Warm Salad of Early Spring Vegetables

Serves: 4

Sauce:

2 cups apple cider

1 each guajillo chile*
(may substitute dried red chile pod)

2 tablespoons dark brown sugar

1 each rosemary sprig

Lamb:

4 each lamb racks *(approximately 12 ounces each)*, halved

2 tablespoons minced garlic

4 each small sheets of lacy caul fat**

Vegetables:

2 tablespoons extra-virgin olive oil

2 tablespoons butter

8 each baby carrots, peeled and blanched

8 each fingerling potatoes, quartered and blanched

8 each red pearl onions, peeled

8 each white pearl onions, peeled

16 each sugar snap peas, blanched

24-32 each English peas

4 tablespoons finely sliced green garlic *(may substitute 1 tablespoon chives plus 1 tablespoon garlic)*

1 each roasted red bell pepper, peeled and julienned

Salt and pepper to taste

Finish:

8 each tendrils from green and yellow peas
(4 green, 4 yellow)

Kosher salt and fresh cracked black pepper to taste

For the Sauce:

- In a heavy saucepan, bring the apple cider to a boil and reduce in volume by 1/2 *(to 1 cup)*.

- Toast the chile, then break it apart by hand and place it in the cider. Add the brown sugar and the rosemary to the cider. Return to a boil over medium heat and cook until reduced by 1/3.

- Strain the sauce through a fine strainer *(or a chinois)*. Cover and set aside at room temperature.

For the Lamb:

- Remove all bones from the lamb racks except for the bone at the loin end of each rack. Season the lamb racks with salt and pepper and then sear on all sides on a hot grill or in a hot, heavy skillet.

- Sprinkle minced garlic over each rack, then wrap each rack in caul fat.

- Roast the lamb racks at 325 degrees for 20 minutes, or until an instant-read meat thermometer indicates an internal temperature of 135 degrees for medium rare. Remove racks from oven and allow to rest for 5 minutes.

For the Vegetables:

- Sauté the vegetables in the olive oil and butter. Season with salt and pepper.

To Finish and Serve:

- Equally distribute the vegetables in a small mound in the upper right quadrant of each of four serving plates.

- Remove the caul fat from the racks, and slice each rack twice *(for a total of 3 pieces per half rack)*.

- Using 2 half-racks *(6 pieces)* per plate, shingle the lamb around the vegetables with the bone end of the racks at the top.

- Drizzle the sauce over the lamb and around the perimeter of each plate.

- Garnish with green and yellow pea tendrils, placing them on top of the vegetables near the bone end of the lamb racks.

* Makes a very spicy sauce. For a milder sauce, use 1/2 of the chile.
** Available from your butcher or specialty meat shop

Sugar and Chile-Cured Venison Chops with Green Chile Macaroni and Colorado Corn Sauce

Serves: 4

Venison:

1/4 cup granulated sugar

1 tablespoon kosher salt

3 tablespoons dark chile powder

4 each venison rib chops,
   7 ounces each

For the Macaroni:

1/4 cup diced red bell pepper

1/4 cup diced red onion

1/2 cup sweet corn kernels
   (ideally, fresh)

2 tablespoons chopped garlic

1 tablespoon corn oil

2 cups cooked macaroni

3/4 cup roasted, peeled and
   puréed poblano chile

2/3 cup grated hot pepper jack
   cheese

1/4 cup heavy cream

Kosher salt and cracked black
   pepper to taste

For the Sauce:

1 tablespoon unsalted butter

1 cup sweet corn kernels
   (ideally, fresh)

1 teaspoon chopped shallot

1/2 cup white wine

1/4 cup cold unsalted butter,
   cut in cubes

Finish:

1 tablespoon chopped chives

For the Venison:

- Mix together the sugar, salt and chile powder in a small bowl. Evenly rub the spice mixture over the venison chops. Set aside and let cure at room temperature for at least 6 hours.

- Brush the excess dry rub off of the venison chops. Cover the bones of the chops with foil to prevent burning and grill to the desired internal temperature, being careful not to burn *(135 degrees for medium rare, about 7 minutes per side)*.

For the Macaroni:

- Sauté the red bell pepper, red onion, corn and garlic in the corn oil in a heavy pan. Add the macaroni, poblano purée and jack cheese. Fold in the heavy cream. Season to taste. Set aside in a warm place.

For the Sauce:

- Melt the butter in a saucepan over low to medium heat. Add the corn and let sweat for about 2 minutes. Add the shallot and the white wine. Simmer for 10 minutes. Allow mixture to cool, then purée in a blender. As the sauce starts to come together, add the butter 1 cube at a time until all of the butter has been used. Strain the sauce into a saucepan and hold over very low heat.

To Finish and Serve:

- Spoon a mound of the green chile macaroni off-center in the upper left quadrant of each of four serving plates. Rest a venison chop up against the macaroni on each plate. Spoon 1/4 of the corn sauce over the open portion of each plate. Top with the chopped chives.

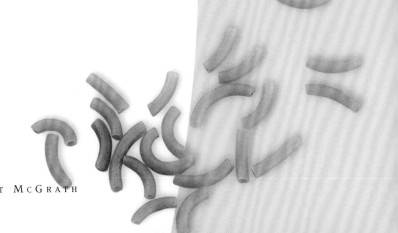

Milk Chocolate and "Cowhide" Turnovers with Strawberry Sauce

Serves: 4

Sauce:

1 pint fresh strawberries

1/2 cup granulated sugar

Turnovers:

6 ounces melted milk chocolate

12 ounces cream cheese

1/2 cup granulated sugar

1 pound moldable marzipan

2 tablespoons cocoa powder

Finish:

4 each long-stem strawberries

1/4 cup fine julienne of fresh mint

For the Sauce:

- In a saucepan, combine cleaned and cut strawberries and granulated sugar and cook over low to medium heat until strawberries break down. Strain and set aside.

For the Turnovers:

- In a mixing bowl, mix the milk chocolate, cream cheese and sugar together until the mixture has a smooth consistency. Refrigerate about 1 hour.

- Thoroughly knead the cocoa powder into 1/3 of the marzipan to make chocolate marzipan. Roll both the chocolate marzipan and the white marzipan out to 1/8-inch thick. Tear the chocolate marzipan into small pieces, place them randomly on the regular marzipan sheets, and roll them into the regular marzipan to create a cowhide effect.

- With a biscuit or cookie cutter, cut the cowhide into 3-1/2-inch circles. Spoon approximately 3 tablespoons of the cheese mixture into the center of the marzipan cowhide. Fold the cowhide circle over in half and crimp the edges with the tines of a fork. Chill in the refrigerator for at least 1 hour.

To Finish and Serve:

- Spoon a pool of the strawberry sauce in the lower half of each of four plates. Overlap the turnover at the top of the sauce. Split the strawberries and place one against the back of the turnover on each plate. Garnish with fresh mint.

Roaring Fork, Austin

Robert McGrath opened his second Roaring Fork restaurant in Austin, Texas on April 14, 2003 in the historic Stephen F. Austin Hotel, one of the very first in the state. Both Roaring Forks integrate McGrath's appreciation for the art world into the design of the restaurants, which feature American Western paintings and sculptures. Local artisans, sculptors, photographers and painters are represented from each respective city. World-renowned Western artist Nelson Boren was commissioned by McGrath to create a signature painting which portrays the flags of Arizona and Texas on weathered cowboy boots. The Austin restaurant features a massive chile hearth, while the Scottsdale restaurant has a massive rotisserie.

JOHNSON & WALES

CHARLESTON, SC

Chef Instructors, students and staff from the Charleston, South Carolina campus of Johnson & Wales University, the world's foremost culinary educator, conducted the recipe testing, editing and formatting for the recipes in this cookbook.

Johnson & Wales University has a long history of commitment to participating in community projects and events within each of its campus communities. The opportunity to participate in the production of this cookbook evolved through this commitment, as a working relationship was formed between the Charleston campus and Tom Stumph, publisher of *Winning Styles Cookbook*.

A number of very talented Chef Instructors from the Charleston campus participated in the formal testing of the recipes, with the assistance of both teaching assistants and culinary students. The two principle chefs conducting the testing were Chef Karl Stybe and Chef Robin Schmitz. In addition, Chef Frances Burnett, Chef Christian Finck and Chef Shane Pearson performed recipe testing. The following members of the Office of Development & Campus Relations participated in the editing and formatting of the recipes for this book: Cindy Parker, Executive Director of Development & Campus Relations; Catherine Huge, Special Events Coordinator; and Barry Rubin, Office Assistant.

Chef Instructor Karl Stybe, M.A.E., has worked for the University since 1998, and holds a number of professional certifications including Certified Hospitality Educator, Certified Executive Chef, and Certified Culinary Educator. Chef Instructor Robin Schmitz, M.A.T., has worked for the University since 1999 and is an ongoing and significant participant in University-sponsored events and projects in Charleston. Chef Frances Burnett, B.S., has worked for the University since 1994, and holds professional certifications including Certified Hospitality Educator and Certified Master Baker. Chef Christian Finck, B.S., has worked for the University since 1998 and is a member of the

Retail Bakers' Association. Chef Shane Pearson, B.S., has worked for Johnson & Wales since 1997, and has served as coach of the Charleston campus's award-winning Culinary Competition Team.

Gertrude I. Johnson and Mary T. Wales founded Johnson & Wales University as a business school in 1914 in Providence, Rhode Island. From its origins as a school devoted to business education, Johnson & Wales has evolved into a world-class institution, providing quality, career-focused education. The University is comprised of colleges of business, hospitality and culinary arts, and schools of technology and arts and sciences, that together offer scores of majors and degree programs at the undergraduate and graduate level. Today, as America's Career University®, Johnson & Wales offers 51 degree programs, with a total enrollment of more than 15,000 students from all 50 states and more than 95 foreign countries; and it has more than 55,000 alumni world-wide.

One of the most far-reaching and pivotal events in the educational evolution of the University occurred in 1973, when the University announced the creation of what is now known as the College of Culinary Arts and the addition of an associate degree program in that field. Since its beginning with just 141 students, the College of Culinary Arts at Johnson & Wales University has quickly grown to make the University the world's foremost culinary educator, with more than 5,000 students enrolled in undergraduate culinary programs at its domestic cam-

puses. Internationally recognized for the quality and variety of its programs, Johnson & Wales became the first school in the country to offer a Bachelor of Science degree in culinary arts in 1993.

While working in the University's own kitchens, J&W students practice the culinary skills they need to succeed in their chosen careers. Beginning with the fundamentals of cooking, culinary arts majors quickly move on to more advanced studies in garde-manger, classical and international cuisine. In a similar fashion, baking and pastry arts majors begin with the fundamentals of baking and cake decorating and go on to fine-tune their talents in working with chocolate and sugar artistry. All students must also complete arts and science course requirements. For one term each year, culinary arts students are assigned to academic classes. In culinary lecture classes, the students are taught subjects such as facility design and layout, nutrition analysis and planning, sanitation, and food and beverage cost controls to supplement their training. For baking and pastry arts majors, academic studies include baking formula technology.

The educational experience itself is quite unique at Johnson & Wales, starting with the upside-down curriculum. Students begin taking classes in their chosen field during their first year. With three terms per year, three or four classes per term, and only four class days a week, students gain a better understanding of each course and may earn two degrees (associate and bachelor's) in four years. This academic schedule also allows students to work in the foodservice and hospitality industries on the weekends.

The hallmark of the University's educational programs is a "learn by doing" philosophy, which makes its students seasoned employees before they graduate. Students may garner experience through University-operated practicum facilities, which include three hotels, a bakeshop and a women's clothing boutique. The University's extensive Career Development Office also offers cooperative education opportunities, where students are able to work at leading hotels, restaurants, technology centers, and businesses as part of their academic curriculum. All of these programs provide students with relevant learning experiences and exposure to all facets of a professional operation, and effectively prepare them to meet the challenges of the work place. Johnson & Wales "best-fit employment" philosophy has enabled the University to maintain a 98% employment rate of its graduates in their chosen fields within 60 days of graduation, for 25 consecutive years.

In addition to the 9,000 students at the Providence campus, today Johnson & Wales University has a significant presence in four other cities around the country and in one foreign country, with plans for a new campus to open in 2004 in Charlotte, North Carolina. In 1981, a J&W campus was established in Charleston, South Carolina, to serve the needs of the United States Navy. The campus was expanded to serve the general public in 1984 and the institution today has nearly 1,500 undergraduate students enrolled in a variety of two- and four-year programs in food service, hospitality and travel-tourism. The Norfolk, Virginia campus also was established initially to serve the U.S. Navy and it opened its classes to the public in 1986. Today, the Norfolk campus has an

enrollment of more than 600 students in two- and four-year degree programs in culinary arts and food service management.

In 1992, Johnson & Wales opened its fourth domestic campus in North Miami, Florida. This campus has more than 2,000 students currently enrolled in two- and four-year culinary arts, food service, business and hospitality programs. In 2000, J&W opened the Denver, Colorado campus, which offers two- and four-year degrees in culinary arts, hospitality and business programs. Located on the former Colorado Women's College in Denver, this campus has almost 1,000 students enrolled in its various programs of study.

In 2002, the University announced plans to open a new campus in Charlotte, North Carolina. This $82 million urban campus is presently under construction in downtown Charlotte and will enroll its first class in September 2004. The Charleston and Norfolk campus operations eventually will be merged with the Charlotte campus operation. It is projected that the Charlotte campus ultimately will have more than 3,000 students enrolled in its culinary arts, hospitality and business programs.

For further information about Johnson & Wales University and its campuses and educational programs, please visit the University's website at www.jwu.edu.

GLOSSARY

Acidulated Water: Water with lemon juice or other acid added, intended to keep raw fruit or vegetables from discoloring.

Adobo Sauce: Seasoning paste used in Mexican cuisine made with ground chiles, herbs and vinegar.

Albumin: Clarifying protein found in egg whites, leeks, blood, and connective tissue.
• Soluble in cold liquid.
• It congeals when heated and traps impurities.

Al Dente: Cooked to the point of tenderness but with some texture remaining.

A la Minute: At the last minute, just before service.

Au Jus: Served with unthickened pan juices, often with the addition of stock or other flavorings.

Bain-Marie: A hot water bath used to insure gentle cooking. Water is placed in a pan and other foods, in separate containers, are set into the water; the whole is then usually placed in the oven. Also, a double boiler insert for slow cooking over simmering water. Also, a steam table in which smaller pans and their contents are kept hot.

Barding: Wrapping meats with thin slices of fat or fatty meats, like bacon, before cooking.

Bechamel: Basic white sauce.

Beurre Manié: A 60/40 mix of whole butter and flour used as a liaison.

Bird Chiles: Slender, straight, chiles, bitingly hot and resembling the arbol.

Blanch: To immerse food briefly in boiling water, either to help loosen the skin or to precook briefly to set color and flavor.

Boil: To cook liquid rapidly so that bubbles constantly rise and break on the surface. To cook food in boiling liquid.

Bouquet Garni: Little bundles of herbs and spices, usually wrapped in cheesecloth.
• Classic combination – parsley, peppercorns, thyme, and bay leaves.

Braise: To cook a seared product in a tightly covered pan with varying amounts of a flavorful liquid for a lengthy period of time.
• Best for tough cuts of meat.
• Usually completed in the oven.
• Braised vegetables are usually not seared.

Bread: To coat with bread or cracker crumbs before cooking, usually after first dipping food into beaten egg or other liquid so crumbs will adhere.

Brine: A salt solution. Also the act of soaking a product in a salt solution.

Brown: To cook in a small amount of fat until browned on all sides, giving food an appetizing color and flavor and, in meats, sealing in natural juices.

Brunoise: To dice vegetable minutely, or the resulting diced vegetable mixture.

Capon: Castrated and fattened rooster.

Carryover Cooking: The cooking that takes place after a product is removed from the oven.
• Remove roasts from the oven at least 5 degrees below the desired temperature.

Chard: A member of the beet family that produces large leaves and thick stalks.

Chèvre: Goat's milk cheese.

Chiffonade: To finely cut greens to produce thin strips.

Chinois: A metal, conical strainer with fine mesh. Sometimes known as a "China cap."

Concasser: To chop roughly – often used to describe a rough chop of blanched, peeled, and seeded tomatoes.

Confit: Meats cooked and preserved in fat. Fruits preserved in sugar or liquor.

Consommé: Clarified stock that has been fortified with lean ground meat and additional mirepoix and bouquet garni.

Coral: The roe of lobster or other crustaceans.

Court-Bouillon: A poaching liquid that contains water, an acid *(wine, citrus, vinegar)*, aromatics and other flavorings.
• Acids help flavor and coagulate the proteins of the products being poached.

Cube: To cut into small cubes *(about 1/2 inch)*. In meats, to tenderize by pounding with a special tool that imprints a checkered pattern on the surface, breaking tough fibers to increase tenderness.

Darne: A thick slice of a large raw fish.

Dash: A very small amount, less than 1/8 teaspoon.

Deglaze: To dissolve and pick up the flavorful bits left on the bottom of a pan after cooking.
• Acids like wine work best because they help extract flavor.
• Stock, water or other liquids can also be used.

Demi-glace: "Half glaze" — a brown sauce reduction.

Depouillage: To skim the impurities off the top of a stock, soup or sauce.

Dice: To cut into very small pieces.
(about 1/8 to 1/4 inch)

Dredge: To coat or cover food lightly but completely with flour, sugar, or other fine substance.

Emulsion: A mixture of one liquid with another with which it cannot normally combine smoothly.

Farce: Stuffing or forcemeat.

Fat: Generic term for butter, margarine, lard or vegetable shortening; also the rendered drippings of meat or fowl.

Fat Cap: Layer of fat that surrounds muscle tissue.

Fines Herbes: A fine mixture of fresh herbs used to season meats, fish and sauces.

Foie Gras: Fattened goose or duck liver.

Fry: To cook in hot fat — pan-frying in a skillet *(very little fat)* or deep-frying in a heavy pan *(food immersed in fat)*.

Fumet: White stock with other flavorings added, simmered and reduced by 50%.

Galanga: A root that is a relative of ginger, used in Thai cuisine — sometimes spelled galangal.

Glacé: Brown stock reduced by 85% to 90%.

Grease: To rub fat or oil on a cooking surface or utensil to prevent food from sticking.

Grill: To cook on a rack over direct heat - gas, electricity, or charcoal; to broil on a grill.

Haricot Vert: Thin French green beans.

Herbs: Leaves of plants used either fresh or dry.
• When substituting dry for fresh, use 1/3 the amount.

Hydrogenation: A process in which extra hydrogen atoms are pumped into unsaturated fat.

Ice Bath: A container of ice water used to stop the cooking process or cool foods or liquids quickly.

Jus: The natural juice of a meat, vegetable or fruit.

Jus Lie: Pan juices thickened with a slurry.

Julienne: Matchstick pieces of vegetables, fruits or cooked meats.

Kale: Curly-leafed vegetable from the cabbage family.

Kohlrabi: Root vegetable that resembles a turnip but has a more delicate flavor.

Larding: Threading strips of fat into a piece of meat before cooking.
• Larding needle – hollow needle.

Liaison: Thickening or binding agent used in the preparation of a soup or sauce.

Liaison Finale: Finishing or enriching agent added to soups or sauces at the end of the cooking process.

Madeira: Fortified wine, either sweet or dry, from the Portuguese island of Madeira.

Maillard Reaction: When natural sugars and proteins react to heat by caramelizing — browning and forming a crust.

Mandoline: A slicer with adjustable blades.

Malanga: A starchy tuber with brown skin with crisp flesh, similar to taro.

Marinade: A flavorful liquid used to tenderize and flavor products.
• Usually includes an acid, oil, herbs and spices.

Mince: To cut or chop very finely.

Mirepoix: Rough cut flavorful vegetables – traditionally carrots, onions, celery and sometimes leeks.

Monder: To blanch, peel and seed tomatoes.

Monter au Beurre: To swirl small chunks of cold, whole butter into a sauce at the end of the cooking process.

Nage: A light sauce created from a court bouillon.

Napper: To lightly coat with a sauce or to cook a sauce until it coats the back of a spoon.

Pan-Fry: To cook in a moderate amount of fat; sauté.

Pan Gravy: Pan drippings thickened with flour.

Parboil: To boil until partially cooked; remainder of cooking is done by another method.

Poach: To gently simmer in liquid.

Purée: To sieve or whirl food into a smooth, thick mixture.

Quenelle: A dumpling made of meat, poultry or fish. It also refers to the basic quenelle shape — An oval formed by using 2 spoons that have been moistened in water.

Ragout: A rich stew.

Reduction: The result of boiling down liquids in order to concentrate flavors.

Remouillage: Second, weaker extraction made from the remnants of a stock.
• Half the water, half the cook time.
• Used to start another stock.

Render: To liquefy the fat from a meat product over low heat.
• Product should be diced or scored.

Resting: Letting a roast rest for 5 to 15 minutes after cooking.
• Equalizes internal pressure so juices can be re-absorbed.
• Allows for carryover cooking.

Roast: Oven-cook foods in an uncovered pan to produce a well-browned product with a moist interior.
• Dry cooking method
• Best for tender cuts of meat

Rondeau: Heavy pan with straight sides that are less than the width of the base. It is commonly used for braising.

Roux: A cooked combination of fat and flour used to thicken sauces and soups.

Sabayon: A mixture of egg yolks and an acid whisked over hot water just until the yolks start to thicken.

Sambal: A chile paste, often with garlic, salt, sugar and other spices, used in Southeast Asian cuisine.

Sauté: To cook quickly over high heat in a minimal amount of oil.

Sauternes: A fruity, sweet white wine from the Bordeaux region.

Scald: To heat milk just below the boiling point (tiny bubbles appear around the edge of the pan when it has reached the proper temperature).

Sear: To brown meat quickly either in a hot pan with very little oil or in a hot oven.

Shock: To stop the cooking process by plunging a food in ice water.

Simmer: To cook in liquid over low heat just below the boiling point *(bubbles form slowly and burst before reaching the surface)*.

Singer: To dust with flour after sautéing or roasting – flour mixes with the fat to create a quick roux.

Skim: To remove fat or scum from the surface of a liquid with a spoon or ladel.

Slurry: 50/50 mixture of cold liquid and refined starch – most often arrowroot or cornstarch.

Smoke Point: The temperature at which oils begin to smoke, burn and/or break down.

Spices: Buds, fruits, flowers, bark, berries, seeds and roots of plants and trees, used as seasonings.

Star Anise: The brown, fragrant pod of a Chinese evergreen used as a spice.

Steam: To cook in water vapors, on a rack or in a steam basket, in a covered pan above boiling water.

Steep: To infuse in liquid.

Stew: To cook a product barely covered in a flavorful liquid until the product is tender.
• Good for tough, small cuts of meat.
• Usually completed on top of the stove.
• Stewed vegetables are usually not seared.

Stir: Using a spoon or a whisk in a broad, circular motion, to mix ingredients without beating or to prevent them from sticking.

Sweat: To cook slowly over medium/low heat without browning.
• Good for flavor extraction.
• Moisture development encouraged.

Tamarind Concentrate: A sour-flavored paste made from the the pod of a tropical tree.

Texture: The structural quality of a food — roughness, smoothness, graininess, or creaminess.

Truss: Tie products prior to cooking.
• Helps maintain a product's shape.
• Promotes even cooking.

Tuile: A thin, crisp, curved wafer.

Turmeric: The root of a musky-smelling tropical plant, used as a spice — usually used in powdered form.

Whip: To beat rapidly with a wire whisk, or electric mixer, incorporating air to lighten a mixture and increase its volume.

Whisk: To beat with a wire whisk until blended and smooth.

Whitewash: 50/50 mixture of cold liquid and flour.

Zest: Outer colored peel of citrus fruits. Also, the act of removing this outer peel.

RECIPE INDEX